Other Publications

Toward a Revised Philosophy of the Paper Machine. Des Plaines, Illinois: *Paper Industry*, 1964.

Editor, Sylvia Bliss, *Quests.* Montpelier, Vermont: Capital City Press, 1965.

Return From Enlightenment. Adamant, Vermont: Adamant Press, 1971.

JOURNEY AMONG MOUNTAINS

FOREST K. DAVIS

ADAMANT PRESS
Adamant, Vermont
1974

Printed at the Pine Hill Printery, Freeman, South Dakota 57029

Published by Adamant Press, Box 7, Adamant, Vermont 05640

ii

To
Margaret and Arthur, William, Charles,
and Katharine; in the wisdom of youth
they have labored greatly to bring up their
parents; if they hang in there they may just
possibly succeed.

*What doth the Lord require of thee, but to
do justly, and to love mercy, and to walk
humbly with thy God?*

—Micah VI, 8

Foreword

Appreciation is expressed to the following journals which have courteously granted permission to revise and reprint papers which appeared originally in their pages:

to *Community Education* of the George Junior Republic, Freeville, New York, for "Characteristics of Religious Thought I: Community As Belief Point" from Vol. II, No. 1, Spring 1965; this paper was a response to a request from the late Paul Martineau, Editor, following whose death the journal was discontinued;

to the *Crane Review* of the former Crane Theological School, Tufts University, Medford, Mass., for "Christianity As Hypothesis" from Vol. V, Spring 1967;

to *Philosophy Today* of Celina, Ohio, for "The Fundamental Questions In Philosophy" from Vol. XII, No. 4 / 4, Winter 1968;

to *College and University*, Journal of the American Association of Collegiate Registrars and Admissions Officers, Washington, D. C., for "The City Education Center . . ." from Vol. 44, No. 1, Fall 1968;

to *The Journal of General Education* of the Pennsylvania State University Press, University Park, Pennsylvania, for "Image-Suffusion In The Small-Group . . ." from Vol. XXI, No. 3, 1969;

to *The Journal of the Liberal Ministry,* c / o Rev. Arthur Graham, Editor, Oak Ridge, Tennessee, for "Ground Notions Toward A Liberal Ecumenism" from Vol. XI, No. 1, Winter 1971; and to James Luther Adams of its Editorial Advisory Board for useful comments;

to *Education* of Milwaukee, Wisconsin, for "The Plunge Through Law . . ." from Vol. 92, September-October 1971;

and to *Improving College and University Teaching,* Oregon State University, Corvallis, Oregon, for "American History Revisited" from Vol. XIX, No. 2, Spring 1971.

As with earlier instances these and other papers derive from personal and professional experiences at a variety of times and places. The first was a position paper within the disciplines of that most distinguished of liberal assemblies, the Greenfield Group, meeting in semi-annual retreats at Senexet House above the shores of Roseland Lake, South Woodstock, Connecticut. The twelfth was a discussion topic in an informal colloquium of CHERS-connected persons in Dayton. The fourth and seventh were considerations during happy years at Wilberforce University as were the two consortial studies. Others stemmed from less precise and more general concerns, themes recurrent from time to time as may be characteristic of this type of reflection.

People in education are forever in debt to their student and faculty colleagues. The Long Island Center of New York's Empire State College has provided the warmest of settings for development of a new and different educational mode. More than four hundred students and some thirty faculty and staff took part in this during its first year of life in the green and horsey country of Old Westbury where colleges seem often to begin and sometimes move away. Although this fascinating experience is too recent and immediate to emerge in these pages its time will come. There is a good deal to be said for working through the establishment of a new college, particularly one with programmatic differences. It does not happen every day, or every year. Most new colleges opening in this period are not very different; they tend to be standard institutional types transplanted to other places. Perhaps people want a lot of traditional colleges. It could be argued that if such colleges are founded and if they succeed in remaining open, in a sense they are wanted, that the public is in effect voting for them. Then why bother to innovate? But there are always individualists looking for new things to do, in education as in other fields, and some of them are willing to face the burdens of uphill struggle to try out the unusual. It is amusing to observe the anxiety with which traditional institutions watch their newer neighbors, even the anxiety with which institutional governors monitor the emergent modes which they have themselves created and which presumably they mean to support, providing of course they find they can abide them. One is reminded of the old drawing from one's childhood of the astonished hen staring in unbelief at the little gosling she has just hatched.

More of this at another time and place. For the present, the public welcome extended on the populous and burgeoning Island to Empire State College with its format of independent study with faculty-student dialogue suggests that people sometimes do vote for new and different ways of doing things in higher education. Already the rapidity with which older institutions are meeting the challenge with comparable programs of their own, and the firmness of the grasp with which Long Island citizenry has seized the opportunities offered by the State University of New York in its Empire State College program, indicate that a thing has been done in college-level education which cannot any longer be undone. If this should turn out to be the case it might be an argument for trying new things more often and worrying about them less. Be that as it may, deepest appreciation is owed to student and faculty colleagues on the Island as elsewhere for great times spent most congenially in the evolving of educational modes. This was a drama in which all had parts to play.

Reflecting once more on the putting together of a group of papers, the second such affair in several years, one has to remark that it is a relief to have caught up with some parts of what one has wished to say. No doubt there will be other things to say; habit is strong, and that of writing gets to be, justifiably or not, an element in the processes of thought. To be sure, the general or reflective essay runs counter to the interests of the time. It is no matter. In the long view that will take care of itself. In all the arts one must work in one's own way, and trust the future.

A word of appreciation remains in connection with the metaphors around which this book is built, in the large and as focused in the concluding paper. In 1928 the poet Abbie Huston Evans of Philadelphia published *Outcrop*, a small book of poems. For more than forty years a four-line section of one of the poems has lingered singularly in mind, gathering in briefest compass much of the matrix from which a lifetime of thought derives. The correspondence need not in such a case be detailed or precise; the communication is rather a kind of resonance, so that general attitudes and matrices articulate somehow with each other. Expressions of them can be of different orders. So the thought and art of a poem are called again from the depths in reflective re-descriptions of

vii

the nature of things. Referring to this relation the poet once wrote in another place of her "wonder at the tight-knit scheme of things within which we live." The present age has tended to lose sight of commonalities and connections in its concern with separate entities. One would do well to remember that forgotten articulations may exist between instances, realities not immediately visible in obvious ways, appearing when appropriate questions are formed and left as landmarks among which and in response to which ideas may move whither they will.

—Glen Cove, Long Island, New York
September 30th, 1973

viii

Table of Contents

I The Religious Universe: A Foreshadowing

It is not uncommon in our time to expend great energies on the supposedly important task of modernizing religion with respect to natural facticity, which most often means adapting religious thought and practice to scientific views of nature. To do such a thing it must be assumed that science offers a modicum of stability, a degree of certainty in the region of the object, and a reliability of methodology, in the face of which the gossamer threads of religious assumption must blow forthwith away. The summary position of this type, applied to the history of ideas, is probably J. H. Randall's *The Role of Knowledge in Western Religion,* which concludes that the scope of factual knowledge is widening while the scope of religious ''knowledge'' as such is contracting with the movement of time in western civilization.

Not much of this is so. The stability of the sciences is strictly definitional and operational in its nature, the degree of certainty in the object an evanescent dream, and the reliability of scientific methodology no lesser and no greater than the reliability of supposedly different and supposedly less well-founded ways of knowing with which in actuality it is very nearly identical. These things have been said often enough, and many are willing to agree to them. The difficulty lies in accepting the consequences of such conclusions.

What is being pointed to here is the subjective fundament of scientific knowing, and the reluctance of contemporary man to accept its hypothetical character. Leonard Nash in *The Nature of the Natural Sciences,* among numerous others, is well aware of the subjective fundament. Yet like many more he is reluctant to live with its consequences. Not only is there a world-out-there, he observes, but there is no need to justify it, since the enormous and very obvious results of scientific effort justify it far beyond anyone's need or capacity to do so.

What happy and reassuring nonsense this is. When the nature of knowledge is constructional, assertive, creative, definitional in its nature, as it is, imagine believing that supposedly scientific knowledge

1

which is constructed in terms of operations is accounted for by the effects of those operations. One does something, and one gets a result, so that the result can be used as an explanation of the event. The whole thing is constructional effort; all of it depends on the several stages; the result is simply an endstage; to claim that the procedure of achieving is explained by the results of achieving is only to bite one's tail. It is circularity at its pleasantest and least obvious, but it is nevertheless very, very round.

Liberal Thought Adrift

American civilization is still living in large part on the philosophic bounty of Europe. It is not even Europe in the main which provides the renewals of thought on which the English-speaking world subsists, but specifically a small section of Europe, a golden triangle the apices of which lie at Copenhagen, Paris and Vienna. And even this can be narrowed still further, for Kierkegaard and Grundtvig have been dead for a hundred years. Germany continues to be a powerful source of intellectual energy; France, only slightly less so. In a curious way, however, it seems to be Vienna which dominates Western civilization in these decades. It is this relatively small region in "the heart of Europe," as Matthiessen called it years ago, pivoting on the city of the vanished Hapsburgs, which in an unending torrent pours forth the great philosophic movements which have rolled westward across Europe, England, the Atlantic, and the states and provinces of North America. If it is proper to think of Vienna as the intellectual centre of modern times, then England and America must be regarded as developers and consumers of philosophy rather than as originators or manufacturers of ideas.

How difficult it is to see these things in perspective! The United States may now be one of the most powerful nations on earth. Persons who travel in easy stages about the New England landscape or in other regions of the country, going from place to place more or less as they please even though they see themselves as driven by the pressures of job or home, may be living in the Augustan age of American civilization. America has ruled sea and sky, her influence determinative in many quarters of the globe, even in regions which intensely disliked her. Her hegemony may have been greater than the power of the British Empire in the 19th century, partly because more power and power of different

2

kinds is available in the 20th century. America should, however, be conceived of as an articulated continuation of that earlier phase of the English-speaking power, for all its differences and its new awarenesses. In a very real sense apart from the political, America has not ceased to be a region of the British Commonwealth. What Britain and America have done in the 19th and 20th centuries may some day appear more nearly as one thing.

What this means, of course, is that political events are surface waves, convenient measures, modes of passing times, undeniably interesting in their own right but only contributory to fundamental understandings. If at most they constitute a legitimate form of understanding having its own disciplines and methodology, there will be some value in spending time on them. If one is attending to the grounds of things, however, the focus has to be on the assumptions involved in particular political events, and so one is forever cast back into the realms of reflective thought.

Consider for a moment the welter of thought systems which the English-speaking world has received in recent times from the German-speaking world: idealism, relativity, Freudianism, Marxism, positivism, philosophical analysis, phenomenology, and some group process theories; if one wishes to distinguish German and Danish, then existentialism may have been Danish; otherwise, as Maritain observes, it is German, French, and Italian. It would be interesting to know whether the roots of social democratic thought stem at all from the German-speaking realm. Notice that liberal religion itself, now so perversely unsure of its own strong roots, also took its rise in part in Transylvania, close to the golden triangle of European thought.

It cannot be said that a culture which produces new ideas is always the culture which welcomes them. Not infrequently Holland, England and America have played host to ideas which have been rejected by their cultures of origin. But unwise cultures which originated ideas and then rejected them have after all had the intellective energy to inundate the Western world over and over again in a magnificent assertion of the majesty of thought and of its fundamental role in the adventure of human development in the West. Nor need it be puzzling that reflective thought and political thought are frequently disjuncted. Pools of ideas and energies tend to be localized, so that larger significances of one or the other go unperceived.

3

A consequence of this is that the political errors and even the moral crimes of the German-speaking realm must probably be seen in a new perspective. The shame, the tragedy, of political Nazism is inscribed forever in the history of Europe. But the chances are that what it represented is in a sense more basic than political superficiality could disclose. Obscured by social perversions and brutalities may have been the irresistible drive toward unification of the peoples of Europe, that same region of continental civilization which constitutes the geographic seedbed of Western thought. Perhaps not so strangely, it was Otto Lyding, Unitarian minister in the classic mold, German by birth, a grim proponent of democracy, who remarked precisely this in the 1930's. "The unification of Europe has to come," he said, as he stared out the diamond-paned windows of his New Hampshire study; "it is just too bad that it has to come in this way." Well, it did not come in the Nazi way; the cost in human suffering was too great, the moral injury to society too painful. So cruel an effort could but destroy itself. Unification will come, however, and again when it does come Germany re-born and reconstituted may well be in the forefront of it. Is it too harsh to consider that the excrescence of Nazism may really have been another in the halting efforts which Western civilization has made toward a unification of cultural groups geographically closest to each other, a false step, an unacceptable and hateful step because of its particular assumptions and methods, yet with its meanings clearly pointing in the direction of the gathering of peoples, steps that civilization in the course of time and in more congenial modes cannot help but take?

Philosophic movements like these are simply systematic positions involving theories of the real, divided regrettably into theories of nature and theories of the self or human nature. Liberal religious thought partakes of similar systematic forms. Questions will turn on the source of the liberal forms and on any individual differences among them.

Liberal religious thought has been over-responsive to scientific theories of nature, but this condition would not have derived from European positivism. More probably it stemmed from 18th century empiricism reinforced by 19th century English and American naturalisms. One may wonder whether the relative rootlessness of these naturalisms may have contributed to a certain incapacity to deal with reality in depth, a tendency to be content with surface phenomena, and with techniques of managing phenomena which remain closely moored

4

to their surfaces. In terms of general ideas, liberal thought has been adrift in America for most of the 20th century. It has forgotten that its genius does not lie in 17th-18th century contemplation of nature—a system of understanding not very distinctive at best. The universe as knowable had been a mediaeval idea and there was nothing new in the notion that knowledge of it could be achieved. It has been rather that liberal thought adopted a direction of address to nature and a vehicle of communication with nature which led toward reliance upon limited entities of nature directly known, as in empirical awareness of the larger scale physico-chemical phenomena. It has tended to specialize itself down toward smaller and smaller points of reference, until the world it was willing to reflect consisted only of bright points glancing off the revolving sides of physico-chemical minutiae. At this level of perception or apperception its way of knowing inevitably went out of focus without its being aware of the implications of its predicament.

The Genius of Liberal Thought

The genius of liberal religious thought in America, so far as the Unitarian part of the tradition was concerned, lay in 19th century rational transcendentalism, in rational romanticism, if we like, which asserted the capacity of the individual to rise above himself and his environment, eventually enabling him to recognize that man could and did create the world in which he lived, using the term ''world'' to refer to his own immediate world, brought forward out of the groundworld. This is the great gift of American liberal thought at its best, more poignantly and more personally developed, more immediately gathered about the nucleus of each individual life than was or would have been possible in Europe apart from England and perhaps Holland. This is the genius which American liberal thought has allowed itself to forget.

Liberal religion does not now have a theory of human nature at all, unless a simplified physico-chemical notion derived from naturalistic origins or a semi-religious cloud of unknowing derived from Judaeo-Freudian sources can be said to provide one. Both of these types of theory represent reductionist patterns by which a distinctive individuality or a precise metaphysics of human nature can be escaped through re-description in terms of other disciplines.

Liberal religious education still maintains a progressive approach implied in which is a residual romanticism expressed in confidence that

5

the individual can learn and be effective. Trust in the individual is then one of its assumptions. Notice, however, that 20th-century progressive education along with pragmatism has adopted a poor relation of the natural sciences, to wit, physico-social environmentalism, and permitted it to abstract from itself any romantic and rational content. Thus liberalism has been left aligned with determinist philosophies. Environmentalism has seen human nature as creature of its surroundings. In the education of the child the conditions of learning were in theory varied to produce a desired result. Where adult originality comes from to vary the environment in ways that are educational is less clear. A philosophy of originality is missing. Change is ascribed to random physical and social motions amid selective forces and circumstances.

Liberal religious thought has the same reflective problem that other philosophies have, and it has to resolve the problems in the same way. It has to decide what man is, what the world is, and what the relation is between the two. Presumably in the 19th century conditions of inheritance from the 18th century and conditions of origination of new ideas happened to be just right for the development of a theory of human nature which was highly effective for the settings in which it was operative. Rational-and-romantic-man was a concept of great promise, close perhaps to a creation of genius. But the notion declined from neglect. Liberal thought has made a practice of leaving to traditional scholars or to semi-independent professionals (as Spinoza in an earlier time) the working out of comprehensive and systematic philosophies. Why this has been so is hard to say. The large questions necessary to the philosophic enterprise have simply not been asked among liberal philosophers. It may mean that liberal interest has been directed to social or practical issues rather than to reflective questions, leaving the latter so to speak as space unoccupied. Inevitably the work of reflection would get itself done, for it is a major and recurrent interest of the human mind to do it. Neglect by liberal thought has simply meant that reflective philosophizing would be accomplished elsewhere, in other viewpoints and disciplines, with the added consequence that it would increasingly become the custom for interested persons to look away from liberal thought to find it. What then has happened is that the liberal view of man has been pre-empted by deterministic or scientific views of man, which is to say, by views of human nature as creature of a universe defined as physical or social.

6

There are two things to be said about this, as usual. The first is that the supposedly firm scientific view of man will not last, as we already know from the existential and phenomenological inroads made upon its assumptions, and therefore that liberal thought will be left sitting in mid-air. The second is that the general ideas of liberal thought are in demand. Development of a religious view of human nature as recommended in this sketch requires intellective ski-steps anyway, that is, long asseverational strides taken in particular directions because clearly the situation is at hand to require them. A comparable reason was given by the bee-keeper of New Zealand for his having gone to the trouble of conquering Mount Everest. It was there to do. Ideas, too, are there, and they make demands on men. Since such projects tend not to be philosophically planned the haphazard assertions which do get made often lead institutions or positions first in one direction and then in another, often omitting the systematic asking of prime questions which would be imperative for the development of broad prehensions.

For present purposes the crucial concern is the redefinition of human nature and the relation of the self to the object. In this fundamental realm liberal religious thought, if it wishes to work with serious reflective questions, must have the courage to reassert its classic heritage, producing the general ideas necessary in metaphysics, to the extent of denying even its present positions if that were called for. Should that occur, perhaps a philosophical negativism could become affirmation. There might then be some gain over the profound philosophic silence to which liberalism is otherwise accustomed.

It makes little difference where one begins—whether with the reality of the universe, the nature of man, or the theory of knowing. Each involves the others, and each depends on the others. The parts to follow make up simply the taking of a general stance, hopefully on sufficient ground, in the belief that this is an aspect of reflection seriously demanded by the times. Everyone is aware of the common view that systematic thought is out-moded and to be discarded in the interest of cultivation of aspects of restricted disciplines, as for example, language, logic, mathematical reasoning, and other forms of analysis. In undertaking the present effort this view is in turn denied, and in its place an assertion is made that systematic thought is indeed called for, even that it is returning anyway whether one agrees with the change or not.

7

Rational-and-Romantic Man

Rational-and-romantic-man is to be conceived of as a thinking and deciding being, full of the capacities of intellect and art, moved by emotion but not commanded by it, subsuming physico-chemical constructs but not at all their victim or their creature, selector and organizer of his universe—a particular universe drawn from the abyss of possibility; engaged with phenomena but aware of the ground of being, and able to plunge to its depths; a moral, caring being, recognizing good and evil, unwilling to discard the moral categories or to reduce them to other dimensions; able to transcend himself and his environment, to rise to challenge, especially to challenges he sets himself; presuming with fair confidence that his apperceptions of reality achieved by the several knowing operations reflect actuality and real things, and not illusions, so that the world can be known and the ways of knowing peculiar to the self can articulate effectively with the ranges of the universe.

In turn, the universe with which human nature remains or comes in touch can be known so to speak by extrapolation from the equipments of the self. It can be known obviously by sensory selection, that most limited of the knowing dimensions, which can be conceived of as projective operation rather than as passive reception. It can be known more fundamentally in a rational dimension through the operation of reason, the faculty of rational thought. And it can be known intuitively, which suggests a rational-spiritual dimension of reality subsisting in its own right. It is not necessary to delineate sharp separations between these dimensions of understanding or the realities toward which they move. It is enough to observe that they represent phenomenological superstrates for which metaphysical grounds can be assumed. In remarking on these aspects of the real one obviously does not forget the efforts of the Freudian half-century to understand reality in strictly emotional terms. If this powerful current of interest is omitted here it is because it has not appeared that the effort to reflect emotionality in cognitive terms has ever been very successful. This dimension does indeed appear to be one which reduces to other modes of understanding, even granting the large influence it can wield from time to time in particular sets of circumstances.

Of Mind and Its Knowing

A conceptual theory of knowing appears to present the most useful picture of the subject-object relation. By this is meant a description of the individual as instrument, and of the several knowing means as sub-instruments or derivative instruments, so that the relation of subject and object is an instrumental or selective relation of an active kind, choosing, defining, even in a proper if special sense creating, the universe of reference. In this view the knowing relation is a vigorous, moving relation, not a passive receptivity; in it the content of knowledge is a constructed content; it is not detached from the real; it is not a pure projection, for there is an objective, continuative reality articulated with the self. It is rather the form of the knowing of the self. Given the heavily rational content of the self the knowing relation can be conceived of as itself conceptual in nature, but the weight and reality of the realm of the conceptual must also be allowed. It is intended to leave the individual self in a determinative, formative position, in command of more than he knows, in a conscious sense.

A case could perhaps be made for the notion that the individual actually decides a great many more things in his own life than we commonly allow in the determinist fashion of the day; it may be worth some thought that more frequently than is suspected the individual may decide the moment and circumstances of his own death, quite apart from anything ordinarily referred to under the heading of suicide; this is to say, the individual may well decide, in long range terms and by innumerable decisions, the circumstances and moment of his demise. That such things seem difficult to conceive in these terms may be the consequence of fashion in outlook rather than of any reliable correlary of some inescapable theory of perception in the empiricist cluster.

We have said that psychology and metaphysics necessarily assert each other, in the sense that a view of human nature entails a certain kind of world in which it exists, and conversely, that a certain kind of world has obvious implications for the nature of life with which it is functional. The connection between these two facets of the real is of course the dimension of awareness, some part of which is traditionally theory of knowledge, variously defined.

In the effort to develop a system representative of the periodic human interest in systems which will also apply in the realm of liberal

9

thought, where is a start to be made? It can be made in any of the three parts of a system—the subject, the object, or the epistemological connection—and the question of where a particular system should begin is in the present judgment a function of temperamental concern. The point of major concern or interest in a system is not necessarily its first principle; the systems of Newton and Descartes have been given as examples, their points of primary interest not coinciding with their notions of ultimate responsibility. The existentialist systems—using the term deliberately, as the existentialists would hardly care for it—each begin with a psychology, and their psychologies remain their major foci. Positivist and analytic systems hinge first around methodology and then around content, while their psychologies trail weakly in the rear. Empiricist and naturalistic systems center their primary attention on an objective universe, adapting an acceptable method to a notion of objective existence and furnishing a small corner of the cupboard with living dolls somehow constructed from similar materials.

This kind of thing goes on all the time, subject to the fashions of philosophy and to the swings of reflective evolution. It is probable that the times are now ready for a major description of the movements of ideas, as distinct from the construction of particular philosophies of history—which of course men do more or less anyway. It seems likely that enough is now known of the ecology of idea-systems so that their common movements would be predictable, as for example in some such pattern as: romanticism — to naturalism — to positivism — to — existentialism — to — phenomenalism — to — romantic rationalism. Similarly the times should be right for a patterning of intrasystemology, which is to say, for the intra-locutions of parts and aspects of particular systems, metaphysical, epistemological, and psychological. It ought not to be supposed that predictability of philosophic development will ever be complete; there is typically an element of hindsight in such patterning. But even approximate predictability should be interesting and perhaps useful at least in suggesting appropriate lines of reflective effort.

Thus it is indicated that there is no single acceptable rule on how to begin the philosophic or systematic effort. The thing to do is simply to begin. Begin where? Begin where it is interesting to begin, at the point of one's greatest concern. This is what systems do, as noted in their recurrent characteristics. If there is no one right way of doing this, it follows that any system may be as valid as any other system as long as it is genuine in intent and effective in its accounting for ranges of data. Acceptability of a system will hinge in some part around its compatibility with other systems, that is, around the commonalities it holds with comparable systems, or in plain language, its degree of fashion. Whether validity and acceptability of systems constitute quite the same thing may remain an open question.

Consider for a moment how this kind of systemic activity might develop in a cluster of reflective individuals. Granted the immense significance of choice and decision on the part of the individual, granted his capacity, granted his rational-and-romantic character, a group of reflective persons becomes one of the most powerful assemblies in Western civilization. It is made up of specialists in reflective studies, aware of the enormous influences of ground-systems and acquainted with the ways in which they work. Furthermore it is a membership which, granted the premises just noted, represents an unlimited capacity for origination of thought, for initiation of movement in the long continuum of thought and act, and, if one may venture to remark it, which is constricted only by possible self-limitation, by any existing concern that the world should be adapted to rather than be made or constructed. In short, the power of such a group is limited only by its own prior judgment as to the limits of that power. If it thinks it is relatively free of artificial and external limits it is in fact relatively free of them; if it thinks it has little or no freedom of motion within the rigid bands of social or natural process, then it is in fact without freedom to just that extent. Sometimes it is difficult to grasp the enormous power the individual person holds, or, to put it a different way, it is difficult not to believe that individual man is a minor down-post in a universe of forces unbelievably large, of the vast and multi-faceted nature of which contemporary civilization is only now becoming aware.

It is the present conviction that such a semi-popular self-defeatism, spawn of a misdirected approach to philosophic systeming, is straightforwardly an error, to be replaced by confidence in the nature of rational-and-romantic-man settled in a universe which meets the manyed outreach of the self at points without number, a web of actual and potential existence the function of which is to respond selectively and with good effect to the movements of human aspiration.

11

Louis Craig Cornish used to tell an amusing tale of how he raised the money to build the first married graduate students' apartments at Harvard. He told it on himself, and the point was the same. It has to do with the formative nature of individual decision and involvement. Some of the alumni arranged a luncheon for him in New York attended by influential business leaders, lawyers, and trustees. The way Dr. Cornish told this story gave the impression that he felt considerably out of his depth in such company; but he was a good storyteller and this would have been just atmosphere. Anyway, after the luncheon at which nobody said a word about why they were all there, although of course everyone knew all about it, it began to be time to go back to the financial canyons. So someone said something about the purpose of the proposed housing at Harvard, and one of the tycoons turned to Dr. Cornish and asked how much money he wanted. At this point, said Dr. Cornish in recounting the affair, his mind became immobile. All the money in New York was at his fingertips—his mind refused to take account of the possibilities. At last he blurted out the largest figure he could think of in the stress of the moment: ''Three hundred and fifty thousand dollars!'' He could have used three times that amount, he said later, but he simply couldn't conceive of a figure any higher than that. ''Well,'' said the tycoon, turning back to the departing guests and going around the table, ''I'll take fifty thousand, you take fifty thousand, . . .''—and in less than two minutes the three hundred and fifty thousand dollars had been subscribed, the busy wheels had left, a limited objective had been achieved—and the opportunity for a greater thing was gone for years to come.

Reason and Myth

Since the universe of rational-and-romantic-man is known in part through the medium of equipments of the self it may be useful to refer to the component of rationality. What again are we to understand by the rational, by reason? By this it is intended to suggest the self-moving capacity of thought, the Capacity to assess, to judge, to discriminate, to construct, to engage its counterparts in the environing, beckoning universe. It is intended to suggest that there is a continuative engagement of self and object which is of the order of thought or mind, that this order is real and fundamental, and that to attempt to understand the universe without it is to lose oneself among irrelevant byways. Systems which attempt to specificate this order of relation, such as Alfred North Whitehead's, invariably develop problems of their own, no doubt because of the limitations of conceptual operation even in the broadest sense. Concessions have to be made in order to get them to work; perhaps indeed such systems never do work perfectly. They draw together such diverse elements that the mediating construction necessary to articulation of their parts produces a fractioning tension. The principle of concretion is difficult to entertain as an enduring, vivid prehension. Yet the effort to develop systems in this dimension recurs constantly, and for good cause; the order of rational understanding is at the very least one of the major modes in which reality is comprehended.

Reason was a strong word still when Earl Morse Wilbur was writing his monumental history of Unitarianism. It is as if the content of the word had been gradually pumped out, leaving a small logico-mediative function applicable in the interstices of scientific observational process. The decline of reason was probably also part of the anti-facultism which arose after MacDougall in psychology, as well as part of the emphasis on exclusively scientific observation in other studies in accordance with which reality was to be described within increasingly restricted frames of reference. The ground of the decline of reason is of course in the first instance the primary metaphysical decision as to what is real and in consequence what can be accepted as valid human existence. If reason does not exist, or exists merely as a minor bit of adjustive neurological machinery, like the couplers on an old-fashioned train of cars, then essences and universals, Ideas and Forms, Abstract and General Realities, also do not exist. At least there is no need to be concerned about them. The converse would likewise hold, if one preferred temperamentally to begin with the world ''out there''; if general reality does not exist or can never be known, clearly there is little ground for assuming the validity of a reasoning faculty which will never have anything to do other than the minor coupling and uncoupling of freight cars.

The combined and interactive relation of reason and general reality then asserts that essence and universal are real, and are known by a reason within the self which is also real. Forthwith empiricisms go by the board. There are no longer two categories of semi-awareness, the

13

region of certainty on one hand, defined by scientific operations and depending on operational confirmability, its content defined as "knowledge," and on the other hand another region of declining certainty, perhaps in recent times most commonly characterized by felt-valuation, emotional dedication to values of conduct. Randall's position previously remarked is therefore outmoded and cannot further reflect what is conceived to be the history of Western thought.

Reason as constructional, partaking of the nature of definition, of selection, therefore of creation, takes as its objective the establishment of understandable pattern. The pattern can never be complete or fully comprehensive. Reason is individual as well as general; it chooses and declines. Other instances of rationality do likewise, but differently. The resulting pattern is always the relatively thin and partial skin of something. Reality, including the ranges of possibility, extends unreachably and immeasurably beyond the graspable pattern. Logical lines dividing and contrasting the possible and the actual, the potential and the real, seem of little use.

What then is myth? If myth is symbolic reality, or in a more inclusive rendering, symbolic truth, is it not a fine distinction between that and the patterns of the real established by rational process? Language is always confining; to escape it is to write poetry and to loosen the connections of language with its points of reference, to call upon affect for illumination and enrichment of understanding. To erect into a story or personalized form a cosmological theory not otherwise describable is common enough in cultural history. Myths in this sense have been enthusiastically attacked as misleading by virtue of their allegorical or semi-representational characteristics. It is perhaps too easy to be literal about myths as symbolic stories. But is there any substantial difference between this type of semi-story representing a ground-notion of the origin or meaning of human existence and the tentative theoretical constructions around the nature of the physical universe? Operational thought suggests that there is little difference. The role of the individual observer is too much a part of the observational process for the results to be genuinely objective. Construction is an element in natural knowledge. In the natural and social sciences the individual in some part defines and creates his environment.

Myth is used today as one of those convenient escape routes by which the determined empiricist disposes of regions of awareness which

14

cannot be otherwise explained. Myth is somehow respectable; it can maintain itself as a cultural study without requiring allegiance of any other kind. Perversely, the contra-empiricist whether existentialist, intuitionist, or related viewpoint, is also happy about myth. Here myth serves as a welcome solvent of the positivist threat. It tends to be anti-structural, personalized, dramatic, sometimes colorful, humanly interesting—and welcoming. It may serve the same function as the Tolkien . . . *Ring* novels of the mid-1960's among the college generations—it may offer an ersatz theory of the real at a time when naturalistic and positivist theories seem lifeless and cold. If the present approach is supportable it may suggest with entire consistency that there is no accounting for tastes. In this view tastes must account for themselves, and they do.

The myths of the past, says Campbell, are the masks of God, their functions being to reconcile the conscious mind to the great mystery of existence, to interpret totally by way of image, and to enforce a moral order upon the individual. Perversely again the contra-mythologist or positivist who is busy quantifying the procedurally confirmable dimensions of the real has his own means of fulfilling these same functions. He defines consciousness in the first instance so that it need not know its fate, rather so that it articulates neatly with the environment; he has a naturalistic cosmogony to provide a compelling imagery; and he expects sensible man to conform to physical nature. So who is really scientific and who is in thrall to myth? Is it so simple to distinguish?

The Religious Universe of Rational-and-Romantic-Man

Rational-and-romantic-man, it is contended, is the actual liberal religious construct on human nature, although it is a view not often seen nowadays in liberal religious circles. It follows that the universe of selective response for rational-and-romantic-man is a religious universe, purposive, intelligent and moral, in a sense planned yet subject to imperfection, full with possibility and at the same time slow of movement, struck through with numberless modes of understanding and activity the inexhaustible and unbelievably complex involutions of which suggest futures so unlike the past as to be beyond imagining. In this perspective apparent philosophic confusions of the present day should be considered merely as stages of lessening disarray.

Rational-and-romantic-man is then to be described in operational terms, but with the idea of operation vastly expanded beyond Bridgman's original notion of it, allowing for what contemporary scientific thought now knows to be the case, that is, the formative entrance of the observer into the knowing procedure and result; and in still further addition, broadening the idea of operation to include every kind of human awareness and expression such as the forms of art, social decision, or emotional relation. It is conceived that particular universes, drawn from the great ground-universe, are to be defined in these broad and deep operational terms; and the nature of awareness in this mode of understanding is to be termed conceptual—in a new, comprehensive, and profound sense of that notion, less the older, strictly reasoning sense than in a new mode which registers the inexhaustible and manifold dimensions of human understanding and expression, that is, of decisional relation.

To define the characteristics of the universe of rational-and-romantic-man the first and major step is to comply with Whitehead's request to rid the mind of the super-annuated notion of nature bifurcated. The world of rational-and-romantic-man is not a Whiteheadian system, but Whitehead was right about drawing together the divided nature of modern times. Most if not all of the religious and other orientational problems of modern times derive from this once-necessary error in the evolution of Western thought. Whereas it first served to free the sciences from intellectual restrictions of other modes of thought, so pervasive and so subtle have been its influences and so completely has the contemporary world-view become its creature that it is now extremely difficult for the individual to make the necessary change. It is an outstanding attribute of world-views that their ground-assumptions and general ideas become so closely interwoven with their cultures and have so very much to do with forming them that it is difficult if not impossible to make operational allowance for their influence and then to make changes in them. Yet they are actively formative and not merely receptive or consequential, and it is of utmost importance to make changes in them. This is why the work of Lovejoy, Henry Osborn Taylor, Whitehead in one of his aspects, and of other historians of ideas is of such intense interest; they were able to point out in connection with certain ages of Western civilization the assumptions so general that the people of those times took them almost wholly for granted and

16

therefore rarely wrote them down or even mentioned them. The very slight but profound change in the general assumptions of the present time, from a bifurcated nature to a unified nature, is precisely the kind of change which has to be made if the general situation of rational-and-romantic-man is to be understood. The old bifurcation of nature which has served Western man so brilliantly in improving the management of nature, especially in its hither reaches, is now outdated except within its own limited sphere of restricted physico-chemical constructionism.

This is then the major prerequisite of the present effort and at the same time the most difficult condition to fulfill. Possibly it can be enabled only through meditative reflection at intervals over long periods of time. The consequence of achieving the necessary change in the ground-notions of modern times should leave standing in articulated grandeur the monolithic universe struck through with numberless modes of meaning, each new dimension contributing to the significance of the whole.

What is it that makes this universe religious—which is to ask, what makes its meanings significant in religious rather than in secular terms? Given ideas sufficiently general it could not be otherwise. The bents of human understanding and the nature of generalizing intellection require it. Meaningless process on general levels does not obtain in this universe. To suggest it has been a happy sophistry, useful for improving materiality by identification of factors and procedures in physico-chemical plumbery, but not useful as ground for general theory.

For purposes of general theory it is necessary to ask general questions. This is the entire key to the matter. There is no more powerful weapon in the arsenals of Western man than that of the question-posed. It is an infinitely more formidable instrument than that of the position-stated, because it is able—assuming it is applicable—to throw into operation the capacities of the question-posers, who may be large in number, in addition to possible capacities of position-takers which might be addressed to the problem through their strongest assertions. The additional difference is that in the case of the question-posed, the precise answer is not determined; it is open-ended. The question-posed can be set up in a great variety of forms and will be answered in a great variety of ways. A consequence of their posing is the focusing of vast energies into the region of the questions. Definition of the universe as religious does assume that the use of the question-posed has an immense positive value and that it is a good and useful thing to handle issues of general theory in an open-ended form to enable a wide variety of potential solutions.

Assuming the nature of rational-and-romantic-man, and assuming the conceptual and operational nature of knowing in its possible expressions, the general question-posed compels a general answer. One may not conclude what answer; but it is clear that the answer must be general, and that it must be of an order of generality comparable to the generality of the question.

A religious universe is marked by the largest and most general meanings; it is shaped by purpose, albeit also by mystery, for it is in the nature of great questions that the materials for answers are not ready to hand. Indeed, they require ranges of awareness outside normal human capacity to provide; the constructs of myth, made up of imaginative cantilevers of experience and history projected backwards into antiquity, are one type of effort to communicate in realms of general meaning. To assert that the universe is describable as religious is to deny the propriety (in the longest run) of generalizing on restricted ranges of data. Everybody does it; every philosophy, including the present one, is an instance of it. But then, every philosophy, including the present one, is incomplete and therefore wrong. Every philosophy cries out for expansion and further generalization. Bearing in mind the comprehensiveness of conceptual epistemology, there is really only a single fundamental metaphysical dimension—that of lesser or greater completeness, lesser or greater generality. The religious realm is the realm of the greatest possible completeness and generality. The secular realm is that of the lesser, the realm of particularity. Convenience inheres in the lesser; man must live in some part in restricted ranges of theory and practice. Plumbing and moon-rockets do count for something. But human nature constantly surprises. It should be happy in restricted realms, but it is not. It revolts, existentially, phenomenologically, artistically; it bats around for a time in the by-ways of semi-emotional speculation. Inevitably in the course of time the great questions emerge again.

There is no dimension of significance beyond the strictly utilitarian, physico-chemical orders which is not best understood in large and general terms. Rational-and-romantic-man is, so to speak,

18

designed to move toward greater generalism, for he is an inveterate and unyielding searcher after great meanings. He cannot refrain in the long run from asking great questions; he can only delay doing so for a while. In a figurative sense he can preoccupy himself for periods of time along the Broadways and the Boardwalks of limited significance. He can even soberly advance the notion from time to time that issues of general significance are intellectual booby-traps which ought to be ignored in the interest of doing smaller and more precise things and doing them better. But he cannot deny his questioning nature for very long. If one is dissatisfied with a philosophy of the moment, as with a transplanted European viewpoint which delights to dismiss as meaningless the general question-posed because it deals with terms which are not scientifically confirmable, the recourse is not unlike that of the person dissatisfied with New England weather: one need only wait. The human drive to question will soon take care of it.

In movements of reflective thought changes in surface phenomena result from the operation of constant forces beneath the surface, forces more reliable and more constant even than the so-called atmospheric jet-streams which are said to be responsible for North American climate. The latter may have only relative reliability and may alter in cycles of several years' duration, producing periodic variations in this region or that. Currents in reflective thought may not allow for changes of that kind. The more accurate description of change in the movement of ideas may be that of action or inaction, of operation and neglect. Reflective activity calls for greater generalism; reflective restraint or limitation entails particularism. Granted the religious universe of which the chief inhabitant is rational-and-romantic-man, and granted the unidimensionality of conceptual knowing, the phenomena of philosophic cross- and counter-currents may be best accounted for by the notion of reflection withheld. The major reflective interest of men is the urge to know, in the most general sense of that idea. It is possible for the drive toward knowing to be suspended while people engage in busy-work; it is not possible to alter the metaphysical order of reflection if reflection is genuinely taking place. In other words, logical positivism and related schools are what happens when the great questions of existence are simply not posed. In the resulting vacuum questions of restricted range and import are put forward, having a variety of natural, social, and

19

personal uses, real and valid uses, to be sure, adding to ranges of awareness and spheres of control, but uses limited and limiting.

However, in time the major characteristic of human nature reasserts itself. When it does, the religious nature of rational-and-romantic-man drives once more through the welter of things and of process. An expansional movement of this kind may be a mark of the latening 20th century in Western thought.

II Christianity as Hypothesis

Ecumenism is having the effect of raising religious questions in new perspectives. Religious strife in earlier times in the West has taken the form of oppositions among positive beliefs and has followed, when overt hostilities resulted, from the inability of one set of beliefs to tolerate another. Since the main stem of Catholic Christianity has provided the vehicle of religious understanding in Western thought misunderstandings have most commonly obtained between it and its offspring, so to speak, the oppositional sects which broke off from it at various points. Particularly at issue have been those ideas which seemed to the parent position to threaten its standing fundamentally, as for example the assertion by a sect that it possessed direct access to religious truth and therefore by implication that it did not need the Catholic stem as vehicle and interpreter of Christianity. Western religions have tended to take positions rather than to ask questions; the principles of Christianity have tended to be established in didactic forms, respect for which was enjoined; and on the whole the religious complex of Western civilization was set up in Christian terms such that communication more or less had to be in these forms, certainly so if it was to be acceptable within the enveloping church or pervasive Christian society.

The issue now arises as to whether religious positions ought not to be understood as hypotheses rather than as assertive certainties. The sophistication of reflective thought has developed to an extent which may permit religious standings to be cast in hypothetical forms without losing any of their traditional dignity and value. By this means the difficulty can be avoided which has beset Western religious thought for several centuries whereby it has been in appearance repeatedly backed from corner to corner by what was understood—quite wrongly, of course—to be the steady advance of secular knowledge. Philosophic sophistication has taught us many things, among them the seemingly obvious fact that there is no such thing as a fact, and that scientism is a reflective and semi-religious cult like any other such cult. This is not in the least to detract from the enormous and very real progress which science as a discipline has contributed to the development of the West; the recently discharged hospital patient has only to recall his illness to know the closeness of articulation between evidence and treatment. The student of nature can with equal facility call up evidential material which can be as readily correlated with consequential effects by means of an appropriate disciplinary logic. But it is one thing to recognize the articulation between datum and consequence, and quite another to assert that very much is known about either the datum or the consequence or even about the logic which obtains between them. In a philosophic sense, Western science is as far at sea as any religio-philosophic system that was ever invented, even in the remotest antiquity.

It simply does not do to dispense with religious knowledge. Religion does indeed contain knowledge; the religious process is a process of knowing and of understanding, and the object of religious knowing is as metaphysically objective and as real as the ranges of data to which the natural sciences are applied.

What then is knowledge? As has been indicated from time to time, thereby hangs a considerable philosophic tale. Knowledge is to be understood for present purposes as being of the nature of conceptualization of materials into forms, such that they become usable in themselves, understandable in relation to other such forms, and articulatable into systems. This is to say, knowledge of any sort, scientific or religious, historical, individual, or whatever, is of the same order; it is conceptual in its nature, not perceptual, not representational except in qualified part, and it is rational as distinct from empirical. It follows that the knowing self is heavily involved in its processes of awareness. Active knowledge does not exist without such involvement, although the standing of objective records such as those of history need not be regarded as impaired in this view. Conceptualization is the fundament of knowing, and this principle applies in all fields of awareness.

Christianity and its daughter houses are on the same basis of knowing and understanding. Traditional Christianity and liberal religion need have no disagreement as to the nature of knowing. They need only to recognize that they have slightly different extrapolative forms in which are cast those matters which each wishes to regard as being certainly known. The central message of Christianity is that man, having fallen from grace through his own sin as predestined, is potentially redeemed by the sacrifice of Christ who ascended the cross for his sake and took upon Himself the sins of men, offering in their place belief in Himself as Son of God and means of salvation. Various mutations on this theme have been offered by certain of the sects, common elements of which are examinable together with relatively minor divergences. Christianity has traditionally offered a variety of modes of understanding, primarily and fundamentally revelation understood as immediate and final transference of certainty from the Ultimate to lesser beings without use of intermediate modes of comprehension such as rational understanding, numerous mystical approaches to certainty, and on the simplest level, sensory awarenesses by physical means. Revelation and mystical understanding have a certain family resemblance, but they are not to be understood as identical. Revelation must be comprehended in traditional terms as ultimate cognition initiated from and by Divinity and received by man under special conditions and at rare intervals between which he is responsible for striving to understand by rational means, supplemented by mystical means, as much of the depths of revelation as he can. In recognition of the weight which Western religious thought has ascribed to revelation it must be granted status as a means of knowing along with the other more common modes which are more readily available to individual persons.

Hand in hand with revelation goes the Bible conceived of as the Word of God, and History as the working out of the Will of God. Judaism and Christianity have understood these two concepts in somewhat different perspectives, but even with different emphases they have continued to be comparable and interchangeable at need.

There remains central in Christianity the peculiar problem of religion as personal drama. The Christian story is properly understood in one sense as personal drama, and it seems undeniable that a great deal of its enormous persuasiveness and power in Western civilization have derived from its capacity to appeal to individual humans as personal drama. It is as if Western man has been driven once again to recognize that his greatest interest can be most conveniently cast in dramatic personal or human terms, such that issues and principles can be understood less in their rational forms, which undoubtedly obtain within them, than in dramatic and appealing human forms which can perhaps be understood by a wider range of human abilities. It is enough for present purposes to recognize this compelling aspect of Christianity, but if Christianity is to be understood even in brief compass the element of personal drama as the fundamental form in which the Christian message is to be understood may not be omitted.

Whatever suggestion is to be made concerning the understanding of Christianity as hypothesis or potential question, these elements must be taken into account. Revelation, the Bible, History as the Will of God, and Christianity understood as personal drama, comprise major facets of the Christian complex to which the notion of hypothesis must be applicable if it is to stand examination.

Certain general comments can be made at this point concerning the flexibility of understanding in whatever religious tradition it appears. It is probably true that understanding can be set up in terms of nearly any period of drama and history if the range of history selected contains the proper elements in large proportion. This is to say, there is excellent reason why the Bible should be understood as the Word of God, and one of the very best reasons is that it contains such an enormous mass of human experience of highly diverse kinds, such as a wealth of insight, and so many penetrating personalities, that sensible patterns could after all hardly escape emerging from it whether or not the hand of the Lord were said to have stamped it. If other such collections of human experience could be amassed in such small compass, covering such long histories expressed at comparable levels of artistic achievement, it would be fair to regard these also as Bibles in their turn. The Latter Day Saints may have constructed such a Book; various non-Western religious literatures have been described as comparable. The elements necessary in considerable proportion for a collection of literature to be regarded as semi-Biblical are not difficult to identify. It will be necessary to have in such material (1) reference points outside the realms of the subject selves, (2) immediacy and relevance of periodic communication between the points of reference and the subject selves, (3) human lives and situations, the materials of existence, in enormous profusion and complexity, and (4) the potential or very wide generalization of insight and implication.

One method of managing knowledge which has previously been lacking in the consideration of religious systems in the history of Western thought is comprised in the electronic computer, the possibilities of which apparently lend themselves to the enablement of religious understanding among other systems of understanding. It is not in the least bizarre that this is so, since if the nature of knowledge is understood to be conceptual, the computer would have been built by the same instrumentality as Biblical literature and ought to be applicable to it. There should indeed be some reasonable relations possible between them, as has turned out to be the case. It should perhaps be said again, lest mischief be suspected, that these observations are not in any wise to be understood as impairing the standing of revelation, reason, mysticism, or other major elements in the history of Western Christianity.

In this view, to be blunt about it, Christianity is to be understood as true. It is true in the genuine and general sense that a system comprising what Christianity does comprise has of necessity to partake of truth. An assumption is made here that a ground-reality underlies multiple expressions of the real, and that it can emerge in several if not numerous forms. This is to say, truth is hypothetical in its nature and therefore Christianity can be said to be hypothetical in its nature. The opposite of Christianity may also be true, for the same reasons. This is intended to suggest that within some broad valuational frame of reference a number of major formal expressions of the real are possible, and that in the course of time relations and articulations may become evident among them. It is not necessary to understand this comment in the ethical dimension, such that good and evil systems have equal truth-properties. The comment is rather metaphysical and epistemological. Nevertheless it is undeniable that articulation exists between metaphysics and ethics, and a moment's reflection on some of the historic events of our own time, such as the Buchenwald-Belsen complex in Germany in the 1930's and '40's, will suggest that it is a fine line, if any at all, between ethics and metaphysics. It may be ethically valid to say that Christianity is true, and that the opposite of Christianity is also true, understanding truth in this sense to involve ethics as well as metaphysics and epistemology. The point is not crucial for present purposes.

Truth is then to be conceived of as constructional in its nature. Discovery and creativity are essentially the same. If this is so both for Christianity and for the opposites of Christianity, then Christianity partakes of the nature of hypothesis and can be considered and respected as tentative, as questioning, as assertive within limited ranges, and at long last, to be susceptible of formulation in terms of questions as distinct from eternal principles. Hypothesis can be understood as a question in the form of a tentative statement, and similarly, a question of a durable and enduring nature can be understood as partaking of the nature of hypothesis. Christianity can then be understood, with full acceptance of its uniqueness, its special revelational quality, and its articulation of the relation between man and God, in terms of major religious questions which are open to a wide variety of interpretations; yet the questions are eternal questions for all that, corresponding to eternal principles understood as partaking of the nature of enduring hypothesis.

Ecumenism, which raised these issues to begin with, can benefit from them. The problems of understanding among points of view are obviously different and have different potentials for agreement and disagreement if the materials which are to be the subject of communication are cast as questions rather than as objective principles. It is worth re-asserting that the potential of a question is far greater than the potential of a principle. A question can produce answers in any age, untrammelled by previous expressions and yet having successfully channelled the energies of men around its central concerns. The implications of such enormous power can hardly be over-estimated, and seem to be quite in accord with the traditional judgment of Christianity implied in its two millenia of history.

III   Characteristics of Religious Thought I: Community as Belief Point

A new condition appears to obtain, or nearly so, in the present movement of religious thought. It is becoming possible to hold that a great number of belief-points can do duty as foci of comprehensive thought, and therefore can serve as centers of systems of meaning. The consequences of this condition are stupendous. If diverse centers of systematic thought are enabled, with comparable degrees of validity if not of popular support, then a choice can also be made among clusters of systems such that some can be seen as of one order or family and others of another. In a still later stage it can be decided whether multiple foci clustered into families can in turn be clustered into a monolithic category which subsumes apparent differences, even the multiplicity of foci itself, and if so, what the nature of that monolith is. Conceivably the characteristic of multiple foci will not withstand intellectual dissolution into universals. Within this context two possibilities stand out—that the fundamental dimension of reality is religious, or that it is secular. The position taken here again is that it is religious, and that there is no entertainable secular dimension at all. To a continuing consideration of this possibility the present sketch will be directed.

The secular dimension has been adopted by a variety of unidimensional views in recent periods, as for example positivism, Marxism, linguistic analysis in its simplest forms, and several of the contemporary humanisms. Nevertheless it has lately come upon hard times. Each of its forms depends for its validity on a closely restricted knowing relation and on a corresponding, narrow definition of the real. Confined descriptions of reality have their social and practical uses; they enable the accomplishment of certain limited objectives, often very useful objectives. But they do not satisfy the questing mind in an age of widening and multiplying perspectives. This endless questioning is surely the key to much of the modern temper, marked as it is by expanded concern with ways of knowing and with possible dimensions of the real.

The times require vast breadths of interest, awareness in profoundest depths. Unidimensions applied merely to the hither reaches of the universe, which is to say, to the thin surface of the earth which has been until very recent years all that was readily at hand for study, or perhaps to the superficial skim of social process, are too restrictive to reflect the new full ranges of actuality or possibility. Unidimensionality may be a proper characteristic of ultimacy, and no doubt it is. Ultimacy is not, however, the problem of immediacy on which is bent so great a share of current interest. Hitherness, attention to immediate and limited phenomena, appears to be the concern of the later 20th century, whether or not it is equivalent to omission of major significance and meaning, and the question of how attention is to be balanced between the ranges of the now and the grounds of ultimacy is quite generally a center of confusion.

What happens is that a particular local focus of commitment is generalized into a full-blown metaphysic; it becomes the fundament of a theory of the real, so that a comprehensive position is set up and pivoted on what amounts to a local belief-point. It can be re-emphasized that this process is often operationally useful, enabling the movement of a line of inquiry or development. The question may come on whether it ought to be characterized as religious.

The subject of ultimacy can be set apart for present purposes; its nature is inescapable and will come to notice soon enough. It is enough to observe for the moment that religious centrality as focus for individual human energies comes over on several levels short of ultimacy in the cultural complex of a pluralistic time. That this is so may be a matter of singular significance in the traditionally secular realm for the clarification of relatedness among seemingly divergent points of view, and in the traditionally religious realm where as a consequence of it that most difficult of theological problems, the grounds of ecumenical understanding, may come suddenly into perspective.

A primary implication of the fact of multiple religious foci is the comparable standing of varied systems of meaning, short of the range of ultimacy. It has long been customary to consider certain accepted systematic statements as religious, as for example, Islam, Christianity,

Hinduism, Judaism, Buddhism, and similarly general systems—and to regard certain other systematic statements as secular, as naturalism, pragmatism, Freudianism, existentialism in its secular line of descent, and a number of predominantly social valuation-theories. If it is now possible to say that these major systems of understanding reflect functional psychologies closely related in types and degrees of personal involvement and in what might be termed the system-consequents, by which is meant the implications of a given system for certain fundamental categories of meaning, then the distinction between clusters of supposedly religious and supposedly secular systems vanishes, and all the systems, the traditionally religious and the traditionally secular, can be considered as operating in a single dimension. The issue of the religious or secular nature of this fundamental dimension can be bracketed for reconsideration later. For the moment there is merely the apparent fact of breakdown of sharp distinction between religious and secular. As practical an administrative agency as the Selective Service System eventually updated itself to recognize this. Draft deferment or exclusion came to be allowed to persons whose beliefs were genuinely organized around social values rather than exclusively around classical conceptions of deity. Nevertheless the common view remains that certain traditional foci of belief comprise the religious, while the absence of these foci or the substitution of foci atypical of traditional forms, constitute the non-religious. Similarly, religious neutrals and varieties of unchurched positions choosing supposedly secular, non-religious views no doubt often take their stands from positive convictions in a negative direction, making a decision concerning what is not wanted; the understood choice is then to be something other-than-religious, and in such instances this is a choice of something definite.

The secondary point to be made derives from this. The religiously characterized relation of subject and object, which is to say, religious knowledge in a fundamental, constructional sense, is a quality of knowing in all of its possible ranges and at numerous levels of intensity as well. There has been discussion before of the nature of religious thought as concerned with the largest and most comprehensive of questions, that is, with questions larger and more general than those which mark the common, daily ranges of human concern. By means of a greatly expanded definition of the conceptual nature of the awareness relation some apparent differences between seemingly divergent types of knowing are eliminated. This has perhaps been sufficiently done. The effect of it for present purposes is in turn to describe the individual person as taking part in an intricate process of expressional relation previously described in limited terms as one or another of the forms of knowing.

What is this to mean for the focus of Community?

Philip H. Phenix of Teachers College, Columbia University made a significant statement of the nature of community as gathering-point of religious concern and activity in his small volume of some years ago, *Intelligible Religion.* In practical terms what is to be had from this is a developed social focus, that is, an energy center toward which and from which effort can flow. The usefulness of such a center is not at issue; it enables an enormous energy exchange around the idea and fact of community, a source of great difficulty in the urbanized complex of modern life, in which for example enormously complicated cities have distorted America's historic conception of itself as the cities of the eastern seaboard have sprawled into a megalopolitan extension from Maine to Virginia. The necessity of giving careful attention to design and construction of cities and towns in which men can live with most benefit is hardly debatable. Columbia, Maryland, Reston, Virginia, and other planned urban units are cases in point. Hence it is right to say that the concept of community is a highly appropriate value center in American life.

The interesting aspect of the matter from a reflective standpoint of course is that reflection does not stop there. The human mind has its perverse will to know, to understand, and insofar as community represents a moral focus for practical policy development it may also come to represent a reality-focus for purposes of philosophic understanding. A relevant point to be made is that this tendency to generalize a local focus into a far-reaching principle of understanding is a characteristic of the religious mode of thought, that is, of reflectional thought, and that it occurs and recurs in a great variety of instances and types of instances.

For the viewpoint which Phenix represented in *Intelligible Religion* community provides a substitute focus for good feeling, a legitimate receptacle of positive emotionality, or what might be termed an ersatz-religiousness. The chances are that little or no metaphysical effort is present or intended in Phenix's view. But as a matter of course, if the metaphysical question is put the answer has to be given; the implied metaphysic is there if it is demanded.

It is normal enough that this is so. Foci of religious commitment have obtained with respect to far less defensible phenomena or centers of concern than community, which is after all largely a modern notion and which has the welfare of groups and aggregates of people at heart. Few of the older local foci of belief had better or even as good grounds for being as does community in the recent sense. There have been many altars in the religious history of man, and not all of them by any means would be considered respectable today.

The metaphysic of community is necessarily social. It has an implied concern with the individual which is very strong, but its philosophic fundament is relational among individuals. It asserts in brief that the idea of community made up of individuals in partial symbiotic interdependence is a substantial metaphysical relation which does not reduce to other relations or to other substantial entities. This is altogether the center of the matter, and its importance cannot be over-estimated.

Notice that there is no philosophic justification for the establishment of this metaphysical center. There never is, with any such center. It is rather an activous decision in the realm of metaphysics which is based on a constructional awareness of the real extended in the given dimension. The great probability is that there are operative today a considerable number of such decisions giving rise to considerable foci of concern in the reflective realm, allowing committed persons to center their energies around them. The phenomenon is essentially religious. It is accurate to see these foci of concern as most often religious in nature since they provide gathering-points for life-times of personal effort. The focus of meaning in each instance is conceived of variously as a receptacle for loyalty, a center of value, a source from which further good can be derived. This is to say, it is a focus which can and should receive gifts of personal commitment, and it is an objective source from which value is held to flow. It is then a center of validity in the midst of perceived chaos.

In former times such a focus of commitment would almost certainly have been referred to as an Ultimate, and the nature of such a focus would have been in part defined by the conception of Ultimacy. It would have been thought to derive its meaning from Ultimacy as well as being thought to contribute its effort to the final ground, Divinity. Questions of Divinity will be better considered in other studies and in other places. For the moment it is significant simply that one of the marks of contemporary psychological life is just this existence of a number of semiultimates, limited, temporary, or partial absolutes as distinct from final absolutes, around which a good deal of life-effort is personally volunteered, and which serve at once as receptacles and sources of values so that enormously powerful commitments can be made with respect to them.

The psychology of national betrayal, technical treason perhaps in a legal sense, may sometimes exemplify this type of limited, semiabsolute. The idea of community, the perception of its reality, may be for personalities organized in new ways in process of significant change. What may be involved here is the substitution of a larger community for a smaller, more immediate one. It could be that this kind of change is sometimes the essence of the matter in certain transgressions of law. The movement in such instances may be from immediate life to abstract life; that is, the vivid, full living of the small 19th century village may have subtly given way to a more abstract idea of social relations involving a community of distant populations, as for example America and the Philippine Islands, or America and England, or the Soviet Union and Cuba. More developed constructions of community might entertain the idea of community obtaining among nations lately ill at ease with each other, as for example, America and Mainland China, the Soviet Union and West Germany, or America and Cuba. What constitutes apparent opposition to national policy may be in some cases rather the entertaining of ideas of community of different or larger scope than that normally comprised by nation or country. Conversely, contraction of the idea of community may be a reverse instance, as when a small sect such as the Doukhobors in Western Canada appears to oppose national community on behalf of their smaller, more selected sectarian community. The Quebec nationalist movement in Eastern Canada may be an even better case.

Without being able any more to be sure, on account of the passing of time, it does seem likely that in the hill country of northern New England a century ago the actuality of community was a real and vivid thing, often a matter of necessity in that the dependence of people on other people was clearly felt. The sawmills were set up on certain brooks where settlers knew their logs could be made into boards, for houses, furniture, or coffins; district schools were used on the Sabbath for Christian services, an almost unheard-of notion nowadays, schools being then the only public buildings available until churches were built from forty to sixty years after the settlement of the town; violins were handcrafted at a brick house overlooking a winding stream; the general store was in the back ell of the coach tavern, the leather shop next to it, surviving account books showing that between them they sold just about everything then used on a farm. School kept in off-seasons so the boys could work at home on the farms in sugaring and the planting-spring, in summer, and in harvest time; girls could work in the farmhouses. In many ways the common energy was devoted to survival. Community was not an idea, even a good idea, in those days; it was just what people did because they had to do it; it was simple necessity. Perhaps no one even thought about it. Why should they? For the most part they just did their work and liked their neighbors—or disliked them. In any case they told stories about them, with verve and mischief, often with affection, and some of those tales have endured for generations, told and re-told, woven into the fabric of community taken for granted among the simpler, heavier labors of those forgotten years.

There is a story of old Longstockings in a northern Vermont town, so called for the most obvious of reasons, who lived in a little brick house in a clearing on the side of a hill, on a road long since thrown up, across from where the violins were made, and who was inordinately fond of a pig. One night the boys of the countryside decided to plague him, so they went over through the woods to his place, crept up to his pigpen by the barn, and poked the pig with a stick. The pig squealed, and for more than a hundred years the storytellers of the town have recounted with delight how Longstockings put his head out of his door in great perturbation of spirit and called, ''Piggy! Piggy! Piggy! What's the matter, Piggy?''—at which the pig would be quiet, the boys would wait, Longstockings would go back to bed, and then the tale could all be told again.

And there are the sad stories, hovering in the faded airs of history above a country graveyard. Some are shrouded in a mercy of silence,— the rows of little stones for the children of a single family, dated every one within some dreadful week or month, marking an epidemic of long ago when a homestead was suddenly and shortly drained of all its reasons for existence. So hard a tale should be fulfilled in the wordless telling of the stones. But some can still be heard among the tragic legends of the town—the simple stone for a woman in the midst of life whose husband outlived her by thirty years, the pain of which remains in the memories of later generations who have cared about what happened because it happened there and to those people, the woman who had gone by herself to a city hospital for a minor operation of no account, arranging with her husband to meet her at the station a day or two later, and met him, dead and in her coffin, so that he drove her home in the back of his wagon as he would have had to do with anything else brought into that country in those days, and lived with the dulled loneliness of it for more than a generation after, as he had lived before he met her in his early middle years, before that bright, brief, unexpected flash of affection and of home.

The idea of community would not indeed have entered greatly into the awareness of former times. In its modern sense it is surely a recent idea, having little or no history in its role as one of the partial absolutes of 20th century relativism. Its relational affect would have obtained in its purest form in such Scriptural settings as the Fourth Gospel; but this would have been a different matter. Then it represented a phase of ultimate reality working itself out in human affairs, conceived of as part of a fundamental substrate. Its contemporary forms show the effects of transformation by subtraction, a kind of ideological lumbering operation in which scattered landmarks are left as when in a denuded woodland the forest is cut off leaving the bull-pines standing at lonely intervals on the bare hillside. The notion of community is then to be acknowledged as a substitute metaphysic of restricted and local dimensions accidental with interested persons and situations, and applicable chancily over a limited range of usefulness on the basis of human interest rather than of unconditional validity.

If there are indeed numerous possible foci of concern doing duty as temporary or partial absolutes some notable repercussions can be anticipated.

The nature of religious concern is generalized, apart from particular conceptions of Divinity. A good many instances of human commitment become describable as religious, and it should be possible to engage with these attitudes and operations more usefully in consequence. Religious concern becomes a common thing, normal in the

34

great majority of life-histories instead of being a separative system of highly specific focus gathering around conventional expressions. Religious thought and attitudes become the forms of ordinary life, operating in the midst of life instead of on its edge and set apart on single days of the week. Religion becomes visible in the common daily round instead of appearing only in occasional ritual functions.

Concern for community, among the most contemporary of the gathering-points of 20th century affective life, stands identified as one of these partial and temporary absolutes, able to provide a respectable repository for good feeling and sound action on the part of its devotees, persons who feel a discontinuity with traditional religion but who harbor many of its moods and commitments. Community provides embarrassed man with a modernized "secularist" religion which is, so to say, "religious" in its psychology and operation and "secular" in its seeming separation from traditionally religious modes of thought. In the present view secularism in this sense is not a useful or profound conception, but an aspect of the problem which can well await a different study.

To conclude, one far-reaching implication stands forward. Ecumenism, the gathering together of the great church viewpoints of the Western and Eastern worlds, may achieve some significant advantage as well as entertain a certain hazard in the recognition of the multiplicity of possible foci of religious concern. The advantage may appear in the opening acknowledgement of the nature of religious participation as general in human experience, as distinct from being articulated only with particular objects. A corresponding hazard would almost certainly present itself in the tendency to exclusive relation of subject and particular object normally found in the major religious traditions. The point here is not that a solution to the ecumenical problem will have been found in these further reaches of various positions, but that the basis for exchange can have been shadowed forth for what value it may produce.

Community then takes its place in the religious spectrum of the 20th century, a valued and genuine place, full of promise, wide of prospect. If the full explication of religious reality is not contained within it, as it indeed is not, it is surely no restriction on the validity of community as one among the foci of human concerns that this limitation applies.

IV American History Revisited

The historian, it is said, walks backward into the future, taking account of factors and events as they burst into view on either side and move apart in a receding avenue of things and figures. In this manner of speaking the writer (and teacher) of history is less the amanuensis of an age, still less a provider of the grounds of prophecy, than he is a force for recognition and identification of the materials of his craft, an adjudicator of persons and circumstances so that they may take their rightful places in the stately dance of time. History thus has constantly to be re-written. New elements plunge from the curtained present into the visible and patterned past, displacing or partly covering those of earlier days. Perspectives are altered, albeit more slowly with increasing age. Redescriptions become inevitable.

We have now to suggest that the metaphor is outdated, whether permanently or temporarily remains to see, and that the writer and teacher of history is better described as one who strides among the currents of his world, contending with its events, influencing its directions, taking active part in developing the substance of history. Perhaps to a degree greater than in more quiet periods the historian has become a factor in the history he teaches. Let us see how this curious condition comes to pass.

Notice that the problem deals not with the management or manipulation of history but with the selection-factor in the composition of historical records. In two respects, perhaps three, abrupt additions to the range of awareness commonly covered by American historical studies imply that American history has now to be reconsidered and in part rewritten. The first of these is in the direction of a North American or continental history to include Canada and Mexico with the United States in a continuous, contemporaneous mosaic; the second is toward an intercultural history within the United States, enabling amalgamation of minority group with majority group abstractions into more comprehensive general historical abstractions.

Toward a Continental History

That history has its mixtures of mythic qualities and selective strains is obvious enough. These are inevitable parts of historiography; without them it would be impossible to write or teach history. The problem is how to enlarge them as perspective enlarges, how to widen interpretations as required by widening ranges of historical materials and ideas, if adequate understandings are to be produced apace.

Late colonial and early national events in the classic pattern of American history may be especially subject to limitations imposed by tradition, the result of an eastern seaboard, old-colony set concerning what was important in those periods. There is ample reason for this. The Revolutionary War took place after all on the Atlantic coast and not on the Pacific; it revolved around General Washington and not General Custer; it had something to do with Yorktown and not much to do with the Alamo. History is what it is and is not what it is not. Yet there are indeed abstractions in the public mind from which history is thought to be made, points of view which in time may have influences on social and historical decisions of significance.

The preoccupied citizen's idea of the period is that the Revolution consisted of some tax aggravations, the Boston tea party usually not recognized as an early type of demonstration, gunfire at Lexington and Concord, a cracked bell, Washington at Valley Forge, Cornwallis' surrender, and the Declaration of Independence. The Confederation is distinguished with difficulty from the Confederacy. The adoption of the Constitution is a little clearer but its amendments have obscured its stages.

Colonial history may stand in even lesser part. Some little ships brought English pilgrims to that same Eastern seaboard; there was Thanksgiving, suffering, Pocahontas and other Indians. Most of the latter data have lately become embarrassing since the Indians nearly always lost their shirts; early American intergroup relations have had to be overlooked except as passing inspirations for little boys.

It could be contended that Americans have sufficient difficulty grasping their own history and should not be expected to expand their historical consciousness to include neighboring countries. But the real question is whether they can afford not to make such an enlargement of their awareness. Canadian and Mexican history affect United States history, not just because Canada and Mexico are important all of a sudden but because they have always been important and to omit their histories in conjunction with relevant segments of United States history is to understand history less well and less completely than it should be understood.

Canada disappeared from the non-professional American consciousness about 1780 and did not reappear in it again until the 1930's when the novels of Kenneth Roberts suggested that American colonials mounted expeditions into Canada in Revolutionary times. In the 1930's why they should have done so was anybody's guess. It seemed most ungracious and might better have been forgotten. But the novels were interesting and they were not forgotten. University departments of history may not have required fictional aids to remind them of those distant events, but impressions deriving from elementary and secondary school units in American history, regrettably uncorrected by higher education, are a different matter. Is it not those same unspoken "climates of opinion" made famous in other connections by Whitehead and Lovejoy which provide much of the present problem?

Even today the simple way to rediscover common United States-Canadian history is to camp around the Maritime Provinces and points west into Ontario reading the signs erected on historic sites by Canada's alert provincial and federal governments, at Louisburg on Cape Breton Island, for example, on the heights in Montreal, or along the Great Lakes. Persistence may show that enterprising Nova Scotians once returned the compliment by invading the coast of Maine, and with rather a flair, too, since for years as a consequence Maine contributed substantial monies to the endowment funds of Nova Scotian higher education. If it cannot be proved that invasions of Canada from the Colonies were profitable it at least appears that Canadian expeditions in reverse functioned in better part.

Speaking of curious invasions one stumbles now and again on that conspiracy of Southerners during the Civil War who invaded Vermont by way of Canada in the hope of subverting the Lincoln government and ending the conflict. Vermont was the wrong state to choose. When the invaders set up shop in a local hotel near the border to wait for a Union disaster Vermonters apparently went about their business as usual without paying them any mind, and so nothing happened. After a while the conspirators went home. The affair never got to be anything more than a good story with an international fillip, and when *Vermont Life* retold it after a hundred years it must be acknowledged that many of its readers had never heard of it.

To return from good stories to the groundwork of the subject, the influence of the national border probably accounts for restrictions of awareness between the two countries. Whatever the future of such borders may be there was a time when they defined the ranges of history thought to be of prime interest. School children read "Evangeline" in Longfellow but found it easier by far to locate Louisiana—which was within the United States at the time of reading—than to realize that Acadia might be geographically closer by. In these later days when people from both countries cross the border with few or no restrictions the relations of the United States and Canada are in a new and welcome phase. It is as if an early colonial, pre-national condition of free movement and free exchange of ideas were being re-established after two hundred years. Business and industrial ties may even be too close for Canada's comfort. A considerable exchange of citizens as permanent residents takes place each year, some from Canada preferring the larger opportunities in the States and some from the States preferring the smaller, more individualistic and intercultural flexibilities of Canada. Colleges and universities in both countries are establishing regional study centers which cross the border. Is it not time that political influences which national borders have on national self-images should be cut down to size? Conceptions of history as written and taught have a large bearing on this question.

How shall this be done? Is it a bi-national or bi-cultural situation in which the 300-year histories of the two countries should be taken apart and redacted into a single common history, to be taught on all educational levels? But not so fast. There is also Mexico.

Constrictions of awareness apply also along the Mexican-United States border. As with Canada, there are nonprofessional awarenesses of Mexico in the gringo consciousness, but again how limited! The Mexican War of 1848, the film "Juarez" with Lincoln's portrait brooding on the wall, Willa Cather's novel—what else? The expedition of 1916 is remembered only if one's uncle happened to go along. Bandits on television? Volcanoes? Acapulco? Marijuana? Interesting topics, all, but hardly grounds for reliable cultural awareness.

But come off it. From colonial times much that happened in the United States happened first in Mexico. Exploration was born there well before the Mayflower obliged New England with genealogical antiquity. Early visitors had equally difficult times in both regions. If winters were colder in New England there were more bugs in Central America. New England had its Bradford, the Gulf Coast its Cabeza de Vaca; but few residents of either region were socially outstanding. New arrivals were minority groups in one way or another, often ill-prepared and ill-equipped for hardship. If aristocracies resulted they were mostly indigenous, not imported inheritances. Perhaps the upper crust tends to stay home. Why should it leave?

The nub is not yet, however. Mexican civilization conceived of as philosophic adventure, as any civilization must ultimately be, represents a separate cultural development, specialized and sealed off, even a hothouse culture, South European, Roman Catholic, Latinized, later partially secularized, withal something different in its own right. What of the presence or absence of the more familiar North European cultural strains in Mexico? Are there commonalities as well as singularities?

Roman Catholic thought, to choose one major theme which appears in all three North American cultures, has been a powerful component in the three histories as well as being a contemporary presence. While Catholicism is a different thing in different countries is it not also a common thing, possibly a uniting thing, in a diversity of cultures? What changes might be wrought among them if the significance of so great a commonality were comprehended? Might not the cultural self-image of each be profoundly affected over a period of time? Who begins to know the meaning of so vast a thing, unrealized as it remains? If sets of ideas eventually determine history, as an idealistic theory suggests, would not its course be formed in new ways?

To begin the struggle with old ways of looking at familiar things, it might make excellent sense to challenge undergraduate history classes to coordinate materials required for re-writing periods of history on a North American continental basis, to write drafts of such histories, expecting cultural strains, figures and events to be identified and treated contemporaneously in all the cultures. It would amount to re-writing North American and Central American history from the beginning to the present time with no regard for national boundaries except as these may have figured in sets of circumstances as any other component of history may do.

Toward an Intercultural History

The second chief respect in which American history now needs to be re-thought is the less remote, more demanding aspect of Black-and-White intercultural history, where a comparable range of problems forecasts the historiographic dilemma. It is as if two histories subsisted side by side or in layers, one obvious and highlighted, one recessive and only periodically emergent; one a direct, written-and-printed semi-official history, subject to reinterpretation but falling into classical, accepted patterns; the other a folk-history, oral, emotionally conditioned, semi-humorous and semi-bitter, unofficial, even subterranean. Perhaps there are always unofficial histories or versions of histories. Occasional book titles and grassroots publishing ventures purport to show how things ''really were.'' Periodicals have thrived on such stocks-in-trade. Columnists become masters of the inside story. Unofficial histories are not new. The issue may turn on the degree of dislocation, the seeming distance, between official and unofficial versions and the likely influence of the distance on social decisions implied in the two positions. This is the problem now.

In this subsurface, unspoken, unwritten way, it is fair to say, a substantial segment of Black Americans today simply do not believe American history as it is commonly set down. That this is so may not be immediately obvious to other population groups. It is necessary to be around for a while, to pick things up informally, to be where talk flows more freely than common, where tongues are not self-conscious, where a degree of confidence is established, where sets of assumptions can appear out of the dusk. A subterranean version of reality may then appear on the surface, sometimes in the form of a straight story of the inside truth, sometimes as a wryly humorous twist referring to much that is understood among conversants but rarely described verbally. Gradually the listener becomes aware of the existence of a view of history different from the standard one of school and college courses.

Were some of the colonial and early national fathers financially interested in the slave trade? Muckraking and scandal-mongering are considered to be in poor taste so that if American patriarchs had been in the slave trade it might well have been played down as a matter of form. To the Black American it is not a matter of form; it was his ancestors who were sold on the block. Who sold them? Whose ancestors sold them? What do the answers to these questions mean to the validity of

41

the abstraction which constitutes American history in the period in question? Or in our own period? Abstractions, remember, are the stuff of history.

Did George Washington take advantage of the slave women on his plantation? Did so-and-so have a racially mixed son whose physical characteristics or family connections were never mentioned? Was Lincoln a racist? The latter query, obviously, written down, became a weapon in the attempt to engage racial groups with one another in conflict. Other such questions have not been written down, or if they have been, are seldom read where they can affect the historical abstraction.

What it boils down to is that when one's forebears were born slaves, sold periodically among white masters, functioned nowhere visibly above the field or plantation house, never dealt with ideas, principles, documents, decisions, property, travel, position, respect of self or associate, American history as usually set down does not look complete to one if its principal groups. Above all, the emotional component of history is missing. To the nonblack who "knows" the facts about slavery in a statistical way the perspective of American history does not include slavery as an emotional presence, vivid as people are vivid, real as they are real. For him slavery is even more of an abstraction. He feels no shame or guilt (if he resides in the North), for was not all that wiped out by one of the bloodiest wars in history? How can he see out from inside a Black American whose visible family history began only after the Civil War, sometimes long after, and has taken a century to settle into form—if indeed it is settled? Conversely, how is the Black American to understand the view of the nation's history held by English-Americans whose forebears arrived on the earliest ships, helped write the national documents, contrived the institutions of democracy, and managed the social apparatus of earlier times? A dislocation is hardly to be escaped. It could not be otherwise.

If the proper name for this condition is provincialism it at least applies as directly to one side as to the other, to the English scion and to the African scion, slave or free. Both viewpoints partake of the provincial. Each must labor if it is to achieve understanding of the other. The study and writing of history are efforts to overcome the limitations of provincialism in the interest of approximating objectivity. It is also true that historical data are winnowed by socio-cultural habitudes which determine what is to be kept as record and what is to be discarded, and winnowed also by historiographic methodology which determines secondary historiographic selection and interpretation.

Until William Styron's *Confessions of Nat Turner* perhaps no serious artistic attempt had been made to study the personality and worldview of the slave, so to speak from the inside. Twentieth century Black literature has had a deal to say of minority life in recent times, and there have been studies of slavery as a social phenomenon, all having important things to convey. But there has not been ready access to the mind and world of the American slave prior to 1860, or to the outlook of the Black American during the Reconstruction and later when restrictive patterns were being hardened into social policy. It may be less than remarkable that the Styron novel appeared in 1967 when emotional components determining historical viewpoints through conditioning of formative ideas and methods were everywhere rising to the surface. It may be part of the new romanticism in which the energies of the self are bursting forth everywhere in new ways.

The Black American then does not really believe American history, for his own part in it, real enough in actuality, does not appear in the account. It is to him a half-history, omitting the roles, the thought, and most of the persons of his lineage. He knows that the antiquity of his line is as great as that of any human, else he could not be here to draw breath. The issue turns, then, on the problem of cultural data selection and on additionally selective historiography.

It would be well to eschew anger in this matter. The blank columns of American history are the loss of Everyman, White as well as Black. If history is an effort at objectification it is also a system of abstraction; it has to be, for the data are too numerous to be treated individually. They must be clustered and categorized to be manageable; patterns must be introduced. In the present set of circumstances the categories have been badly conceived. And that is the nub of it.

If historical method and historiography follow upon conceptualization and selective methodology, then it is right to speak to viewpoints and to the grounds for selectivities which are their consequence. Historical and historiographical criticism become exercises in criticism of personal philosophies, decisional commitments by individuals and groups in advance of the operations of history or at most constituting its earliest stages. This is to say, history is written out of conceptual awareness, and if historical positions are limited they are so limited by conceptual awareness. When a conceptual awareness begins to move, previously accepted history will appear in disfocus and must be rewritten to redress the clarities.

With respect to their own historical lines Black Americans have had an enormous advantage over other group outlooks upon Black history since necessarily they have been aware of that history from the inside. They may have had other conceptual limitations, but those concerning their own inheritance they did not have. That these factors have been so largely omitted from American historical awareness could not but persuade them that American history has been little more than half written.

When the balance is redressed by the rewriting of American history it will be because the fundamental change will have taken place in the American consciousness and common self-image, not alone because certain changes are made in the pages of schoolbooks or in the standard versions of certain heroic national tales. History will continue to be the reflected mind of man, so that when conceptual awareness of major strains in American history is expanded to include neglected elements historiography should fall appropriately into place.

The role of conceptual awareness in forming views of history is demonstrated with pathos in the concentration camp rumor of 1967. Beginning about then, among Black Americans it was commonly believed, but rarely stated in mixed groups, that federal concentration camps had been prepared in the Southwest, in Oklahoma, Texas, Nevada, Colorado, or New Mexico, to contain summer rioters from the great cities. It was not clear in the rumor that all the detainees would be rioters; there was some willingness to believe that Black Americans in general might be subjected to containment.

By 1967-68 this rumor had become part of vernacular exchange. It appeared in a variety of forms, as a joke, as casual reference, as a type of self-raillery. For some who did not really believe it, it was still viable communicational coin. It was taken semi-seriously by persons who would never riot under any circumstances. The next stage was for it to become more specific. Younger campus minority groups and the militant black power national organizations became far more specific about it. By midwinter 1968 the rumor, then 12 to 18 months old, was being sent around in mimeographed form for posting on campus bulletin

44

boards. The circulars were about Orangeburg or other specific tragedies; the concentration camp rumor was being woven into the materials as something additional which the writers and readers also "knew" to be so.

Elements going into the rumor could conceivably be recollections of the detention camps for West Coast Japanese in early World War II days, federal preparations for city riots in the summer of 1968, widely reported in the press, pointed news stories of suburban firearms classes directed toward anticipated violence in the summer of 1968, and large doses of folklore. It became at once part of the self-consciousness of a minority group and part of the raw material by which that self-consciousness was supported. One of its consequences was inevitably reinforcement of disbelief in history. Majority groups do not assume there will be concentration camps for Black Americans in the Southwest. Early in World War II the United States detained a group of several hundred thousand Japanese Americans in camps inland from the West Coast. Nevertheless the majority self-image is that the United States does not do this kind of thing. Thus does an unofficial view of history develop; things are quietly assumed to be different from official or majority group versions of them. There - have - to - be - official - versions - and - we - know - about - that - but - we - also - know - they - are - not - real. The issues are seldom discussed because they are difficult to raise across color lines. An assumption follows that differences in group awareness and group versions are deliberate, purposeful, for exploitative or destructive ends. And why should such an assumption not be made? Was not the institution of slavery exploitative? No Black American will ever forget the nature of slavery. White Americans commonly do forget it. They may not have felt personally or directly involved in it if they lived outside the South, although they certainly tolerated it, and then there was that bloodiest of internal wars which somehow gets to be conceived of as an exculpation. It is not unlike the problem which Americans have had with modern Mainland China. Americans once put great effort and self-commitment into missionary movements operating in China. China as a whole was polite about this for a while, but did not really like it much in the long run. It was a rude surprise to America to find that China would as soon run the West out as not. It was additionally shocking when China adopted a rival set of Western ideas as a social experiment of its own on a grand scale. Motives get to be mixed;

undeniably there is a difference between the ways the United States is seen and the ways in which it sees itself. It is hardly astonishing that a smaller scale instance should develop in internal group relations, where assumptions of intent in both directions are soon being made which ought not to be made.

Far from being ivoried off in towers in these days the writers and teachers of history are drawn toward mid-battle. Professional historians and historical educators must realize that they come near to dealing with the living stuff of history. Events of a century and more ago brood among us, presences vividly in mind, forming the attitudes, decisions, and events of today. Along with the streets of cities, classroom and campus may become the arena, if hopefully not in a physical, surely in an intellectual sense. On the premise that conceptual ideas are formative in the construction of viewpoints history is being made even while it is taught. If determinative viewpoints in American history are indeed dislocated, as they appear now to be, at least two major historical interpretations are developing side by side concerning the same social and historical material, interpretations different in content and import.

In quieter times this would not have been so. ''Official'' versions and minority versions there would have been in plenty, for these are merely functions of large-groups and small-groups; in time the normal processes of social reflection would have combined them into a pattern of interpretation acceptable in general. The difference now lies in the immediacy of articulation of idea or historical theory with act or policy, and in the scale of application. Thematic strains are enormously influential at present in the determination of what is done. Majority groups have been accustomed to workable approximations of theory and policy. Interpretive differences have been small in the long view and have been settled by periodic voting at the polls. What is at stake now is more profound. It is not clear whether the yawning chasms of opinion can be kept bridged by democratic process. Fortunately the matter need not end on so dubious a note.

The answer could still lie in the classroom where versions of history, vivid, active, influential, may be found and considered. Again the soundest approach may be to invite younger generations of students to take part in the intellectual and artistic re-writing of history. In the doing of it they may learn what history really is, and their elders too may learn, for history is never done. In days of danger and uncertainty resolution of a national problem may yet take place in the minds of men. While guns snap and buildings crackle, in the realm of ideas peace may yet be aborning, transforming threats of crisis and disaster into new leadership and new conceptions of historical movement, heroic themes stirring to life like the figures of legend, as when in Hawthorne's brooding tale the Gray Champion of long ago strode once more in King Street.

V   Ground Notions toward
a Liberal Ecumenism

Under the general rubric of "Issues Toward a Liberal Ecumenism" immediate concerns tend to focus first on traditional Christian themes. Ecumenical discussions on the local church level show the extent to which individual anxiety can hinge around conceptions of Jesus and the resulting necessity of working out some basis of common understanding if the discussion is to move. The position taken here is that ecumenism is indispensable and inevitable and therefore that the problems arising in connection with it such as that of a Christology, a natural philosophy, a theology, or a theory of human nature are simply the next problems to be resolved. There may be many reasons why liberal thought has not done this in recent times. Liberal religion has been very busy getting used to modern ideas of the world, and has invested effort in the direction of becoming scientific. It has also been preoccupied with social responsibility. Perhaps any cultural group has only a certain amount of energy at its disposal, and some things go by the board while others are being considered.

A justification from history suggests that because so much of Western culture is made up of the substance of the Christian tradition and of echoes from it, it is impossible to understand Western civilization without a working knowledge of the Christian position on man, nature and God. This is a good idea. But it will have its greatest appeal to persons already committed to history as a mode of understanding and a source of value; perhaps regrettably, the liberal church comprises viewpoints that give relatively little attention to the significance of the past.

A systematic approach to a liberal formulation of major Christian themes then becomes necessary, in part to serve as basis for ecumenical discussions and in part to provide a ground for communication among sub-groups. By a systematic approach is meant the resolution of the problem in its own terms and on its own grounds rather than simply for facility in understanding other points of view. It may be suggested that liberal derivations from the principal themes of Catholic and Protestant thought were worked out in the nineteenth century and that the liberal church ought to get on to modern problems. There is no need to subscribe to this. Much of the excitement of the study of religious questions comes from the fact that they are not settled with finality in any age but remain open to rediscovery and reformulation amid the changing elements of each succeeding time.

Considerable difficulties do, however, stand in the way of thematic studies in Christian thought for any group, perhaps particularly for religious liberals. Foremost among these is the problem of primary assumptions. Perhaps at one time it was possible to take for granted the nature of the world in which man lives, and to assume that if one knew certain things about it these were known reliably in ways which would be commonly understood and accepted. This is to say, the general ideas underlying a variety of philosophical positions would have been held in common. It was a considerable advantage if this was so, but it is not so now. Even a generation ago, to remain within the present century, it would have been possible for liberal groups in general to agree that some kind of scientific naturalism ought to underlie most positions they would take on most issues. That this uniformity has evaporated is simply a measure of the rapidity of intellectual change and the diversity of ideas that have come to be regarded as significant. The implications for liberal religion are as significant as those for any religious viewpoint.

A special difficulty does obtain in working with very general ideas. If a general principle cannot after all be taken for granted it must be made clear that this is so, and the fact is that in many cases this is not done. Assumptions are made which either ought not to be made or, if they are to be made, ought to be specified so that it is possible to judge what is involved. If these ideas become sufficiently general they approach the "climate of opinion," and this too is not infrequently a factor in the difficulty, being certainly as awkward to make clear as are general ideas of lesser scope. It is as if it had been common practice until recent times to deal with surface levels of the real, while making assumptions concerning the levels or grounds beneath, whereas now it is indispensable to deal with what might be called vertical wholes, so that even the most general assumptions underlying a point of view must be explicated if reasonable understandings are to be expected.

Any effective philosophical position requires a primary decision in metaphysics. That is, the nature of the universe required for the taking of a particular reflective position is ordinarily prior to the taking of that position and a part of it; without this there is no position and no philosophy. Notice that the primary decision in metaphysics is prior also to evidence as such. It rather defines the nature of the evidence to be accepted, so that if it is said to depend upon evidence the reasoning is inevitably circular. The primary metaphysical decision is properly a clear, clean thing, an aspect of individual personality, and a vector of individual human life. To take the contrary view that a philosophy to be accepted is based on a certain kind of evidence is again to make a very general assumption and then to forget that one has made it. The effect is self-deception. The philosopher who moves to take a given position should know in advance the nature of the real presupposed in the position; he should know how he knows it; and he should know the presumptions concerning the nature of the person who knows and decides.

The Issue of the Existential

Accordingly, it is now necessary to state some aspects of a general position to indicate the rationale for an approach to liberal Christian themes. Since the issue of the existential is in the forefront of New Testament thought it may be well to begin with this.

Demythologizing the New Testament has two major drawbacks and one considerable advantage. Its first major defect is that it depends on a world-view defined by contemporary science and makes assumptions concerning that view and contemporary reactions to it. Its second major defect deriving from the first is that it requires a definition of knowing which will probably not hold water. Its considerable advantage is that is provides a fresh view of New Testament thought and of the Christian theme and greatly assists in the shaking up of elements of these at a time when intellectual elements are generally fluid and when new views are therefore especially useful.

It is quite right to say that the contemporary popular view of the world is conditioned by naturalistic methods and elements, and therefore that it is difficult to understand the New Testament when so much of recent thought is conditioned by old scientific forms and is struggling to master new scientific forms. The fact is, however, that modern popular thought is conditioned by what amounts to an eighteenth-century notion of the world and of the forms of knowledge necessary to understand it. There is a tremendous intellectual lag in such matters, and there are enormous lags in the scientific realm as well as in other modes of thought. It does not follow, however, that this condition is a good thing or that it ought to stand as a set of categories in terms of which contemporary understandings are to be cast. What does follow is that scientific modes and methods present highly useful ways of constructing cantilevers out into the unknown. Since these methods of study, experiment, and understanding are built to do certain things in their particular terms they must be expected to work. This is because there is a certain reflexiveness to the interaction of subject and object which can result in effective articulation of man and nature in certain of these modes of understanding. What is involved here is a conceptual epistemology which must be explicated elsewhere. It must be realized, however, that epistemological modes are constructional in nature, that they depend upon human decision and effort, and that knowledge is not simply a process of going out and breaking one's foot over the real in some segment of irreducible matter.

The scientific mode of understanding should therefore be regarded as highly useful technology, with philosophic or reflective implications, while the mind remains open to other modes or to modifications of the scientific mode. By implication the comment that modern man does not understand the New Testament appears as a fleeting consequence of contemporary intellective underbrush. It is by no means clear that this misunderstanding will or need endure. To establish a school of New Testament criticism and a religio-philosophic view of the nature of Jesus principally in response to so evanescent a condition is dubious at best. It may have the advantage of bringing fresh light to bear on the problem; this can be of great value. But to allow religious thought to be continually elbowed and crowded by the deceptive and illusory encroachment of pseudo-scientific modes of thought must be quite as disadvantageous as to allow some antique conception of the New Testament theme to stand forever without question at all.

There is as well a consequence for the analysis of thought. Knowledge is to be divided into myth and existential awareness. Myth is to be eliminated; it is allegedly contrary to things somehow known and somehow certain. The remainder is to be existential understanding.

Conceptualization is to be defined as limiting, abstractive, falsifying, and of no use to understanding in depth. Conveniently, old ideas can be called into question or eliminated by this means, and questioning of this kind has obvious uses. In its questioning of conceptualization as ground of constructional thought such analysis miscarries, however, and leaves the substance of awareness to be accounted for by some other means. Of course it immediately looks around and discovers the possibility of existential awareness.

The great question in all the existentialist positions is how they know what they know. There are several possibilities. It is possible to go into the analysis of consciousness, in which case one is probably approaching a neo-idealism of some kind; intuitionism offers an avenue if one is uncertain whence knowledge is to come; and then of course there is always the inelegant gut-type awareness that somehow precedes knowledge in any conventional sense and derives from an unspecifiable union of neuro-chemical and psychological sets. Existentialisms are commonly based on varieties of stomachy understandings that are extremely difficult to study and document, and which can be said to provide convenient escapes from the unwelcome precision of rational and intellective methodologies. Existentialisms have then for present purposes to be regarded as interstices in Western intellectual history, providing periodic readjustments of the subject-object relationship, enabling fresh views of major elements in the human condition, calling usefully into question standing concepts of the real, but in no way furnishing an enduring answer or even a method for the purpose of doing anything that would not otherwise be done by fundamental means in the course of time.

Knowledge is to be considered of the nature of the conceptual. What has been termed a New England approach in philosophy will require a greatly broadened definition of the conceptual to include much of the emotional as well as of the intellective. Reason will be established as the mode of understanding which gives rise to the conceptual. Individual human nature will find its best description in the person of rational-and-romantic-man, the definitive substance of the self which operates over the entire range of religious and humanistic concern.

As prologue therefore to an evaluation of New Testament thought, to attitudes toward the life of Jesus, or to other major Christian themes in the present time, it is necessary to remark the not inconsiderable philosophic swing that seems appropriate now, in the light of which it becomes once again the responsibility of the individual human life to recognize itself and to function as decisional entity. This is simply to recognize what has been observed before, that a reflective position is in the first instance a highly complicated decision taken by the self, and that the evidence that is then adduced to support the position becomes admissible as a consequence of the prior metaphysical decision rather than being antecedent to it. The expansion of the concept of the individual from that of neurologically responsive animal to the decisional human being in turn requires revision of various conservative notions of the self into the broad and deep conception of rational-and-romantic-man. Rationality and reason are here understood as referring to the capacity and instrument of judgment, involving the full range of the natural and spiritual self, able to strive for understanding and accomplishment, capable also of recognizing the limitations of the human self in its relation to the Ultimate. The term romantic is used here to convey the notion of man as striving and effortful entity, yearning always for greater understanding and accomplishment, aware of the emotional range and resource of human life but not confined to it, aware of the enormous capacity and power of the intellective reach of the self while constantly mindful of the Unreachable, profoundly sensible of the delicate balance of self-confidence and humility which in some strange way provides human life with its capacity to move most usefully within the receding ranges of its limitations.

Consequences for New Testament Thought

Evidently the maintaining or demitting of myth in the New Testament will depend heavily on the nature of knowing and in turn fundamentally on the view of the real or the metaphysics which underlies knowing. The individual student of such matters must decide whether knowledge in this field may be properly divided into myth and stomachy understanding. If myth is to be maintained in New Testament thought, then perhaps knowledge in other realms can equally well be divided into myths and intestinal awarenesses appropriate to them. There would be a Heideggerian myth; reference has already been made to the myth of natural science in a general sense; myths should also be identifiable in the separate sciences, such as psychology, chemistry, physics, and biology, as may very likely be the case; there would be the myth of history and the myths of other disciplines. The problem of stomachy understandings might present some difficulty in several of these modes of understanding but would presumably be significant in most of them. It is more probable that demythology in New Testament thought should be viewed as a belated response of New Testament and theological thought to the scientific mythos, under the mistaken presumption that there is something definite about the latter and that some sort of response ought to be made to it as to something certainly real. Any major swing in the conception of a field of study is interesting and even exciting, and it may be that intellectual progress can only be made through these major sweeps of the pendulum back and forth across the ranges of possibility.

There remain the two traps for intellectual heffalumps—the ignoring of the nature of knowledge and of knowing, and disregard of the generality of myth. Once it is recognized that the eighteenth century naturalistic view of the world which goes to make up so much of the contemporary popular world view is illusory, heavily made up of myth, and so similar to what the demythologizers have described as the state of awareness of New Testament thought, a very large part of the certainty concerning positions to be taken in New Testament as well as other realms of thought must vanish. For all of its uses as a way of shaking up and refreshing the contemporary intellectual complex obtaining around and about the life of Jesus it is probable that we are today in the midst of an interstitial situation, from which the way lies open in many directions.

The liberal religious decision is probably to be in the direction of what has been called a New England approach to the conception of human nature and of its living frame of reference. To take this position is of course to over-turn a very large part of the modern mood concerning the "scientific" approach to the nature of the universe in which man lives, and to throw open for redetermination practically every area of intellectual endeavor. The chances are that the remonstrance of a generation or two ago concerning the bifurcation of nature which was characteristic of the 17th and 18th centuries has only reappeared in another form, and that from it there depends a similar implied remonstrance that the nature of knowing must be suffused again into a broad conceptual whole. Achievement of such wholes is undoubtedly an end to be striven for though it is not likely to be accomplished, at least not in the present time. It can be an ideal because it can be conceived; in practice it will continue to be enormously difficult to bring about simply because in defining what something is, it is helpful to be able to say what it is not. Categorization into opposites or into a very few major classes of possibility may be inevitable within the foreseeable future, until a great deal more is known about the behaviors of philosophies, which is to say, until the reliable and repeatable patterns of philosophical evolution and change can be more clearly identified. Another point to note is that major ideas and forms of ideas tend to recur, often in new forms, so that there should be no surprise if the pattern of bifurcation should be repeated in subsequent sets of idea systems.

A New England Approach to a Liberal Ecumenism

It may be that there are times in the history of a well-defined culture when the organic union of Idea and Object enables the emerging of Spirit in new ways. Spirit will be understood as the happy articulation of idea with thing, subject with object, universal with particular, will with substance, such that there appear perhaps in new forms original and functional understandings of means and ends. The sombre imagination of Hawthorne has described such events in the early history of New England, occasions when over-arching purpose became clear to men if only for brief moments. To produce again a period having the characteristics of those early times there must be also in contemporary times a conception of the individual as entity of decisional capacity and power, profoundly aware of his limitations in relation to the Ultimate, aware too that movement in fact and relation, progress in the modern phrase, is a resultant of a receding, ever more majestic conception of Divinity in conjunction with a singular combination of power and limitation on the part of the individual Self. For man to imagine himself alone on the face of the earth or in the void of the heavens, or to see himself as the highest form of animal life on some wandering globe, is to limit his own capacity most cruelly, since he will then have no standards by which to determine what his capacities are nor any conceptions of great purpose by which to determine what he might become. If the great religious questions of our time are to be resolved again in ways appropriate to these times it will be necessary for the under-described and awkward figure of homo sapiens to recognize himself anew in the benign commitments of rational-and-romantic-man, to become aware in new ways of the extraordinary capacities that are his, and of the conceptual nature of knowing which goes far toward defining his astounding ability to realize the ranges of possibility.

A major question remains concerning the truth-value of the decisional process of rational-and-romantic-man. This is a fair question. How is one to judge between conclusions in conflict resulting from varied decisions that seem to follow with every appearance of validity from the stance or being-toward of different individual selves? In part the answer to this question may derive from the nature of Spirit, in which organic union obtains between Will and Object, as is surely the case from time to time in the periods of a culture or civilization. But Spirit too may be in error, as certain cultural episodes in Germany will suggest. Beyond this, there is the appeal to History, in which are hidden clues to the nature of the real that become audible when rung against the interpretive substance of historical knowledge in conjunction with tested and confirmed valuation.

A still newer possibility is, however, operative in several of the disciplines of knowledge. Pragmatic requirements of immediate tasks to be accomplished have conditioned until this time, except for the peculiar phenomenon of unresolved paradox, the limitation of understanding within the disciplines of the social and natural sciences and the humanistic studies to relatively straight-line derivations in accordance with demands of particular studies. A phenomenon can be understood in economic terms, in political terms, or perhaps in biological terms, and heretofore this has been sufficient for adequate description. Now, perhaps for the first time, it appears possible that seemingly contradictory conclusions can be regarded as being true at the same time. The sorting out of contradictory evidences and conclusions will remain the necessary result of the working out of the prior metaphysical decision within the welter of the several disciplines, subject to the corrective interpretations of history. Undeniably, however, it now becomes clear that seemingly contradictory conclusions can indeed be asserted and maintained from the same evidential base, the implications of which run counter to each other, the effect of which is simply to enlarge truth-possibilities rather than to blunt or twist them and so to destroy their natures.

If the drift of the present position is at all clear, it will be obvious that different theological ideas are examinable and allowable in this approach. The traditional idea of Christ as Son of God, sent to earth as Teacher and to become the Sacrifice to atone for the sins of fallen men, can exist alongside the nineteenth century liberal idea of Jesus as greatest of the prophets and best among men of good will, and likewise with other possible views. The interpretation presented here is that what is called for is a new look at the liberal idea of the religious status and stature of Everyman, so that the earlier religious conception of each individual life as one among the sons and daughters of Divinity can acquire again in its new context some sensible standing. This notion, once commonly held among the liberal churches, has necessarily been dislocated by the cultural divergence into scientism in the first half of the twentieth century. It could not have been otherwise, for there was an enormous amount of scientific work to do, and it was entirely to be expected where so large a portion of energy was consumed in those labors that there should have resulted some metaphysical limitations accurately reflected in philosophic writings and in popular ideas concerning the nature of the real. As this large but perhaps unavoidable error in American intellectual history is now at last beginning to be outmoded, it should be possible to reexamine the general idea of the religious significance of each individual life in the quite different context of the wholly religious significance of life in general. In this perspective Jesus may appear truly as Son of God, in special case, as indeed every individual person is son of God in a universal sense.

What then is needed is the context of the religious significance of human life as ground notion, as distinct from the bifurcation of life and nature into the religious and the secular. In this view there is only the religious, which is to say, life and nature are seen as purposeful in the largest sense. If men insist on cutting themselves down to the level of the secular, they rest on the level of rejection of the fullness of self-development. The freedom to choose belongs with the self, and Grace— sometimes in obscure form—is ever present.

The reason for the long way around must now be clear. It will require a considerable effort of mind to entertain the reflective ground notions toward liberal ecumenism briefly sketched in these pages. A New England approach, involving so profoundly the stance of the individual self toward some tested and validated position, perversely provides for equal or added weight to opposing interpretations which may well carry the day in the course of ecumenical history.

The notable point is simply that this is again a time when the powerful individual bent for being-toward can possibly be determinative in great ways. Granting all the need for checks and limitations, for tests of value and validity, still Everyman can stand for great ideas amid the confusions and alarums of these days. Indeed, in the realm of ideas Everyman is the best advocate of a particular position, as distinct from some form of group advocacy, and if the spirit moves in him he may even be the major advocate on behalf of others for such a position.

There is this difference from earlier times, that then resistance to oppression faced outward against governments and nations, whereas now the tyranny is more nearly a self-restriction imposed individually from within, a rejection of possibility as if by choice. If the burden seems heavier for that it may be because restraints of self are selectively less necessary, applicable within the framework of social order, taste, and valuational self discipline, but often not required as artificial limitations on the natural and conceptual outreach of the self. Social freedoms may be within reach. Rational self-determination, that incomparably greater end, may still be far away.

VI   The Plunge through Law: Education in the New Romantic Age

Among the most difficult of reflective issues is that of the general idea. To put it differently, the general philosophic assumptions of a given cultural period go far toward making up the intellectual stuff of that period because so often they underlie the positions taken, attitudes held, and directions or vectors of significant components of outlook.

Among the great swings of the pendulum which eventuate in one or another of the major reflective questions appears now the basic one of What is Real?—Although it is somewhat seeing matters after the fact, it is not improbable that such a metaphysical mood can follow on a series of questions which have been uppermost in the Western mind for a century or so, issues clustered around the natural world contributed to substantially by the several sciences, other issues centering around human nature contributed to equally substantially by Freudian-psychological traditions, and similarly involved social issues the implications of which are not yet explicit. It is as if in some subterranean fashion the common mood of Western civilization, or at least of the visible segment of it, appears to know in advance of being explicit about it when a particular line of investigation is approaching its end, so that investigative allegiance tends to shift to a new line. Another way of saying this might be that if it were possible to delineate a behavior or behavioral description of the histories of philosophies it would be clear that new philosophic strains tend to begin in advance of the conclusion of old ones, and that in some peculiar way the behaviors of persons who may not be philosophers at all reflect a general awareness of philosophic relevances to such degree that various levels of operation, feelings and actions can be said to reflect the idea-condition of the time. Still another way of saying this is that certain types of behavior on the level of action can be interpreted philosophically, as for example the incident of the Laconia motorcyclists in the summer of 1965.

In this occurrence a convention of motorcyclists spilled over into anti-social behavior in Laconia, New Hampshire and more or less tore up the town. Similar instances occurred among motorcycle clubs in California. More recent student behaviors in campus upheavals have been subject to frequent analysis from a similar standpoint; in these the intellectual or idea-dimension is nearer the surface, though variously interpreted. Behaviors of these types can be seen as representing efforts to discover what is real in a new period of time, or in another expression to determine what is worth doing. To describe instances of behavior as purposeless or senseless may only mean that it is purposeless or senseless within a given frame of reference. Once the frame of reference is called into question, as it may well have been by the persons engaged in the behavior, it is possible that the antisocial behavior would be seen as "making sense" in a manner of speaking, albeit also illegal, physically dangerous, or in other respects unacceptable in traditional continua.

The underlying idea here is that action and notion are interwoven and articulated, perhaps best understood as a single dimension, so that where a notion or general idea is concerned it should be possible to figure out what actional consequences might follow, and where a course of action is under examination it should be possible to figure out what philosophic position it represents. In taking such a position one is not unaware of emotionality as a ground of explanation of behavior; this is simply to suggest that there may also be modes of definition of notionality as general idea and action, behavior subsuming emotion.

The Complicated Nature of Romanticism

Romanticism can perhaps be understood as renewal of the process of unfolding possibility. In terms of the articulation of notion and action and the overlapping of old and new reflective positions in a given cultural context, it may be said that from time to time man becomes bored with the forms of thought, the ideas, the institutional practices in which his interests have lately been expressed, and so seeks for new ones. Search may be equivalent to construction: it may be necessary that he actually build new forms or modes if his restless energies are to find appropriate expression in a puzzling present age, when violence lurks around every corner and when so many public and private events seem to contain destruction as one of their forceful elements. It may indeed be worthwhile to reflect that the things we see may be embodiments of a new surge of the human psyche emerging from a culmination of revolt and re-assertion. Perhaps they represent in the final analysis most simply a new outreach of the spirit of man, blinded and blinking in the daylight, its assumptions unsure, its capacities and powers untested, its objectives still veiled in uncertainty—but withal grasping for new realizations in the worlds of today and tomorrow.

The central question—What is Real?—may indeed be the essential query of the hooded and booted motorcyclist who strikes down a pedestrian and does not stop; of the urban revolutionary who overturns police cars, sets buildings on fire, steals goods, and pelts onlookers with stones; of the college-age experimenter who takes mind-altering drugs as part of a deliberate campaign to widen his perceptions and awarenesses, to peer, perhaps, around the corners of consciousness into new corridors of existence and potentiality; of the anti-hero and the anti-man, the youthful Citizen Genet who commits crimes because he likes to and because to him there isn't any reason why he shouldn't; of the campus rioter who siezes buildings in the hope that the arrival of police will help to polarize his community and bring him power; even of the subtle avoider of taxes, speed laws, or similar social expectations, who may mean well but is in a hurry or has other matters on his mind, or who just hasn't taken time to define his relation to the common country of which he is a part. Perhaps the question expressed in these behaviors is ultimately the same—What is really real?—And then, since the ethical appears to follow the metaphysical, a second question would be—What is to be done about it?—All this is to say, the franticity of young people may be more a series of efforts to grasp the reality of things than simply to rebel against the adult world, as is often suggested, or to indulge the self with pleasures as has also been thought to be the case. Perhaps the moral quest should always be formulated in terms of the consequences of a metaphysic: to be right one does what fits the real; one does not normally work against the laws of the real, assuming that the objective is the Socratic and of doing the right thing if one knows what that is. Therefore, the ground of an ethical inquiry is a metaphysical formulation. To devise a moral code it is first necessary to discover and construct a judgment of the real.

The present purpose is less to repeat a ground of moral theory which has been described often enough before than to remark the ways in which the ethico-metaphysical situation works itself out in the cultural turmoil of the present day. For persons concerned with education the point may be significant, for it is on some such grounds, however the issue of the metaphysical resolution may settle itself, that the educational policies of the immediate future are likely to be decided.

Education, let us suppose, deals with idea and practice of the idea, more with idea than practice, for there is a lifetime left for the evolving of practice and action even if education is conceived of as continuous in later life. The relation of education to law may then be a sensitive one, for law may be said to be concerned with the same relation in reverse order, that is, with the dimension of practice articulated with idea, more with practice than with idea, the exigencies of individual existence in society being what they are. In problems of technical or actual breach of law by young people of college or near-college age the field of legal philosophy may come to be of more than customary significance, since the decisions and actions of young people appear to stem directly from ideas they hold and since the resolutions of conflicts may in some cases involve the realm of ideas more immediately than the realm of practice. In some instances this involvement might make a difference in the disposition of a case at law.

It should be clear by now what the characteristics of this neo-romanticism are. The 'beat' phase of a recent decade was a minor episode in the passing show; it was no more than a first stage of withdrawal from old concepts, followed by lethargy or at best by a disoriented thrashing-around, for the most part disarticulated from any real problems beyond personal whims of the moment. The so-called 'beat' philosophy consists of descriptive materials, sensational dramatizations of allegedly new modes of life, but essentially without understanding, basically dull, uninteresting, and ephemeral. In the 'beat' or hippie mode there is no place for the ''lost'' to go, because going somewhere involves purpose and commitment, and these in turn involve structure. Movement is not possible on a foundation of simple withdrawal and non-involvement. And in the long run human nature cannot be kept contented in a condition of emptiness. Whatever the price in wasted years and useless lives, in the end human nature will insist on gathering itself up and moving off anew.

If romanticism is to be understood as the endless surge of the Self, as in its earliest phases and to some continuing extent the effort toward self-understanding, certainly in its middle and later phases as the drive toward conquest and accomplishment involving expansion of understanding of the self as basis for expanded articulation with the environment, then in turn the partial objective of education has to be in the direction of meeting the surge of selfhood with structural channels of expression and experience such that the Self can develop its competence in the realms of being and doing. Structure is nearly always rational. This is to say, it partakes of some kind of logical arrangement of space and time and of the content of space and time. Rationality and structure have to be closely interwoven, so that it is proper to describe human nature in the hyphenated phrase ''rational-and-romantic-man.'' Structure will have been conceived by man and implemented by him; structure is perhaps a natural product of the rationality of human nature. Yet it is also the nature of man which fractures structure, which rebels against it by a variety of sensible or nonsensical undertakings, and which in the end may move beyond given levels of structure into new opennesses into which in turn additional structures may be introduced to become formative and disciplined receptacles of early wildness and untempered self-expression. Human nature, it appears, works in both these modes—the structural or rational, and the romantic.

Descriptions of rational-and-romantic-man are numerous enough. Heretofore it has been common to characterize an age or a century as being predominantly one or the other, rational or romantic. No doubt the characterizations were reasonably accurate and did describe an alternating emphasis on one or the other, the length and intensity of the phases of which depended in some part on the rate of change in social and intellectual characteristics in general terms of a given period and on the relation of this rate of change to the working through of particular sets of ideas. At one cultural stage it might well take two full generations spread over a time range of three generations to work through a set of assumptions, while in another epoch due to a differing rate of change the length of time consumed in such working through of assumption-sets might have been considerably more, or might some day be considerably less. The presumption in our own period is that the time consumption in the working through of assumption-sets is indeed markedly less than it was a century or two ago.

Human nature at the college age then presents a built-in romantic constant, by which is meant a fundamental and recurrent drive to be and to do more than it has been or has done. Education has to expect this; it may well expect all kinds of bizarre behavior as manifestations of it. If it is accurate to describe the present period as romantic or neo-romantic, whether partially or predominantly, this observation will be reasonable enough. The problem will be rather how to understand rationality and the attitude toward structure.

Education and Law

In common expression romanticism and rationality tend to be opposed, or to be at best extreme polarizations of an attenuated continuum. This is no doubt a consequence of the emphasis on biology and psychology from 1850 to the present time. Knowing is held to be rational, and knowledge to partake of the nature of rationality. Romanticism is seen as somehow demonic, made up of that which is left over in human nature, of the uncontrolled, the wild and passionate, the non-rational and non-structural. There is also a tendency, perhaps stronger rather than weaker even in our own self-conscious day, to equate the creative with the demonic, and to oppose the creative and the rational or structural. That is, if one can be said to know something somehow the knowing and the known are lessened in the universal standings of value; that which can be characterized is weaker than that which cannot; what can be managed or administered is somehow poorer than the untamed energy of nature in advance of its conquest by man. This view is very old, having come down to us from early Greek times and is no doubt rooted deeply in human understanding. But it may be worth noting even in this latter day that rationality itself may partake of the romantic, the demonic, and the creative and may in truth be one of the fundaments of position and of movement. In the nineteenth century Kierkegaard revived the notion of the power of the irrational and gave to it an enormous impetus which has been felt in the twentieth century from the heart of Europe throughout the West. It may be extremely difficult to change the contemporary tendency to polarize human understanding into the rational on one hand and the demonic or irrational on the other. Yet the power of rationality and the capacity of reason to range at large over the face of the universe is surely as amazing a phenomenon as can be discerned in any formulation of demonic energy, fully as amazing as the purely irrational or non-rational. It is not just that the magic of the unknown can be said to obscure the wonder of the known.

These are cultural positions and they will change. Rationality will not always be regarded as the systems of inert formulations into which the surges of the Self are cast after they have lost their living qualities and their mysterious motivating force. Reason itself may come again to be regarded as an originating force in its own right. How long this may take may be a function of the length of time consumed in the working through of reflective assumptions in a particular set of circumstances.

If something like this takes place the philosophic approach may shift. In the dimension of order and disorder an enormous advantage always accrues to rebellion. The upstart mode, the attack from below, the intrusion from small-group sources polarized against the accepted formulation, against the old, the previously established, and the traditional, is invariably a species of tweaking the lion's tail. This being so, that which is new or radical or revolutionary subsists in part on the sufferance of that which has been. The attack is pressed from the standpoint of disorder upon the positions of order. In most cases the substance of the new is discovered in a new reading of the real; that is, the effort of criticism is to look within the aged husks of reality to discover its true nature and formulation apart from the encrustations attached in the course of time and of human operations. Originality is ordinarily thought to be found in the mysterious and the unmapped. A phase of the ultimate resides so to speak within the newly discovered nature of things, so that the object or end-purpose of rebellion is to bring it to light and to generalize it over its range of applicability. The effect of all this is to deliver to disorder or to the demonic the tactical advantage of initiative. It can engage the fight, select the ground and the conditions of contention, and function for a long time without the normal consequences of opposition. It is as if every new idea were cast freely to the winds in some convenient Trafalgar Square, unencumbered for a time by the risks of consequence.

Law partakes of order. It stands, it protects, it expresses what is and has been—all of this at least in common thought. If creativity is seen as residing elsewhere than in the rational, then the nature of law remains essentially conservative rather than creative, receiving and passive rather than giving and active, and in the end comes to be regarded as inert, defensive, subject to successful attack from new angles much as a

Maginot line in generations past was turned by a technology which it had failed to note.

If however rationality embodies creativity, at least in some measure, then the nature of law too may be different. It may be regarded as a centrally creative and constructional formulation jutting forward into the uncharted regions of time and relation, the very vehicle of change, perchance the actual substance of active knowledge. Popular views of things are difficult to combat and yet they do much to shape conceptions of things. Law is too often seen in the dimension of the great obstacle fractured by the obstreperous individual, the consequences played out in court and press, the results often some period of detachment from common life for the person concerned, or a different penalty otherwise defined. This may be the obvious facade. The essential content of the drama may be elsewhere; it may be better interpreted as an expression of knowledge and of knowing, applied from the general to the particular, for the common or social good.

A lag exists in the law as in other human spheres, and some laws surely become antique when they no longer represent what is known. They must be changed, and usually they are. Knowledge can range beyond particular laws; but perhaps it cannot range beyond law in general. The old problem of universals no doubt rears itself amid these observations. Opinions may differ temperamentally as to whether there is such a thing as law in general. The question is at least debatable, even in law; one may note it and pass on. It may not be necessary to raise the questions hinging around the three major schools of legal philosophy,— natural law, positivism, and historical jurisprudence. Conceivably the approach and the consequence where education is concerned may be the same in effect for all three.

There would, however, be a philosophical problem underlying this approach, and it would have a consequence for education if not for law. The problem lies in the general assumption that rationality and reason constitute a real and formative mode of human operation and understanding, and that the faculty referred to by these terms does engage with aspects of the universe which are significant and dependable. Undeniably it would be simpler to rule reason out of account and take a strictly empiricist stand; one would then have merely to record the data of sensory reception and responses made to them, and ultimately to devise laws representing as large a number of particular cases as is convenient for a given sphere of operation. The question which inevitably comes to mind is whether the empiricist approach is over-simplified to the extent that it no longer represents the nature of things and of process.

If on the other hand reason and rationality are to be regarded as valid modes of constructional understanding, and if law in general and to some extent laws in particular are to be regarded as extensional dimensions of rationality then it is possible that the natures of both education and law are affected in the direction of turning towards discovery of new ranges of understanding as distinct from mere defensive assertions concerning what has been understood to be real in particular times and places. If the major concern should be the nature of law, then it would appear that a position of what might be called tentative idealism might emerge in which the uncertainty of actual law would be recognized even while its general nature were being acknowledged as idealistic or partaking of the fundament of the idea. If the major concern were the nature of education, then it would be necessary to re-address the educational effort in some part to the nature of idea as realistic and formative, withdrawing some emphasis from behavior, statistics, numerical evidence, and the like.

It has certainly been true in the past that rebellion against ideas has been an element in educative development of young people. Perhaps this has been so in part because of the mistaking of particular ideas, even of particular systems of ideas, for the general nature of idea. Idolatry can arise in any context and in any mode, and the mode of the idea should not be an exception to the expectation.

Behavior can certainly be an evidence of idea. Indeed, the argument presently is that behaviors can be strong clues to ideas, and that a common error in recent times has been the neglect of interpreting behavior such as that of the Laconia motorcyclists or other law-breakers so that the ideas inherent in these manifestations have been obscured or missed. To come at the matter from another side, to take a tentative-idealistic (conceptualist) position is to recognize that idea underlies all behavior, and that behavior can be used to discover it. In the end this is just another way of attempting to overcome the "false dichotomy" or bifurcation of nature, in which empirically perceived events or things are regarded as one type of knowledge whereas other types such as the rational or the intuitive are regarded as generically different, less reliable, weakly imaginative or simply threadlike rather than substantial.

The Plunge Through Law

Law is then to be regarded as consensus among structural decisions. Law-breaking in the present context can be described as the quest for intensification of subject-object relation, as a kind of quest for knowledge. The "plunge through law" is a drive to touch the real, or short of that, to test the real. Certain types of extra-legal endeavor may be more difficult than others to describe in this context. Violence can be understood in strictly pathological terms, and some cases of it should no doubt be so understood. But even a psychopathic frame of reference may convey a species of groping for what is solid, which is to say for a reliable mode of comprehension. It is as if anti-social behaviors were in some part to be seen as forms of search for the substantial.

There should be some means of confirmation of the actual condition or case, by operational repetition, by simple concatenation of events, or by social agreement. There cannot be certainty, but only tendency, probability, greater or lesser likelihood that one interpretation properly supervenes another.

A great many problems of law will continue to be settled in the most practical of terms. Similarly educational policies will continue to be set in accordance with one or another of several major educational philosophies. The point to stress for present purposes is that behaviors and ideas should be regarded as closely articulated, such that the one by implication conveys the other. Because of the pressures of events in these several spheres there is an enormous temptation to deal with each strictly in its own terms and to ignore its conveyance. If the articulation is noted rather than ignored there may be considerable consequences for philosophy of law and of education, and in the long run for implementations of policy in these fields.

Inevitably and reassuringly, the general problem remains open-ended. Questions to which it may be useful to turn at some convenient time are: What are the grounds of law in a subjective or conceptual universe? What factors contribute to the relations of education and law in particular situations? How tentative are we willing to be in the face of the multiplications of individualistic absolutisms? Remembering always that recreating the world in hypothetical reference frames is a heady thing, indeed, how open-minded can a culture and its educational system afford to be in these crucial regions of thought and decision? And not least, what is the metaphysical reality of the social or group dimension in terms of which so much practical law is cast, and which the violent inquiry of today denies by its intent and affirms by its existence?

VII   The City Education Center:
A New Institution for a New Task

Two variant solutions are being advanced for the development of higher education in the inner-city. The first suggests that selecting-out as many capable young people as possible and sending them to college and universities will eventually modify the depressed nature of the central city. The second advocates the founding of new urban universities to place educational opportunities where they are needed. It will be contended here that modification by extraction will not affect the central city, and that while new urban universities may indeed be needed these alone will not include enough people, in the city or out of it, to make the necessary difference. These two considerations have in common the question of whether selective admission to the necessarily abstract and verbal communication systems which constitute a college or university, brought to bear at that admission level, can provide educational channels sufficiently open to encompass the rising social energies of these times.

The Selecting-Out Proposal

A familiar type of conceptual fallacy appears to be restricting social policy with respect to inner-city or depressed-area urban education. The selecting-out proposal suggests that if enough units of a kind are subtracted from an aggregation of units, the remaining aggregation will in time be fundamentally changed, its problems resolved, its illnesses cured, its unfortunate characteristics transformed. It may be so for plant or animal groups where pervasive management techniques are applicable. It is hardly close to a practical policy involving the predictable characteristics of large human groups. The interesting old study of the Jukes and the Kallikaks which most psychology students once read about in college, thinking no doubt that it uncovered something reliable about social evolution, contained a similar error. It assumed that the statistical forms of the study, its conceptual notions and methodology,

70

encompassed the capacities and behaviors of the two families of individuals and therefore that their futures could be predicted from them. This was not so. Individual human capacities are not represented in so strict a statistical mode. The evolutionary increase of one family type over the other, generalized into a form of the overrunning-of-the-earth motif, does not reflect a comprehensive range of actual human mobility, nor does it describe the complex range of individual and group relations. It is an interesting idea, but that is all.

Urban educational pressures may lead now to comparable self-deception. Selecting from inner-cities a range of students who can qualify for admission to the residential colleges and universities of the country is a good thing in itself. It is worth doing; it cannot do serious harm; it will add to the capabilities of the students, to the potential of the families and communities they later form, to their own professional achievements and to the level of the general culture. It will add to the educated and competent majority, self-sustaining, contributing, creating. It would be convenient to assume that as the competent group expands the inner-city residues will contract and die away and that the inner-city problems will disappear with the generations from which they arose. It is characteristic of human thought that it should comfort itself with the notion that difficult problems will go away if things continue in some promising direction. Some problems may oblige in this way. Many will not.

Human aggregates do not readily remain within statistical categories. The inner-city groups, those great collections of social protoplasm, are living too. They will remain alive, creative, full of promise, operative where and as they are—enormous reservoirs of potentiality. They can spare the few hundred or few thousand students selected out each year to attend college in the country enclaves of educational peace and possibility. Departing students will not even be missed, except in a friendship way. The inner-cities will remain unaffected and untouched, closing their ranks, flowing to and fro over the pavement, boiling among the bricks and brownstones.

Residential colleges and universities are moving very much as they should to admit as many students as they can educate, with representation from all parts of the population. By and large with very few exceptions the higher education institutions in America are integrated, open-minded, and socially responsive. They are doing what they can,

71

and as they see what more can be done, whether this involves admitting more scholarship students, or simply doing a better educational job with the students they now have, they will do these things. Educators are honest people dedicated to their life-work; they are also harshly self-critical, constantly berating themselves and their fellow-educators for not doing better than they do. Indeed, the critical function in American education may be better served among educators than among the interested laity.

Residential colleges and universities, great as they have been and still remain, are simply not intended to achieve major social transformations of a specific sort, in type or region. Their work is different. It is unfair to expect a residential higher education system to enable rapid social transformation when its own chief commitment is to individual learning, teaching, research, and intellective reflection, often at locations remote from centers of social difficulty. The question of the durability and practicality of the residential college can certainly be raised on other grounds, social and communicational. But this is another story. It is simply unreasonable to ask higher education institutions to do something which they were not set up to do, and which, if they were to try to do it, would interfere with other fundamental responsibilities.

That higher education institutions have responsibilities more fundamental than social reform would not have been news to earlier generations. Hopefully it is not news now. The issue is philosophic. The life of mind and idea is real and formative; otherwise the major preoccupations of higher education should be replaced with physical and emotional self-culture. Philosophy is subject to fashion along with dress and vehicular design. Just now it is entertaining itself with matters apart from its central nature. Reflective institutions, educational and religious, have been misled by these ill-founded fashions and may have begun to doubt their kind. They should return to philosophic reality and get on with their true business.

What then is a workable relation between education and social development—specifically, the development of inner-city populations into happy and satisfied contributors to life and thought? For education in general does have a social responsibility, or more properly, an educational responsibility which carries with it a social dimension.

72

The City Education Center

Imagine for a moment a new educational institution of indeterminate threshold among the elementary or secondary grade-levels, continuing through the first or second year of college, a City Education Center. It should exist in the midst of the city; its boundaries should be unclear, its exclusiveness nonexistent; it should maintain the educative function in all needful regions, communicational, conceptual, self expressional, and it should do so within the immediacy of urban life and pressure. It should be open at all times of day and night. People of all levels of preparation, of all ages, and of all vocations, the employed and unemployed, should move freely in and out of it. Almost no one should be denied admission. Guidance and classification should assist the student in discovering what he can do best and what he does least well. Counseling services should help with decisions and choices. Valuation study should be immediate and constant. Education for the good of oneself and others should become visible as a value above negative values—values associated with human dignity as above values of social disintegration and criminality. The presence of value contrasts in the inner-city, in settings open to all and closed to none, would introduce useful confrontations of relative valuations in formative as well as in adult years.

The question of the relation of the City Education Center to other divisions of the educational system will come to mind. Its relation to elementary and secondary, vocational, technical, pre-professional, para-professional and other special educations would have to be worked out functionally to diminish overlap and to provide educational services not otherwise present in a given city context. There should be some common ground with higher education systems, although not by more than a year or two, to enable flexible transfers of students from Center programs to terminal or continuing higher education programs.

Types of education to be available in a City Education Center above the varied preparational levels should surely be general liberal arts, vocational and technical, pre-professional, para-professional and continuing. The Center should provide any or all of these as needed, with arrangements for transfer of students to established liberal arts and professional institutions of higher education as early as practical. It would be of prime importance that community relations and community services be parts of the City Education Center. Competitive implications are not the point and would be highly undesirable. Education is a beneficent tension between abstract reality and human development. There is little point in denying one important function of education in order to do a better job at another.

In an original survey of his own from the former Rodman Job Corps Center staff in New Bedford, Massachusetts, Douglas Osborne has suggested from his experience with residential vocational education some interesting points of variation. He observes that to meet the long-range educational needs of a community it is necessary first to meet the short-range needs. In addition to continuing educational and vocational training he points to the possibility of an experimental program in preparing teachers' aides. Community parents could be trained at the Center to assist in the school and to encourage community involvements in education at several levels. He also sees connections between City Education Centers and agencies such as Neighborhood Youth Corps, Head Start programs, Distributive Education programs, and after-school tutorials. Some form of subsistence allowance or educational stipend he would see as desirable if this could be coordinated with public agencies so as to encourage rather than discourage individual initiative.

Clark Kerr has spoken of the need for urban colleges and universities to be founded in urban centers where education is needed, rather than for existing institutions to be overtaken by embarrassments resulting from their accidental submersion in urban problems. The question here is whether the standard college or university is what is really needed in the central city. The Antioch-Goddard "beach-head college," later referred to as the system or "network" unit, is a variant approach on a small scale, applicable either to rural or urban settings. Higher education institutions planning expansions in the next few years may think of coordinate non-residential institutions in urban centers, or technically oriented coordinate divisions, or any combination of these with other educational vectors. There are some indications of related concern among the great private foundations whose task it is to enable pilot efforts in new directions prior to the commitment of major public investments through federal and state funds.

The proposed City Education Center is conceived of as a new educational institution—if indeed any institution or suggestion can ever be new—paralleling the pre-college and first college years, departing flexibly from existing school systems at those points where local community conditions indicate that there is work to be done, and returning students to existing colleges and universities at the first or second college year or at convenient points thereafter, for completion of liberal arts or special education if those are their educational needs and if the means to meet them already exist. The Center would be new in its flexibility at both ends and in its conception of itself as multiform, not exclusively liberal arts, not exclusively technical or vocational, not exclusively anything, but rather inclusively all of these as might be required in particular settings or required from time to time in those settings. Certainly it should provide great freedom of movement for students among its numerous educational modes.

A Balance of Institutions

The temptation to educational apocalypse should be resisted. Existing colleges and universities in America are not and should not become primarily agents for social reform. Their truth-function, so to speak, and their individual educative functions, long tried and found of value, can be interfered with only at peril of eclipsing modes of understanding and operation which stand at the heart of American life. They are also, of course, abstraction systems necessarily requiring that their entrants satisfy conditions of admission appropriate to particular tasks which institutions have defined for themselves. Educative needs have broadened now so that the residential liberal arts college may itself have become a special kind of institution where once its lines were classic and very general.

To set down new higher education institutions of standard kinds in urban settings as Dr. Kerr suggests, assuming they would admit some and exclude many, seems not to the point. More colleges and universities may be needed, some of them even in urban settings. But this is far less likely now than in earlier years. The futuristic learning industry, infant giant of the planning boards, with its radical ideas of the Edunet variety, will likewise have a thing or two to say on the need for multiplying higher education institutions, as it may with respect to every level of education. For present purposes the notion of the City Education Center is directed rather toward the need for educational institutions which will invite into their flexible and capacious functions all who wish to learn, and who will teach in whatever modes and contents are required by the conditions of those who come to study.

75

Clearly there is common ground and a close relation between the proposed City Education Center function and the existing American college and university function, however the communicational forms of these functions may develop in years to come. It would be unnecessary for them to conflict and unwise for them to be mutually exclusive. Each would have its purpose, however intricately articulated they might be.

It is encouraging to see these problems coming under heavy discussion. Useful ideas commonly rise in several contexts at the same time, helpfully so in complex societies where vast energies are roaming in the search for things to do. The consensus of concern, if not yet of policy, points surely to a genuine focus of need. Whatever the ultimate solution, it is certain that urban education, especially inner-city education, will draw to itself major private and public energies, with enormous general consequences.

VIII Image-Suffusion in the Small-Group as Limitation on the Bio-Social Ethic

The bio-social ethic, a common contemporary position in ethical thought, discovers a hitherto unseen limitation on its systematic nature and operation through the agency of image-suffusion in the small-group setting. It appears that study of the phenomenon points to a general limitation on the operation of philosophic systems, with particular reference to ethics as illustrated in the bio-social sub-system.

An ethic described as being of bio-social origin, such as that attributed to John Dewey, Max Otto and comparable figures, refers to the biological or social orders of reality for the fundamental categories of the system. The implication or assumption is that the biological order, to take one aspect, provides the basic reality underlying human nature and its behavior. Ethical problems can be referred to this biological order for resolution in cases of conflict, indeterminacy, or other uncertainty. It is necessary to understand that every reflective system has its order of final responsibility into which its systematic problems are referred for decision. The ethics of Dewey and Otto were heavily social, but with a biological frame of reference such that a combined category becomes a practical description in brief of their primary positions. Inevitably, enormous questions remain; as with the ethic of Ralph Barton Perry, ethical conflicts can frequently be settled so-to-speak by resolution of forces. That is, if two forces are opposed in an ethical conflict, one being of the order of 80 and one of the order of 20 on a scale of 100, an ethical resolution can be reached often enough by drawing the line between the principals at the 80 / 20 point. Dewey is more complicated than this, but his ethic is clearly social in its nature; he sees the composition of human nature as largely social and biological in a broad sense.

It is not often that the consequences of operation of an ethical position can be examined with anything like completeness. The present instance is problematic, and yet withal provides an interesting setting for examination of a particular ethical position as well as of the operation of systems in general.

One ordinary assumption in ethics is of course that each ethic rests on the foundation of a metaphysic. That is the assumption here. Ethical problems become immeasurably more difficult in a cultural period characterized by metaphysical flux, as has been the condition lately. To examine an ethical problem it is necessary to isolate the root metaphysic as well as the consequential ethic which is under study. A metaphysical assumption is one that is appropriate to make prior to any specification or derivation from it. The dimensions of metaphysics, like the incidence of logics, are substantially on the increase in our time and their multiplication cannot be ignored in the considerations of sub-fields such as ethics.

The probability is that image-suffusion is a relatively rare phenomenon in American society because of the commonly high degrees of intercommunication usually operating among small groups and constantly increasing with technological improvements in communications methods and also as a consequence of heightened mobility among American social groups. It may still occur in occasional instances of cultural isolation, as for example where a social group lives in a remote region with little contact outside, but obviously this is increasingly unlikely as a cultural characteristic. The case which lends itself to study is less likely to be of an anthropological type, and more likely to be a social accident deriving from contemporary conditions of life. By image-suffusion is meant the relatively uniform distribution of the self-picture of the small-group diffused throughout that group with notably rare occurrences of rejection or disagreement. The result of image-suffusion is that the group can behave substantially as a unit, can conceive of itself as a unit, and can project itself into the future as a unit.

Image-suffusion will, however, take place only when the small-group is isolated. Articulation between the small-group and the large-group will inevitably mask the limitations of an ethic operative in the small-group, since ethical cases and problems will constantly be referred out of the small-group for resolution in the large-group. As articulation is all but universal in American society it is the more interesting to observe what happens in its absence.

Modes of articulation are several, such as socialization, customs and codes, and law. For articulation to be absent or nearly absent at least these three ranges of relation must be in short supply. Socialization involves the active social relation of persons in different groups. Customs and codes involve modes of behavior within restricted referential fields, such as might belong to professional groups, age groups, or other moderate divisions of the social order. Law, the most powerful of articulations, will involve the decisions of the large-group expressed by the various appropriate means of common decision. For these three types of articulation to be absent or in short supply is surely an unusual circumstance, but it may obtain in some measure occasionally on the American college campus.

Silence among the generations has been a problem since Biblical times and need hardly surprise anyone now. It has, from time to time, however, been replaced at least in part by an active, virulent anger between the generations which is no respecter of families, as in a type of striving and conflicting in the highly communicative, urban life of late-20th century. It often appears that a young person asserts his or her right to decision-making power and the right of command well in advance of any ability to contribute to the common life or to assume responsibility for the consequences of decisions made. A notable characteristic of young people in this group is their inability to bear without anguish any form of denial. To bear any kind of ''No'' is to provoke resentment and conflict, or intellectual escape through rationalizing of the ''No'' into meaning ''Yes'' for someone's supposedly devious reasons. Obviously the connections of this phenomenon are very wide; the decline of family life, communicational impact, the drum-beats of urban existence, and the like all contribute to a transformation of the environment of young people with consequences which cannot yet be foretold. In any event, for present purposes socialization as a mode of articulation of the small-group to the large-group is a casualty of the process.

Customs and codes are likewise residual, attached as they often are to many of the groups represented in the decline of socialization. Customs and codes are always ultimately referrable to metaphysical underpinnings. In most instances the referral is not needed and is not made, since customs and codes are essentially shorthand ways of managing multitudes of cases in which profound thought and analysis are unnecessary. They become, however, flimsy in structure and residue when the metaphysical underpinnings are not firmly accepted, or when the groups upon which they are based are called into question. It must be expected, therefore, that codes and customs will not be great sources of strength for order in the present circumstances.

Among all the modes of articulation law is the greatest, the most interesting, the most profound, and the most complicated. Law, too, derives from a metaphysical ground; to derive it socially in a Holmesian manner is merely to defer the question; to derive it historically, grounding it in the history of previous formulations of law, is again interesting and partly justifiable, but ultimately this too is a deferral of the final grounding of law in a metaphysic of some kind. In the long run human understanding is dissatisfied with the grounding of law in any of the cultural halfway houses such as the social order, history, or custom. The ultimate question arises in the end: what is the final ground of law? And once this question arises, while the final answer is never within reach, it is clear that a half-answer will never satisfy. It will then be no surprise that in a situation in which articulation declines, the decline of law is a prerequisite to it. This, too, may have occurred in the small-group in recent times. Two factors appear to be at work. The first is the multiplication of metaphysical dimensions previously noted as characteristic of the understandings of this day. The second is the practical revolt against law conceived of as a facet of the cultural "old world" of adults, the yesterdays, the "over 30's", the squares, and the "not-with-its." What then happens when these modes of articulation decline and the small-group falls heir to the consequences?

The resulting creation of the Golding society of youth in isolation from adults alters somewhat the general comment to be made about the nature of human nature. If it is to be acknowledged that American culture is a function of the ordinarily constant articulation of the small-group with the large-group—and so on out in successive layers of small-group into something approaching the 200,000,000-member society which stretches from ocean to ocean—then by implication the distinction of the potentials of human nature must be differently described in a circumstance in which atypical isolation is to be characteristic of a fragment of the social order. Human nature has evidently been evaluated upon an assumption of socio-cultural context which has been taken for granted, but which may now be called into question. It may be necessary at present to state that the potential of human development in any direction whatever, positive or negative, up or down, north or south, good or bad, and in other contrasting dimensions is unlimited by any knowledge which civilization now possesses. The two characteristic Western interpretations of human nature, the liberal optimistic interpretation of human nature as capable and positive, and the traditional pessimistic interpretation of human nature as limited and negative, are very likely both equally in error. The probability is that both have made cultural assumptions which will be seen to have dubious justification when cases are properly introduced so as to provide perspective on the full ranges of possibility.

To return to the condition of image-suffusion in the small-group, the consequences of cut-off in articulation are of intense interest. It will appear that human behavior in isolated small-groups uncontrolled by any reference to any large-group socialization, customs and codes, and law do not achieve controls or achieve them relatively little. All kinds of behaviors can be tried. While it is difficult to imagine that cultural controls can ever be totally eliminated in any human society above that of the legendary childhood of Romulus, and while isolation in any small-group will always be relative, some characteristics may be identifiable. For the most part these must be the subject of future study, the cases of social isolation being so few and studies of them so rare. One characteristic more immediately noticeable is however that of drift. By this is meant a slow, unperceived movement of the small-group with respect to the large-group. This is necessarily slow and clouded in obscurity. Things look about the same. New types of behavioral cases arise only occasionally, and their implications are not always clear. It must, however, be expected that if the modes of articulation are smoothed off such that there is little effective relation of the small-group to the large-group, drift of the small-group with respect to the large-group is very nearly inevitable. Given the present cultural complex of American society the probability is that the small-group will drift to the left when conceived of in relation to the large-group, which is to say, since it will have abandoned its roots it will thrash about more or less in ethico-moral space looking for some place to land. In terms of the preceding discussion what it is looking for will inevitably be the appropriate metaphysical base or ground for the new customs and codes which it as a separate small-group purports now to be developing. Metaphysical

81

grounds can sometimes be analyzed in this way from behavior to the grounds of behavior. This is, however, an exercise in intellectual discovery and is not to be confused with the adventure of assertion, where assertion is understood to be a primary facet of knowing.

In sum, the small-group image of itself can now be said to have been suffused throughout itself so that its behavior is relatively consistent, or is at least subject to only minor exceptions within itself and is not marred by influences from the large-group outside which might modify it or its practices. Once this condition is achieved then it appears that persons can move with equal potential and equal capacity in any direction. The small-group can redefine its objectives as it likes. It is not obliged, if it is by chance an educational institution, to continue to engage in study, because it may decide that study is not its objective. It is not obliged to work, if work were once its objective, because it is in a position to decline this frame of reference. It is not obliged to refer in any way to the large-group outside of itself, since it will already have declined the articulations by which relations with the large-group are normally maintained. What now seems in retrospect to have been the remarkably tight conception of the biological-social ethic or ground for human behavior has become something quite different, something loose-jointed and whirring, with unfamiliar noises of machinery and process, unclear of objective, unfettered by purpose, except perhaps the purpose of indiscriminate exploration, a kind of ethical UFO, fascinating and absorbing in itself to those who belong to it, but sadly and decisively out of focus culturally and philosophically with the large-group sources of its very life and existence.

In fairness to this peculiar phenomenon it ought to be made clear that the small-group perceives itself as justified. Its objects are in its own terms indeed exploration and discovery, in some part honest and frank, in some part deceptive and self-deceiving, marked by individual achievements of a notable kind and by individual failures constituting a high cost in human waste. These aspects have surely been noted sufficiently by a variety of observers. It will suffice to mention them again as characteristics of the small-group, remembering that the present concern has to do with the effects of image-suffusion amid conditions of isolation and the consequences for the bio-social ethic.

A reformulation of what might be called the law of extra-systemic referents may now be possible. Surely it can be said forthwith, regarding the bio-social ethic, that this ethic can be expected to work only when there is effective articulation between small-groups and large-groups. If this is so, the probability then is that the bio-social ethic is not to be regarded as fundamental, since there are circumstances in which it does not work. It is perhaps one of those ''partial absolutes'' which serve to describe ranges of phenomena and relation within an effective operational field, with the provision that when that operational field is modified or eliminated, the bio-social ethic is similarly modified or eliminated.

The probability is that the theme of this discussion as applied to the bio-social ethic is only a particular instance of the general law of extra-systematic referral of points at issue which states that no system of understanding can be expected to work unless its grounds of validity are rooted outside of itself. This remarkable general law appears to apply in the fields of nature, mathematics, and philosophy, and it need not be a surprise that it is illustrated in the sub-field of ethics. The present discussion of the bio-social ethic and its limitations is again presumably only a particular instance of a minor sort. It is the occurrence of phenomena permitting its examination in the concrete which alone may be unusual.

To generalize a final time from this local instance of the limitation of the bio-social ethic, it seems necessary to re-define ever so slightly one of the great insights of Western religious thought, that the truth is often achieved by the individual in solitude, or by the small-group in relative isolation from the crowd. From Biblical times through Kierkegaard and Emerson into the contemporary age of the un conscious, this has been one of the major themes of Western civilization. Perhaps this honored and acknowledged principle has now to be restricted. Perhaps it must now at last be said that Emerson was not alone in Concord, or Kierkegaard in the Deer Park, or Stylites on his pillar, or Isaiah in the Temple in Jerusalem. Whatever the genuineness of the insight of the Self alone with its Source or Maker, understanding of the truth has of necessity to be in part a function of the world in which the individual self lives. This is the first part of the law; a kind of systems-analysis is expressed in it; all factors in the situation have equally to be considered. The second part appears to involve a return of the law back upon itself—that the large-group or world-outside also cannot exist effectively in isolation from the functioning separate self. Individual insight is as indispensable as the conditioning environment of tradition or the world around. And these two facets of understanding are subject to the more general formulation of the law that systems by themselves cannot contain the grounds of their own being.

IX The Fundamental Questions in Philosophy

The problem of discovering what is going on in philosophy, understood in its most general sense as reflective thought including the philosophic, the religious, the contemplative, is not so very different from attempting to understand what is going on in education, in the minds of young people, in international relations, or other fields. The objective seems to be about the same: it is to look and see what is happening, and then to assess its meaning.

There is commonly a great fuss over cultural lag in social fields, such that there are occasional wars instead of world peace, or some poverty in place of universal plenty, accidents in lieu of safety, limited human achievement in place of near-perfection. Philosophy too is beset by a lag, but people do not mind this as much, which may be to say, the reflective fields do not matter. But in truth they do matter. The difficulty in realizing this stems no doubt from the limitations of the contemporary cultural setting in which the stance of knowing is to begin with what is, with what exists, and to proceed to draw very limited conclusions. The late-20th century is not likely to be known as a period which depended heavily on rationality for its fundaments of understanding. It is rather a time in which rational process is a tool briefly applied in the process of knowing that begins with perception and ends with a very limited generalization to cover a few comparable cases. Rationality applies in the process of deduction, but not elsewhere and not in general.

The philosophic fields are not different from the fields of history. They must constantly be rewritten, their fundamental categories re-discovered in each new age, the assumptions of which have grown to differ from the assumptions of earlier times, their processes and procedures redefined, and their conclusions, however tentative, reached and formulated anew.

Of the five classical fields of philosophy, the two which are most alive today in the minds of young people are metaphysics and epistemology. Ethics is a poor relation; aesthetics depends upon the interest of the rare individual; and logic, known to be greatly in flux, while often demanded in philosophic studies is commonly disliked and avoided where possible, perhaps as a part of the cultural trend away from rationality toward other modes of understanding.

All this probably means that the fundamental reflective questions which are being asked today, while related to the five classical fields, are not identical with them and extend somewhat beyond them. A brief table or diagram may help to indicate the relations.

Classical Fields	The Fundamental Questions
1. Metaphysics	
2. Ethics	1. What is the real?
3. Aesthetics	
4. Epistemology	2. How do you know what you know?
5. Logic	
_____	3. What is the nature of human nature?
_____	4. What is the Ultimate?

This table is intended to mean that for present purposes the classical field of metaphysics corresponds to the question concerning the nature of the real, and that ethics and aesthetics are subsumed under metaphysics and under the fundamental question concerning the nature of the real. It continues on to mean that the fourth classical field of epistemology corresponds to the second fundamental question concerning how we know what we know. Logic similarly subsumes under this major question as well. The two additional fundamental questions, on the nature of human nature, and the nature of the Ultimate, are additional or expansive questions. Obviously a study of human nature could be considered to be metaphysical and could be contained under the first question. It is convenient to separate it since it looms so large and since such enormous assumptions are made concerning it in contemporary cultural studies. The final question concerning the nature of the Ultimate is equally clearly a separate question not necessarily identifying with the metaphysical, although related to it.

It may be useful to comment on the contemporary experience with the classical philosophic fields. Among these juxtapositions of fields and questions, that of metaphysics with the question concerning the real is perhaps the most direct. Considering metaphysics to be the study of the nature of the real there appears at once a garden-variety of block against the term metaphysics on the part of would-be moderns who believe themselves to have been emancipated from the study of ghosts, spooks and all such manner of non-existent constructs. Persons taking this line are frequently vehement in rejecting metaphysics as unworthy of consideration in the great Enlightenment of the 20th century. It follows that the old distinction is being made in such instances, obviously to no purpose, between physics understood to be the study of nature, and metaphysics, understood to be the study of whatever is beyond nature. If metaphysics is understood to be the study of the real, and if the physicist or positivist or student of nature wishes to limit himself to the positivistic round in some way, then of course this is an entirely defensible position to take. In present terms the metaphysics of physics is physics. If, as is more commonly the situation now, the scientific studies are rather doors wide-flung and to be passed through, rather than collections of things to be weighed, measured, defined, and set straight forever, then metaphysics, still without any connotations of ectoplasm, is a comprehensive and fundamental category of questioning and understanding. To stumble around in these ways over a term like metaphysics without bothering to define it, while applying to it prejudices which are no longer relevant, seems hardly worthy of the luminous understandings of our time. But any teacher of philosophy can confirm that this kind of thing is precisely what happens over and over again. Metaphysics in its general and proper sense remains, for any philosophic position or conclusion, the study and formulation of the grounds for all other positions in all other fields of reflection and contemplation. One has but to scratch a man with an idea to discover by implication that he is a metaphysician. It is a general condition and requirement of thought that there should be, specified or implied, fundamental assumptions concerning the real which make possible the positions being taken which are subsidiary to them.

The Primary Question: What Is Real??

The way to discover a metaphysics is to insist upon asking the ultimate question with reference to any subsidiary or derived position. In the reflective fields, everything depends upon asking the ultimate questions. In our time the multiple philosophic confusions stem simply from neglect or denial of ultimate questions rather than from any positive validity which short-range positions can be said to have. There is of course a practical justification for stopping short of asking ultimate questions. Enormous ranges of understanding have discovered themselves to inquiring minds in recent centures, and there is simply not enough time to explore them and simultaneously to contemplate their fundaments. The concept of purpose is out of fashion, but the fact is that it very much suits the general welfare that ages pass in the development of philosophic short-range perspectives, this way and that, a consequence of which is that in the course of time new formulations of more general ideas can be developed to encompass these lesser ranges in the interest of ever broadening understandings. It is indeed a strange and curious phenomenon that the simple device of insisting upon asking the ultimate question, in a period of philosophic multiplicity and fractionated relativity, has the effect of throwing the inquiring mind into a situation of such general relations that its comprehensiveness becomes over-arching, all-encompassing, and as approximately universal as the inevitable limitation of data and dimensions permits, in other words, in the best sense mediaeval.

Ethics as a field of study is at present largely residual. It often becomes an extension of, or is commonly extended into, related fields of the social studies or social sciences. Books on ethics in the classical sense continue to appear, but who uses them or benefits from using them is something of a mystery. The field of philosophy registered shock in recent decades when linguistic schools reduced ethics to feelings of approval or disapproval together with behavioral imperatives or imperatives of attitude. There was hardly need for dismay. Philosophies have always done this. It was only slightly more crass in this instance that supposedly noble human ideals should be reduced to emotional jags hardly more exalted than likes and dislikes. Contemplative studies in the past have tended to retain the uplift feature of ethics, its orientation toward the ideal in one form or another, whatever the metaphysical grounds used as foundations for particular positions. Ethical positions necessarily derive from metaphysical positions. Any identifiable ethic inevitably implies a metaphysic, an assertion of the real, for if it did not it would be quite meaningless in any dimension beyond that of a simple restricted group code.

This is not to say that ethics has not been or does not remain a legitimate sub-field. It does. But it is a sub-field in the sense that it is an exploration of derivative dimension from a position on the real, again necessarily time-consuming and therefore legitimately separate, even to the extent that the metaphysical implication of an ethical position may be neglected or ignored by the ethicist. Conversely, it does no good for an ethicist to disclaim a metaphysical connection, whether or not he wishes to deal with it or with the connection between the two. Merely to ask the ultimate question—what metaphysical assumption is involved here?—is to establish the connection and the existence of a relevant metaphysical fundament.

If ethics is in eclipse today surely it need be no surprise. The explanation can be found in the fascination of discovery and exploration of dimensions of the real, which is to say metaphysics, an activity which is absorbing enormous energies in our time. Not all of these interests and investigations are creditable or legitimate. Some are masquerades, under the guise of acceptance of things as they are, denial of ultimate ranges of meaning, simple social rebellion or commonly, the extrapolation of limited principles covering relatively few cases into allegedly highly general ideas assumed to cover all available ranges of cases. The study of ethics probably blossoms in ages which are metaphysically more settled. Then there is time to explore the sub-ranges of general positions. Reflective diversity flourishes, not unlike some Western version of the Hundred Flowers, when the compelling, well-nigh irresistible demands of the ultimate questions are held in abeyance. Then indeed the by-ways of philosophy lie open to leisurely exploration, an activity congenial to an individualistic age and time. It is perhaps an evidence of the close connection between ethics and metaphysics that the study of ethics either does not flourish amid metaphysical confusion or else tends to be translated into or reduced to related disciplines such as the social sciences which undertake to answer comparable questions by way of restrictive metaphysical assumptions and derived methodologies. In either case ethics appears to diminish in stature and investment such that its standing becomes seriously impaired.

Aesthetics may be less affected, negatively, by metaphysical upheaval. Interest in art and the forms of aesthetic expression tend to find their own reasons for being; aesthetics as a study may be a highly intellectual discipline directed to the strictly intellectual description of aspects and problems of artistic expression, but the nature of artistic expression is rooted in the self and senses a justification of itself whether or not it is studied or described. Artistic expression is heavily on the increase; it becomes part of the revolt of the young, or the escape from urbanization, a part indeed of the constant metaphysical quest for new dimensions of reality even when intellectualization of these is specifically refused and the expressions limited to congenial artistic forms. Aesthetics as a field may be somewhat at a loss in an environment unfriendly to rational consideration of artistic themes. It can direct itself toward problems of quantification; it can attempt to clarify the polarities of artistic expression, making some effort to relate the roots and sources of art in the self with expressional forms, and the like. If it goes much beyond these types of problems it may expect to fall, as does ethics, back into an essentially metaphysical study where the questions as to what is real come more nearly to the surface and aesthetic considerations are more obviously metaphysical derivation as distinct from the element or the field separately constituted and maintained.

To what extent aesthetics can thrive amid predominant emphasis on the irrational may be a question, but the eclipse need be only temporary. Asking the ultimate question is essentially an intellectual operation; once it is done all manner of subsidiary questions become immediately relevant. Artistic expression as such may flourish in a non-intellectual environment. This may be ample cultural investment to keep alive aesthetic possibility for a time when intellectual or rational study again becomes a primary concern. It is as if the more elemental springs of culture were being preserved, indeed expanded in multiple directions as an intermediate cultural stage, the function of which may again be substantially to expand the available dimensions of expression and study. To the degree that this is so aesthetics will have a substantial advantage over ethics; ethics appears to generate relatively little interest apart from metaphysical connections of particular ethical standpoints, while artistic expression provides immediate human satisfaction of its own quite apart from metaphysical connections. The immediacy and genuineness of the metaphysical connections may be the same in both instances; certainly there is no reason to suppose they would be of different orders of significance. But it seems clear that aesthetics would have the easier time in a culture which does not always apperceive the value of hard intellective labor and the value of having readily available rational understandings and modes of expression of its major lines of human concern.

How Do You Know What You Know?

If the first high point in the realms of thought lies in the classical field of metaphysics and in the corresponding fundamental question (What is the real?), then the second reflective peak is reached in the classical field of epistemology and its corresponding fundamental question—How do you know what you know?—It is as if there were remaining only two classical fields conceived of as major intellective concerns, metaphysics and epistemology, while the other three are subsidiary to these two, for logic will be found to be subsidiary to epistemology as ethics and aesthetics are subsidiary to metaphysics. Of the fundamental questions, of which there will be four, only two correspond directly to classical fields, the first to metaphysics and the second to epistemology. Of the other two, one is a practical reflection of an enormous region of concern in our culture, which could obviously be derived from the first but because of its size does better to stand alone, and the last, which appears at first glance to be also derivable from the first, actually is not but reflects the apparent fact which obtains in philosophy as in numerous other fields that every system must eventually be referred beyond itself for the landmarks which allow it to exist. This is to say, no system is explicable solely in its own terms.

Epistemology and its corresponding question as to how we know what we know represent one of the major and inescapable concerns of human inquiry. As has been remarked elsewhere, often enough, it is in the main a modern question. In earlier times enormous general assumptions were available to students of intellectual fields which for the most part did not need to be questioned but could be taken for granted. When ranges of understanding became multiple and intellection sophisticated then it became necessary to examine grounds of knowing

91

in particular systems, among their other aspects, as a way of judging their validity.

Old as the field and the questions of epistemology now are, it is astonishing how often they are neglected. It is not that there is anything unusual about asking epistemological questions. They have been roundly explored and no reflective person would think of proceeding without them. The problem is rather a cultural one, involving the usual lag, in which epistemological assumptions are made in a given cultural context, such that extensive ranges of cases or data can be considered under the rubric of a particular epistemological principle without the sensing of a need for epistemological examination. The effect of this is obviously to allow extrapolation of the ranges of a system, possibly somewhat naive, possibly not, to which in the course of time epistemological questions have necessarily to be applied. It is nevertheless astonishing that the question of epistemological neglect so frequently arises. As one of the fundamental questions in philosophy it is obviously a facet of the consideration of the real and therefore while it is a separate and indispensable philosophic concern it is nevertheless articulated with and inseparable from ultimate understandings.

However close the articulation, no doubt epistemology stands for a different philosophic process. The metaphysician may be content with his position; the epistemologist is required to indicate how he reached it. Neither can do without the other, and each is a means of judging the other. A useful epistemology can lead to an improper metaphysical conclusion; a metaphysics can reflect closely the nature of the real even while it remains articulated with a limited epistemology which will in the end be discarded as invalid. The metaphysical question and the epistemological question are equally legitimate starting points in philosophical consideration. None of the other three classical fields represents a legitimate starting point in this sense. Of the two, either may lead sooner or later to the other. Neither can stand alone. Neither can operate very long without requiring the other. Any comprehensive philosophic system will involve both.

Contemporary philosophic assumptions outside the halls of academe, and to some extent within, are to a great extent victims of the common cultural myopia to which any intellectual age is subject. A naive scientism probably derives from one of those periods of contemplation of ''brute fact'' to which Whitehead refers as extremely rare events in the history of thought. One such rare occasion occurred in the 16th-17th centuries; the deceptively simple Lockeian psychology reflected this, and recent American liberal thought has been seriously affected by it. It may not be too much to say that 20th century liberal religio-philosophic thought has allowed itself to become the victim of a Lockeian naivete such that fundamental reflective questions have been ignored in droves and very broad and largely unjustified philosophic assumptions have been tolerated. The consequences of this naivete are that liberal religio-philosophic thought has become unnecessarily and unjustifiably separated from traditional religio-philosophic systems, and has denied itself the more profound ranges of awareness which would follow on the allowance of complexity. In turn classical and traditional religio-philosophic systems have tended to deny themselves newer ranges of possibility represented in oppositional systems and similarly have functioned to prevent or forestall the synthesis of new comprehensive statements which would normally follow the development of reflective polarities. In strictly academic circles reflective dialogues are proceeding apace and can no doubt be depended upon to produce their syntheses in the course of time. There is a certain haphazardy about it all, since academic philosophies reflect cultural limitations, personal preferences, or dubious intellective assumptions in response to the cultural burdens and limitations of a time only slightly less than does nonprofessional philosophy. Nevertheless, if a choice had to be made one would choose the semi-deliberate academic diversity as more productive in the end, if one is interested in developmental change, than the relaxed acceptance of unexamined principle which is characteristic of lay culture. It is as if the function of academe were exploration, whereas the function of lay culture were stabilization. There is enough truth in this assessment to relieve the commentator of any lasting anxiety over the philosophic well-being of Western civilization. In the interest of philosophic efficiency an observer can indulge in a certain amount of fussing, but it would be well for him to be good-natured about it.

What Is Man?

The third fundamental question (What is the nature of human nature?) has no concomitant among the classical fields. It is rather the philosophical reflection of the social science of psychology, a field which in its burgeoning decades has tended to operate without very much philosophical assistance, at least in the recent half-century. The insistence of psychology upon its own independence was no doubt necessary in order to free itself from philosophical presumptions reflected in university departments of philosophy, with which psychology was originally integrated. The history and development of universities in the 20th century reflects a good deal of intellectual history; sociology had the same experience, and found it necessary to separate itself from philosophical presumptions and to establish its principles of operation and its procedures as separate disciplines well apart from and outside of philosophy. At the time there was no escape from this necessity. But times change, and although the disciplines are not likely to reintegrate as disciplines or procedures, much less as teaching fields, the recurrent appropriateness of general philosophical questions may soon again call into question the relations among these fields.

Again it must be remarked that universities do reflect their cultural settings. Only occasionally has a university dared to try to organize itself around ultimate questions. The University of Chicago did this at one point in its history; if the assumption involved has fallen somewhat into disuse it is hardly a matter for wonder. Among American educational institutions even the effort to do this is rarer than a hen's tooth. Church-related colleges and universities, although in a sense making such an effort, have tended not to satisfy the criterion, since they have not passed through, for the most part, the stage of acceptance of diverse formulations of the real and multiple modes of understanding to reassertion of the value of comprehensive modes of understanding encompassing quite diverse disciplines and fields. It is possible that church-related institutions will devise different avenues of proceeding to such comprehensive positions, but this would involve great difficulty on their part and it is not yet clear that it is likely to happen. It should be understood that church-related institutions of higher education have nearly unique opportunities to do this, if it proves possible for them to move in their own positions by way of acceptance of diverse dimensions of meaning to new comprehensive systems or questions which enable systems. Quite remarkable results might develop from such opportunities, but at the moment it is difficult or impossible to predict that this will happen.

To return to the fundamental question concerning the nature of human nature, any investigative or supposedly scientific discipline has its philosophic concomitant system. The implied system may change as rapidly as the question under investigation, or even the methodology in use. The result might seem to be a reflective kaleidoscope attached to a scientific discipline, and this would be quite all right. The natural sciences each have their philosophic implications, although no scientist or philosopher at present knows what these are. The social sciences should not seek to escape from the universal burden of reflective responsibility. To choose the nature of human nature as more fundamental than the nature of human society may be in itself a cultural myopia; it must be acknowledged that ranges of understanding concerning human nature and the nature of the real have derived from the study of human nature in social aggregates. Group-minds and objective state-realities, social realities, and the like may be abolished in theory ad infinitum; it is nevertheless certainly true that facets of understanding concerning human nature appear only when it is studied in its limited relations to other human natures, and this is precisely the function of sociology, social psychology, and related social disciplines. The justification for selecting the study of human nature is simply that man remains finally interested in himself and in his individual fellows, and that culturally at least, he insists upon harnessing the social disciplines into their applications to understandings of the self. In this sense social disciplines then become derivative fields to the study of human nature, even though psychology as a social discipline is far too limited and too fractioned in our time to serve as a discipline comprehensive enough to envelop its academic relatives.

It is also inevitable that any emphasis on questions as general as the nature of the real and the nature of knowing will articulate generically with questions concerning human nature. Questions of existence and the setting of existence can hardly obtain without calling up implications concerning the subject who understands and who somehow focuses meaning and understanding around the self conceived of as a kind of lens.

What Is Ultimate?

A final question concerning the nature of the Ultimate remains to stare down the helpless philosopher who knows he can never answer the question but who also cannot avoid asking it. There is a rationale for asking questions when it is impossible to hope that they will ever be answered. Indeed, where the four fundamental questions are concerned, it should be made clear forthwith that we do not know the answers to any of them. It is indispensable that the questions be asked; answers to them will vary with cultural settings, investigative procedures, and language formulations. The effect of asking questions is essentially that of focusing intellective effort around them. This is a matter of enormous significance since the consequences will be to channel energy in the direction of the major themes represented in the questions and in time to produce a variety of answers appropriate to their times and settings. This is consequence enough. There is no need to be concerned over right answers or particular answers or answers at all. The focusing of the energy is sufficient; the rest will take care of itself.

The question concerning the Ultimate is a strange phenomenon which has a remarkable effect upon thought. It throws into systematic perspective the lesser elements which sometimes go to make up a system but which also not infrequently allow themselves to be extrapolated into sub-systems masquerading as finalities, and in so doing introduce elements of order into the midst of confusion. The philosophic masquerade of the partial system as a final system is not necessarily mischief, although it may be. It may even be useful and assistive in enabling the examination of new systematic possibilities. Inevitably there will be a cost to individual minds which become committed to partial systems, minds which suppose that they are dealing with Ultimates.

Asking the final question—What is the Ultimate?—is not entirely fashionable in the present cultural period. There is even a good reason for this, that it detracts from detailed investigative effort among sub-systems when contemplation is focused upon the Ultimate. Religious contemplatives are perhaps the best examples in any age of individuals highly committed to reflection upon the Ultimate, and it might be conceded that to advocate this in the world outside the monastery may be in its effect to apply to the fractioned world of multiple things and processes an essentially monastic ideal and practice.

It is unlikely that asking the final question concerning the nature of the Ultimate will however sweep up the enormous number of sub-systematic efforts and dimensions of the contemporary world. It will be accurate to suggest that the question will introduce a tendency to universalize and systematize units into an over-arching system. The tendency itself will be sufficient. It can be expected to have a profound effect at least upon the organization of thought into systems. Since it is a question and not an answer, and since the answer to this among all the questions will forever remain out of reach, it is hardly conceivable that an effect of asking it will be to create again a closed religio-philosophical system such as that which arched the world in the Middle Ages.

System and direction are needed; a particular system extrapolated into a general or universal system will not be a proper substitute for the implication of a universal question. There is a difference, and the difference is worth remarking. There is after all no more powerful weapon in the arsenal of human communications than the question; to ask the most general and universal question known to the human mind is to approach the situation of human existence with very nearly the most powerful tool in creation. From time to time adventures in expression even with respect to the greatest and most final of all questions can be essayed as long as these expressions are openly defined as tentative and temporary, and are strictly enjoined from being constructed into final systems. This is the mistake which traditional religion in all its ages, and be it added, liberal religion in its recent lifetime, have always made. The expression of finality is always an error, always limited, always incomplete, always subject to the explosive effect of future discoveries and adventures of the mind, the nature of which can never be predicted far in advance.

Certainty enough inheres in the asking of the question concerning the nature of the Ultimate to reflect all the traditional concern of religion with permanence and the enduring nature of the real. It is not necessary that the nature of the Ultimate should be precisely describable by any methodology or combination of methodologies. It is not even necessary that particular symbols or names for the Ultimate should be required in religio-philosophical traditions. It is enough that the enormous power of the ultimate question should be loosed upon the world to work its Will as it chooses, as its nature enjoins, and as the situation of its formulation and its setting shall command.

X Church and University:
Notes on Education and Change

In centuries past, historians and philosophers of education tell us, higher education was in general an off-shoot of the church, and its institutions were administered as arms of the religious. Its gradual emancipation from church control can be documented in educational history, and it has tended to appear that the onward movement of history and the gradual enlargement of educational freedom were somehow one of the same thing.

No doubt at times they were, especially in the context of higher education in recent centuries. To a degree this may still be so, or may appear so, as witness the recent secularization of a number of church-related institutions. The difficulty with which established religion has at times entertained new ideas has occasionally made it necessary for higher education to separate itself from church auspices in order to set in motion the myriad currents of originality in thought and technology which have gone to produce the modern age. There must be some justice in these rather long, slow movements, After all, the benefits of highly diverse modes of thought and procedure are fairly clear.

Yet, in the late twentieth century the relationship of the church and higher education remains an issue. Many American colleges and universities were founded by churches and denominations. A considerable number are still operated under church control or by church-connected boards. Some maintain traditional courtesy relationships. A substantial number, on the other hand, may either have been founded under public auspices without church connections or have gradually come to separate themselves from earlier church origins and inheritances. So, questions remain. In freeing itself from restrictive monolithic control has higher education lost sight of the central significance of commitment to cosmogony and valuation? Is it possible that there has been and still is something fundamental about the nature of a church which should by rights be the inheritance of the college and the university if the reflective functions of higher education are to be served? Hypothetically, does a higher education institution tend to succeed at its task or to be effective in expression of its nature to the extent that it fulfills certain functions of a church, and does it begin to go adrift and lose its sense of itself to the degree that it separates itself from the legitimate functions of a church?

General Functions of Church and University

If a church is to be conceived of strictly as a particular organizational tradition, divinely ordained for the conveyance of salvation to mankind, certain difficulties are introduced, although the problem of generalized definition is by no means insoluble. Conceived of somewhat generically and without reference to particular traditions or absences of tradition, it may be fair to say, whatever else may also apply in particular instances, that a church involves an association of individuals often but not always with appropriate professional leadership, having primary concerns in the areas of cosmogony, valuation, individual and institutional expression, the development of personal understanding, and the encouragement of channeled social relations. This is a somewhat operational and abstract definition; other descriptions might serve equally well. The chances are, however, that in any comprehensive description these major emphases will appear in one form or another.

A college or university could be described in much the same terms. It is obviously concerned with cosmogony, although its assumptions might be different and the divisions of its address to the problem more finely divided and habitually cast in distinctive sub-generic modes. A point of divergence may inhere around valuation. Churches have problems enough with the applications of valuation, yet on general levels the commitment to values, whatever they may be, is usually clear enough. For higher education institutions, at least in the time with which we are most familiar, there is some hesitancy over commitment to values. These reservations may reflect the reservations of a culture highly skilled in technology and as a consequence preoccupied with a particular image of itself.

Colleges and universities for the most part tend to express their commitment to values in terms of academic detachment. This too can be

99

of value, and undeniably it has the helpful effect of enabling great individual divergence in thought and practice. There is the further problem of whether its valuational restraints will cause the educational institution to be outdistanced by its clientele. If the educational community and its sponsoring society should suddenly demand greater valuational commitment than colleges and universities were prepared to provide the effects might be of two kinds: higher educational institutions could adapt, becoming willing to enable valuational commitment of a kind or to a degree not recently familiar as part of the academic context, or the educational or social clientele might be found achieving its valuational commitment outside of colleges and universities. A comparable phenomenon has been observed often enough in ecclesiastical history. When one institutional (ecclesiastical) tradition has seemed to some of its communicants to be not sufficiently inclusive or exclusive in certain respects a common consequence has been the establishment of a new church or sect alongside the old. It is curious in recent times to observe the formation of so-called "free universities" in the shadow of the large established public or private universities, suggesting that for some members of the educational community, both student and faculty, the older institution has proved less than challenging. There may be so to speak a certain natural history of institutions, such that the survival of ideas ofttimes depends on their incorporation in appropriate forms. Whether the so-called "free" institutions can be expected to survive may depend on their ability to develop appropriate institutional forms which can outlast the passing of particular student and staff generations. Bensalem lasted only three years at Fordham; there may be similar situations elsewhere. Bensalem, of course, was not just a "free" satellite.

The characteristics of the church and of the university can then be said to involve assertions concerning the nature of things—which is to say, assertions of a philosophical or metaphysical nature; association for sets of purposes—educational, moral, ceremonial, and social; and greater or lesser commitments to values—religious, social, and educational. It has been remarked frequently in other connections that the several fundamental questions which any reflective investigation asks are those concerned with the nature of the universe, of human nature, of knowledge, and of the Ultimate. Churches and universities alike are concerned with these, with the possible reservation on degrees of valuation. If it is appropriate to say that an educational institution is effective insofar as it possesses the fundamental forms and attributes of a church, it may be even fairer to observe that a church is effective insofar as it too possesses, embodies and expresses these same fundamental forms and attributes. After all, churches do appear to have their problems and if they are not too often noted for their efficiency in valuation and value application there must surely be some simple explanation for it.

Possible Factors in Variation and Change

It may be useful to look at some of the factors in variation and change. What are they and how do they affect change? From this point an assumption is made that certain institutional characteristics are held in common by churches and higher educational institutions and that therefore the question will apply equally among them.

Social habits of group and community, habits of stability or habits of movement or drift, must be considered in accounting for change. Few questions of significance can be effectively considered without reference to context. But why should social or community context be considered as any kind of root? Surely institutions of all types respond to the settings in which they find themselves, but variously. A conservative community may tend to produce a conservative church or college; but if a liberal church or college is placed in a conservative or traditional setting the probable result will be conflict supported by polarization on the part of institutional and community leadership. This is not to express any judgment of either side; it is merely to record an obvious social event. Be that as it may, it is difficult to conclude that social custom is at all primary as determinant of change, unless perhaps in very small, highly specialized groups committed to particular valuational ends. More likely, social habit or custom will militate against change and will tend to conserve existing conditions. Granting that in certain special cases group or community changes can occur in what appear to be strictly social dimensions involving cases of image-suffusion in the isolated small-group, it remains true that the judgment or valuation of these in strictly social terms remains particularly unsatisfying. Judgment seems more usefully rendered, individually or collectively, in terms of some principle which is believed to encompass a

101

considerable number of cases. The social reference point by itself is insufficient to serve as the basis for valuational conclusion.

Intellectual habits short of genuine metaphysical commitment, as for example liberal or conservative positions in relational issues, also appear to be singularly lacking in determinative capability. This category may be simply a type of social habit, even if it is believed to be a genuine intellectual dimension. In particular instances it is unlikely that any form of "habit" can usefully be regarded as a valid source of variation or change. Not even the most radical types of alleged change, in their social or intellectual manifestations, can be considered at all seriously as an actual root of change. Too many studies of the nature of "revolution" have been made which show that it does not produce anything very real in a new dimension for the observer to take it seriously as a means of accomplishing lasting development. The effect of a national political revolution is apparently to produce a convulsion which has the effect of eliminating a particular situation or group of personnel, only to have the form, function, and expression restored after a brief period so that the original institutions can be regarded as having merely endured through a time of upheaval and tribulation. People really ought to stop using the word "revolution"; it describes only a passing social phase and one which does not produce or convey anything of much significance.

The operational and managerial dimensions of institutional development have come in for close attention in recent years. Student interest in taking part in college and university decision making, perhaps comparable to congregational polity on the ecclesiastical side, again appears to be an instance of a very common and often an institutional problem, but in no wise one which resolves the question of the nature of change. Campuses in recent years have been full of requests for broader participation in institutional plans and decisions. Without doubt educational institutions will need to alter the composition of their boards, committees, and modes of governance; more members of the educational community will take part in operational decisions than used to be the case. But does this convey anything of significance with respect to variation and change? In itself it seems not. Power derives from popular consent, remote as the delegation often is. To involve a higher percentage of group members in institutional decision making says nothing about the nature of change: it only describes a larger percentage of participation in that change. Recent tendencies across the United States to involve more students and staff in institutional operation is not of fundamental significance in a philosophic sense. It is a good thing socially, and in some cases it may be a good thing educationally. For present purposes one simply notes that it is not a type of alteration which has any strictly philosophical validity within the operational frame of reference. Whether power is exercised by few or by many, assuming power derives in a social sense from the consent of the governed, does not affect the metaphysics of the situation. It may be a good thing and sound educational policy to involve more individuals in the making of decisions. That more persons are or may be involved in decision making may be reasonably helpful in that a greater number of individuals concerned with a given situation actually do understand that situation. Still it does not appear that such added involvement has anything fundamental to say concerning the nature of change. The power dimension is not fundamental. It may be general but it is not fundamental. There appear to be no new ideas thus far. It may be fair to say that in the instances referred to, what is being dealt with is variation rather than change, that is, gradual, minute alterations not of a fundamental kind and not involving other than limited principles and grounds. Variation might be said to be change of a minor order. Change in the deeper sense will be conceived of as alteration based on fundamental elements, processes or principles the nature of which will not reduce to anything else.

Educational philosophy and method surely need to be considered possible factors in the process of change. Yet this greatly argued category seems only to provide contradictory evidence. Just when it seems clear that one educational philosophy rather than another has proved itself especially worthy of implementation and repetition oppositional evidence will be sure to suggest that quite another philosophy and method are of equal value, or even more frustrating, that a particular philsophy and method hitherto supported really does not do what it was supposed to do, or if denied, that it really does do what it supposedly could not do. A great deal appears to depend on the individuals concerned, teachers and students, and on particular teaching and learning situations.

Ceremonial affairs, academic or ecclesiastic, appear to be complex variable, esthetic, and reflective events. Probably there is no need to consider them as a category seriously affecting change.

Valuation as process has been widely accepted in recent times as some sort of alternate category in the educative process. It is dubious if it is any such thing. It is certainly a highly important sub-category of individual decision; however, its grounds of judgment are only immediately referred outside to the larger frame of reference surrounding the educational institution, whether that reference frame is a set of principles, of metaphysical convictions, or simply of social expectations. The power dimension is therefore again not fundamental in the contemporary perspective on change in higher education. Contests of power attract a good deal of attention; they are noisy and they are frequently disorderly. They are, however, merely typical; the movement from centralized control to broad or generalized control is only a slight progression in the direction of greater participation in governance. Since it only means that more people are involved in decision making, no new ideas are represented in it and there ought not to be any great hullaballoo about its various manifestations. This type of alteration could be defined as variation; it need not be defined as change, unless perhaps in a thin sense.

Metaphysical Assertion as Root of Change

Education has constantly to ask of itself what it is. When something is worked with seriously by serious people over long periods of time and at various points along its way is found asking the question what it is, it is a sure sign that an effort is being made to redefine itself in fundamental ways. Educators never cease to ask of themselves, What is education? As always, it means several things. In the first place, it means they do not know, and they deserve admiration for being willing to admit it. Then, it appears to be important to them to find out what education is, and some more admiration ought to go to them for that. It also means, commonly enough, in matters of this sort, more than ordinarily so in educational thought, that a range of reality is about to be defined in terms of the educational focus. This is not as odd as it sounds, and it ought to be recognized as essentially a religious as well as a cognitive process. It simply means that for these purposes of understanding the

104

fundamental dimension of the real is to be understood in terms of education.

There is no more sense to this, perhaps, than there is to deciding that any other focus of religious and cognitive concern should be taken as the center of reflective comprehension. Like many such foci, it can surely be reduced to other elements. That this does not occur is a consequence of emotional arrest. The involvement of the self in a particular nucleus of reflective energy determines that momentarily at least or for particular individuals for the time being the dimension of the real shall be understood in terms of this or that other dimension. Education itself can and does become what amounts to a metaphysical substance. An assertion concerning education can be no less than a metaphysical expression. This too is not so odd; educational thought-in-depth must involve a theory of human nature, a theory of learning and knowing, and a theory of what is to be learned, which is to say, about the objective of learning, which can include the subject as object; it also involves, at least by implication, a theory of the ultimate, although commonly the latter is implied rather than specified.

Now it follows that the root of any change which amounts to anything is metaphysical in nature. That is, it involves assertion concerning the real, and learning theory and practice is properly to be derived from that, whatever that is. Change in a fundamental sense can then be seen in quite a different dimension. It is no longer the social education of additional persons, students, faculty, or staff, who may be taken up into the decisional process. All that is merely ripple on the surface of the deep sea. It is not of the nature of ceremony, or of intellectual or social habit. It may not even be of the nature of valuation. Change may in the end prove to be better understood as a dimension of greater or lesser depth. Change in any obvious or surface range is called into question on legitimate philosophical grounds. Change in the skin of things, the thin phenomenal surface, may be of only passing interest and perhaps ought to be catalogued by those who care to do such work. Fundamental change is to be understood as hopefully the increase of understanding in depth, and only as that. It follows that philosophical positioning is the real root of change, and that change cannot be understood apart from metaphysics.

This is not to assert that any particular metaphysical position is required. Of the numerous theories of learning extant in our time

105

probably not one is without a genuine metaphysics (theory of the real), and no philosophy of education could exist without one. Some have tried to ignore their own metaphysical assumptions; this only has the effect of permitting the analytic observer to deduce the particular metaphysical theory involved and to make it explicit in whatever form it can best be understood. On the whole it would be better for philosophies of education to acknowledge their metaphysical positions of their own accord and to describe them in what seem to them to be the most appropriate terms. A few decline to do so on the amusing ground that there is something peculiar about metaphysics and therefore that one ought not to associate with it if it can possibly be avoided. The present position is that metaphysics understood as the philosophy of the real cannot be avoided and must be directly encountered. Without a metaphysical theory a simple declarative sentence becomes by implication impossible, and communication ceases. All of this is only to suggest that neglected questions of metaphysical significance ought indeed to be raised again explicitly rather than merely implicitly if one is to understand the nature of change.

The relation of value to a view of the real remains puzzling. Logically valuation should follow upon metaphysical theory. It is possible that some day the nature of will or decision may be understood as the obverse of metaphysical assertion. That is, value and commitment to value may lie very close to the head and source of the nature of things. It may be the smallest of steps or no step at all to pass from metaphysical theory to valuational commitment. It is more than possible that metaphysics and valuation intertranslate back and forth, and that allowing for temperamental preferences expressed in various degrees of attention to each, nevertheless each does entail the other and cannot be fully understood without it.

Thus far it has been convenient to point to certain characteristics which higher educational institutions have in common with religious institutions, such that the metaphysical nature of learning activity can be understood merely as specified and finely divided cognition. The emotional element is more commonly involved in the church; nevertheless it seems equally clear that the religious function of understanding commonly appears masked in educational process whether or not it is readily recognized there; it has also appeared that among the numerous factors often referred to in movement and change only metaphysical assertion lies close to its heart. The relation of valuation and metaphysical theory is recognized as quite possibly closely articulated and difficult of separation, and as a question to be considered elsewhere.

Implications for Institutional Operation

The conclusion of all this appears to be that fundamental change does not take place casually in a college or university any more than it has ever done in a church. Minor variations and innovations in the programs of higher educational institutions are common enough, particularly in the late 20th century. These are good variations for the most part and can be expected to improve educational effectiveness by replacing outmoded conceptions and practices with ideas and methods closer to the needs of contemporary times. Educational innovation as ordinarily conceived of is certainly useful even though it is open to criticism for being in some instances superficial rather than rooted.

Nevertheless the present point is that genuine change and development is a rooted thing based upon philosophical clarity and conviction, explicit self-awareness and self-understanding. Indeed, consciousness of self is simply indispensable to the rooted self-maintenance of a college or university. The importance of the self-awareness factor is difficult to overestimate. Colleges and universities should acknowledge that their natures, like the nature of a church, require that they be committed metaphysically and valuationally, which is to say, philosophically, to a position which they wish to defend, maintain, and develop, as a major part of their purpose in existing.

Problems introduced by the notion of institutional commitment are not inconsiderable. Institutional commitments tend to be very general at the present time; there is some advantage to this in that quite diverse viewpoints can exist with reasonable comfort alongside each other while providing for students a great range of educational experience. The advantage of this should be maintained even while attention is directed to the further uses of institutional commitment of a more explicit and deeper kind than has recently been common. Several consequences follow. Institutional diversity and commitment are not contradictory. Institutions should differ, while within each of them degrees of commitment to common objectives should be measurable. The particular kind of commitment is of some interest. It is not the social reform dimension which is of use in the community of learning, in any immediate sense. Colleges and universities may occasionally stray from the business of understanding, and there may be reasons enough why they do. But in the Western context, at least, where so much of life is activous, the central function of education is not political. Institutional commitment in higher education is to principle, to idea, to reality, to discovery, to learning, even while some learning involves some kinds of implementation. The community of learning is not the seat of politics.

Campus upheavals in this perspective similarly cannot be considered as amounting to very much in any permanent sense. They may have succeeded—usefully—in adding to the number of persons, including students, who will normally take part in institutional management. This is however not a fundamental or new type of change. Centuries ago students hired and fired the faculty and indeed migrated about from city to city as seemed convenient. In those days the educational groups were small, just as the societies were perhaps simpler, and standards may not have been high. Nevertheless the idea of student participation in the operation of colleges and universities is not new.

The current tendency to feel that students and faculty should be individually free to "do their own thing" is probably some sort of mild disease. Individual development of new ideas and new directions will continue to be as necessary as the air one breathes. Nevertheless an accentuated institutional commitment even on a general level suggests that individuals on campus should no longer have the latitude to move in any direction at all. Institutions should differ among themselves, there being no proper prescription concerning their institutional commitment, so that further ranges of possibility will derive from colleges and universities committed to widely variant philosophies. The present position concerns primarily the nature of genuine change as based on the philosophical commitment of educational institutions to a degree comparable to the commitment of a church. It does not suggest any uniformity amongst institutional commitments, even though it foresees within human institutions considerably greater involvement of students and faculty in the particular purposes of the institution.

Institutions of all kinds today are sadly beset by accelerating administrative and communicational requirements. Everyone is aware of the serious problem of finding faculty and staff time to reflect, time to choose policies on clear grounds and to move ahead carefully in full awareness of what is being done. There is no easy answer to it. Presumably an enormous degree of faculty and staff loyalty to institutional purposes must be assumed if genuine progress is to be made. Whether the fractioned faculties and staffs of our time will gladly contribute this degree of loyalty may be a question. Some sorting out of professional staff members among institutions in accordance with accentuated philosophical commitments may be a necessary part of the adjustment.

These reflections suggest, in conclusion, that among higher educational institutions which have the advantage of being church-connected deliberate attention should be given to the implications of their relation to their sponsoring churches. It may prove in the course of time that church-sponsored and church-related institutions of higher education have a notable advantage in terms of eventual philosophical commitment and contribution to American society. In short, if anything like the present position is to be considered seriously, a college or university which is at present connected with a church denomination will do well to think long and hard before it breaks the relation. Conversely, it could be of great use to American society, indeed to the American adventure in civilization, if careful and precise study could be directed at length to the possible values of church-related education which still remain to be realized.

Institutions which are not church-related and which for practical reasons do not wish to take up the relation may reflect on how institutional philosophy and valuation can be intensified to a degree that the church connection need not be missed. Institutional reflection and commitment on this level is surely not a new thing for some colleges and universities, and need not be unusual providing the necessary faculty and staff commitment can be obtained. If it is awkward to suggest in a day of individualistic diversity that institutional philosophy and valuation should be intensified it is also maintained that the best of individual access to the real should also be central. The conclusion derives from a view of the nature of philosophy and from an application of it to the problems of American colleges and universities, private and public. While cries of anguish may be expected from the pros and cons of the application to educational and institutional problems it will be wise to attend to philosophic foundations. When the philosophy is argued fairly, the rest should follow. If philosophical revision is advisable that, rather than the practical ranges of institutional management, should perhaps be the focus of discussion.

XI Conceptualism

For two reasons philosophical systematics, understood as the formulation of reflective systems rather than simply as the science of classification, has been in eclipse in recent times. First, the rapid expansion of information has naturally led to apprehension; the construction of comprehensive systems appears to entail closure in the face of continuing change. Second, more centrally and less obviously, the construction of systems has been prevented by prior metaphysical decisions. It is the latter ground which is the present chief concern.

Systems have necessarily been formulated in abstract media. They have had to be idea-systems, whether strictly idealistic, naturalistic, or a variant between. They have been built of ideas, as indeed they needs must; but in addition they have tended to take for granted the value and reliability of ideas. This being so, in an intellectual period which has gradually come to distrust the general idea it is understandably less likely that systems would emerge. Ideas are useful in any age, but for differing purposes. In the present period they have for the most part been applied to relatively restricted ranges of data. Partial systems may have been fostered in certain areas of interest. Systematic thought, conceived of as an idea-system arched over relatively wide ranges of data, has however receded as a commonly held concern of professional philosophy and theology. It is as if the touted economy of explanation deriving from Ockham and generally if dubiously regarded as scientific had in our time been applied to representational thought rather more firmly than used to be the case. Systems can be done without, the explanation might run; so let them be eliminated. It has been part of a philosophic mood or climate of opinion, a fashion in thought, so to speak, to restrict speculation to the lesser ranges of intellective prehension. Not the wide-spreading system, but the piercing and precise formulation-in-depth of much reduced scope has repeatedly been the focus of attention.

There is no harm in philosophic fragmentation if it produces analytic intensity. There is always the possibility of learning something more or something new about a restricted range of consideration.

Analysis must be followed by construction, however, if general apprehension is desired; nevertheless, even restricted ranges of comprehension are useful. And the question remains, what happens then? Eventually one of two things happens. Either the restricted ranges of awareness are conjoined, forming a system, if the ranges chance to fit each other, or, more likely, a constructional extrapolation takes place from some convenient partial range resoluting in a system assumed to apply over the entire range of constructional possibility. A partial systematic construct is then assumed to be valid for the full range of understanding.

Simple philosophic restraint may present one further, though temporary, possibility. It may be practical in reflective periods of brief duration—a few decades, perhaps, or a century or two, for philosophy to withhold itself from systematic thought of broad dimensions. If this happens it will be a function of some sort of principle of sufficient attention: because there is enough hard work to be done in immediate ranges of applicability to occupy the time and interest of investigators and philosophers sufficient attention is absorbed in the effort and there may not be energy to spare for systematics. It will not be because of anything new or fundamental in the nature of thought. And in the long run the larger questions will reassert themselves. They cannot be avoided nor will the stubbornly questing minds of men indefinitely permit them to pass by. Constraint of thought from speculative dimensions into analytic dimensions is then a socio-cultural phenomenon, not a characteristic of intellection. If it happens it happens because people are temporarily busy doing something else, not because there is anything special about what they are doing.

It is difficult to say when the times are ready for reflective change. The philosopher, like any other life form, follows his nose. He asks what it interests him to ask. Perhaps there may yet turn out to be ecological successions among types of philosophic position, such that when one set of interests or questions occurs, a predictable next set of interests and issues will follow. Certainly there are fashions in thought; it should not be surprising if styles in ideas were also successive and identifiable.

The Question Poses Itself

Developmental or historical behaviors of philosophies may then be somewhat predictable. Whether a system starts with a general principle or with a truncated particular may not matter. At some point by its very nature it must connect with a fundament. A fundament is that element in a system which does not reduce to anything else. Other elements may reduce to it; the system as it is constructed is then based upon it. When the fundament is reached the definition or the analysis of the system which is in process has nowhere else to go. The recognition and acceptance of a fundament is a peculiar affair, difficult to describe. One simply seems to know when the philosophic situation in which one's meanings are set has been sounded to its depths. It is as if there were an internal logic to the recognition which would not readily entertain denial.

Some say that the present age ought not to be concerned with systems, that it is properly taken up with shorter-ranging investigations in thought as for example in the several scientific fields. This is a ridiculous notion. There can be no comprehensive thought without system. It may happen that a system is not developed or explicated; the system is however there, implied if not specified. There is no escaping it, whether or not any attention is expended on it. Investigators in any field, philosophy and the sciences alike, can of course choose to restrict their studies to any particular range of interest or data, however foreshortened. It is often necessary and even indispensable to do so. But any studies take place within a set of assumptions, and these assumptions, strung out and elaborated in accordance with their natures, constitute a system.

In a real sense a system forms itself. This is to say, the fundamental question asks itself; it cannot do otherwise, and when it asks itself it is irresistible. It cannot be ignored. To live in a supposedly sensate or empirical age is therefore to be self-deceiving. There is no such age. Ultimate questions and the systems associated with them are everywhere about—in every man's mind, streaming in the winds of his passing, attached to his every act, casting themselves like a shadow, yet formative of act and direction, determining rather than determined, active rather than passive, enabling and encouraging in the myriad manner of thought.

Man's nature has probably never been otherwise. Although different ages of thought appear to emphasize differing principles of human nature, and may in fact do so, there is a sense in which human nature is

113

responsible for variant phases of itself. To this conceptual aspect of systeming it will be convenient to return.

The problem of the really-real is then a double problem with a double consequence. One effect of it is to entail (always tentatively) the particular implication of the particular inquiry, that which takes place within a given system. This helps to make the particular system operational. In a more general sense the other effect of the problem of the real or of its solution, whatever that may be, is to establish the nature of the world for which the system is operative. This is to say, it describes or it constructs the full scope of the system conceived of as enveloping, forming and comprising that mode of itself which is the subsisting universe. This may be to say that every system has its operational problems and its substantive problems.

It may be considered that fundamental questions have metaphysical systems of their own. That is, there is a compelling quality which inheres in their nature such that to ask them to create a vector which must then proceed on its way in accordance with its own peculiar characteristics. Furthermore, fundamental questions appear to possess the privilege of compelling that they be asked. If, then, the question contains within itself a compelling quality, and if in addition it appears to require that men ask it, it follows that some sort of objective substantiality has been introduced into or recognized in the human situation and that there may well be a degree of uncontrollable self-management within the human-intellectual situation which has something to say about the nature of things. If this should turn out to be possible or even likely it would be a point to remember in the face of the position being taken here that to a considerable extent systematization is a subjective and human activity required by the nature of mind and of human understanding. It may also be required by the nature of that which is understood.

The requirements of a system are not very complicated. They must include a theory of the subject or of the human self, a theory of knowing (epistemology), a theory of the object or of nature, and a theory of the Ultimate. A system can start with any one of the four major questions. Where a system does start is largely a matter of temperament or of the interest of the systematizer. With any system, however, the question of its fundamental assumption (metaphysics) must eventually be asked, and the same basic questions must be covered in one way or another. For temperamental reasons most systems do not systematically cover all four questions. They tend to fall primarily within one area or another, or to be a limited combination of several. In these cases the remaining major elements must be open to reconstruction or extrapolation from whatever is provided in the substance of the system. It is not difficult to work out missing areas when some areas are reasonably well known. In the long run these are the four fundamental questions which will of necessity present themselves and which in turn will be answered, if not explicitly then implicitly, if a system is to be conceived of as in any sense complete. The four fundamental questions in effect reduce to one: What is the really-real? Or: What is fundamental?

The Sieve-like Nature of Contemporary Naturalisms

Contemporary naturalisms comprise the outlook of certain influential sections of Western society. By this is meant that the intellectual assumptions of numerous Western viewpoints are naturalistic. Within this general type of outlook there may be some variety, even some contrasts, among smaller systems. This is quite all right and is not necessarily contradictory. It still does follow that two general assumptions of that society tend to be that sensory evidence is determinative, and that nature is about what nature appears to be as perceived by the senses; it follows that human life can best obtain in settings derivable from these two assumptions. The world outside is free to be simply what it seems to be—that is, the world outside, containing all the objects, substances, forces, and directions with which one is familiar.

It is hardly surprising that these assumptions are made. After all, enormous practical and very obvious gains have been achieved in the development of human life and its cultural settings in a wide variety of geographical locations seemingly as a direct consequence of this simplistic approach to the nature of things. In cases of this sort the fundamental questions appropriate to a philosophic system have been answered in relatively obvious ways, depending upon fairly consistent means of confirmation for support of the particular naturalistic system. In assuming that the fundamental nature of things is physical and that knowledge of them is obtained by sensory means, even if in some orders removed by a dimension or two with the discrepancies being supplied by calculation and rationalistic deduction, a system lays itself open to

115

criticism in case any of these dimensions prove less firm than they have been assumed to be.

There are indeed some fairly obvious infirmities. It is generally acknowledged now that although men live and move in a world of tables, trees, motor vehicles, and buildings, and although the nature of these is in one modality fairly obvious it is in another and microscopic modality anything but obvious. The term "matter" is no longer even used in a respectable reflective sense. It does not mean anything for the very reason that what used to be regarded as matter has been replaced by a series of extremely minute particles subsisting in electrical orbits in relation to other particles, all of them too small to perceive and therefore requiring that their nature be deduced from more readily measurable phenomena. It is also coming to be acknowledged that the examination of these very minute particles, assuming that they really do exist, is extremely difficult to pursue since the intrusion of the observational process very often affects (defines, constructs) the phenomena supposedly being observed. It may then be fair to say that the role of the observer or his subjective contribution to observation may even be determinative in microscopic and sub-microscopic ranges of awareness. Is it possible that perception of sub-microscopic ranges of nature can occur at all except in this subjective dimension? The answer is not at all clear. Conceivably it may not be possible in other than subjective modes. If then there are ranges of the natural world within which perception is necessarily subjective in its nature, does not the question arise as to whether all perception even in more obvious and humanoid ranges is also subjective and constructional in nature? It may be generally true that the subjective epistemological mode of observation controls and defines (selects, creates) the objective natural dimensions seemingly perceived.

How about the normal ranges of concern? In the strict definition of perception, the ranges of nature perceived are those selected by the five senses. It is the custom in Western scientific observation to feel relatively secure about definitions of nature described in terms of the perceptually confirmable. There is some pragmatic justification for this in that it is of course possible to invent motor cars, improved housing, and moon transportation simply by operating within restricted normal ranges and assuming that the universe will respond in predictable ways the directions of which have been induced from a very great number of previous observations. Predictable natural "laws" have been constructed out of the evidence of large numbers of individual cases and it has indeed been found possible in a pragmatic sense to rely on the universe to continue to respond without undue aberrations. Therefore whenever astronauts are sent to the moon it is practical to expect that they can be recovered and returned to Earth without any more than the usual hazards. Even an unfortunate intervention by collision with an asteroid could be classified as a predictable and even normal event in a very low probability range. Hence no "law" would be transgressed in the event of such an accident.

There is, however, a circularity to this class of naturalistic definition. It appears to mean that within restricted ranges of applicability naturalistic constructional theories prove reliable as long as one does not step outside of those definitional ranges. When one does move outside such a range, as with sub-microscopic investigation, the nature of the process of knowing appears to be modified. It may also prove to be modified in macroscopic ranges of the awareness relation. The more sophisticated relations of space and time may belong in this category. In the past the circular character of naturalistic definition has been regarded as a strength rather than a weakness. After all, it did work in a great number of instances; as a type, it was simple, or it appeared simple; and in accordance with the old principle, if one did not need a complicated definition why go looking for one? Everything may depend on what kind of information one wishes. This is to say, everything may depend on what kind of question one wishes to have answered. It may in the end not remain at all clear that questions ought to be held within the recently traditional or fashionable restrictions of the naturalistic order. And, as noted earlier, once the larger questions are posed they have a tendency to get up off the ground and run off whither they will.

What are the implications of these perspectives for a definition of nature, of human nature, and of the relational process of knowing which obtains between them? It appears likely that theories of nature may have to be recognized, in the popular view as indeed they already are in sophisticated scientific views, as far more of the order of intellectual constructs than they are of the order of hard data units joined by solid linkages. That is, it may be proper to say that there really are a nearly infinite number of worlds or universes constructible from data acceptable to a variety of cultural ages and situations. There may not be just the one initial world or universe of generally confirmable elements linked in confirmable manners into a system describable by a variety of means which in the end approach by one avenue or another some single, central essence. Conversely, human nature may require that it be recognized as the primary channel through which the awareness of ''objective'' nature is made available for intellectual and practicable uses. Thus human nature becomes definitive, controlling, formative in its influence on, selection of and construction of data and data-linkages.

The awareness relation may similarly take on a different cast. Rather than being the 18th-century, Lockeian category of unrelieved reception emphasizing the imprint of the stimulus on the receiving mechanism, and rather than being a 19th-century, purely abstract form of ideational extrapolation, the knowing relation may take on a genuine complexity involving subjective and objective rootage, selectivity and response perhaps on both ends, and a mutual reliability and interdependence among the subjective and objective loci. In place of the tendency of contemporary popular naturalisms to conceive of the world-out-there as firm or constant, and of the world-in-here as comprising microcosmic human nature, the relation between them being largely that of dependence of the human microcosm upon the universal macrocosm, there would instead be a world-in-common constructed out of the capacities of the objective world to respond to the subjective selectivities of the assertive self conceived of not only as individual but also as cultural.

Older Conceptualisms I: Abelard

Conceptualism may be taken to mean the view of the subject-object or knowing relation as rational in its nature or essence, that is, of the order of reason or idea, as involving the idea as rational prehension and extension, and as noted earlier, constructional in its nature. In different periods and intellectual ages the position has expressed itself variously, with greater or lesser emphases on this or that phase of the subject-object relation. What the concept was, what it could absorb and what it could not, and how it served and supported the knowing relation, were central problems in several older views. It may be of interest to sketch one or two of these.

It is interesting to see classical philosophic problems reasserting themselves in new configurations of philosophic elements after long

118

periods of recession. No doubt it was supposed that the old problem of universals had disposed of itself along with the cultural ages dominated by various forms of Platonism. Such problems often do not stay disposed of, and are very likely to reassert themselves as for example when rationalism in turn reasserts itself in different forms and contexts. The early Middle Ages was still Platonist, the intrusion of Aristotelianism being yet to come. Perhaps any age dominated by a rationalism will eventually turn to consideration of the reality of abstractions. Perhaps too, there may tend to be a fine balance between a nominalistic solution and a realistic solution to the problem of universals. This was Abelard's problem and the classification of his solution as either nominalistic or realistic in tendency has depended in the history of thought upon who was doing the interpreting. The period of the 11th and 12th centuries was also one of swift transition in intellectual history, and it may be that reflective motion may always tend to be especially rapid across intellectual divides. That is, where the problem at issue concerns the focus of intellective attention and the ascription of metaphysical standing there may tend always to be a relatively rapid philosophic change and alternation of intellectual viewpoints. There may, in short, tend not to be even a relatively permanent resting place for intellectual conclusiveness in this realm of concern.

In Abelard's 11th to 12th century position which is now referred to under the name of "conceptualism" he was attempting to establish the degree of metaphysical standing to be ascribed to the universal as represented in the abstraction which could apply to a plurality of instances. In the case of similar instances did the notion of class or type have a standing of its own or did it inhere simply in the object as Aristotle was to be heard maintaining? The earlier Platonist view had been that the class or type did have realistic standing of its own; therefore the intellect was genuinely in touch with something real in its dealings with the order of ideas. Some say that Abelard's solution to this problem was nominalistic—that is, the name of the abstraction or universal comprised the main reservoir of reality which the universal possessed. The word or name could be constructed but it might not thereby necessarily refer to anything substantial or which possessed realistic standing in any objective sense. Abelard got around this to some extent by proposing a prior standing, an archetypal order of universals obtaining in the mind of God, so that it did not become necessary for universals to supply their own complete realistic status. A universal was therefore not a thing for Abelard, but so also it was not a word. A word could acquire universal meaning by becoming a predicate. Those elements which could take on degrees of objectivity by their natures as shown through intellectual comparisons could constitute universals. Predication becomes possible only through human thought, which is to say, through conceptualizing. It is this capacity to establish universals which makes thought possible. There is therefore in Abelard's view a genuine reaching out toward ultimate reality.

Abelard advanced the notion that God had created the Universe in accordance with archetypes maintained in the Divine mind. Then universals could be conceived of as existing first in the mind of God, second, in things, and third, in human understanding by way of comparative thought. He was therefore not a true nominalist and his position was a compromise position.

It is difficult to assess Abelard today for the excellent reason that times and settings do make a difference even if classical themes in reflective thought return normally from age to age. Abelard lived at the crest of a wave of reliance upon dialectic, by which is meant the discovery of truth or the achievement of touch with the real by means of intellect. This occurred, one remembers, at the brink of a many-sided cultural period in which human attention was to be turned to the world outside, not only intellectually but also artistically and culturally, and in which the renewing of attention to the intellectual real would recur occasionally rather than constantly. In one of those peculiar configurations of intellectual and cultural history it is possible to see again today in the midst of the new romanticism of the late 20th century a new reliance upon what could pass for dialectic modified perhaps by intuitionism, and certainly confused rather than clarified by the residual persistence of scientific rationalism, partial dependency upon supposedly sensate empiricism, and some straightforward mysticisms.

Older Conceptualisms II: Ramism Re-Visited

In his monumental work on Petrus Ramus (1515-1572) Father Ong remarks somewhere that it is almost impossible to tell whether Ramus was a nominalist or a realist, and notes the strands in his thought which alternately suggest first one conclusion and then the other. There may not be much to be added to this description. Ramus flourished as ostensibly an anti-Aristotelian and a Platonist. He thought of himself as a Platonist and in reaction to medieval scholasticism pursued through much of his professional life a philosophical method designed to ''short out'' the Aristotelian syllogism and the logical structure which it entailed. His view seems to have been that nature itself was laid out in a discernible contrapuntal structure which lent itself readily to discovery by intellectual means. If ideas could be set forth in such ways that they met the natural structure of things at significant points what amounted to an intellectual avenue to the truth became immediately available. The juxtaposition of Platonist ideas with aspects of the discernible world may belong with Abelard's and similar views involving archetypes in the mind of God which somehow balance with instances in the world of existence.

Father Ong notes that Ramus was not an observer of nature in either the Baconian or the modern sense; and yet it seems inescapable that his complicated and well-stretched position went far toward preparing the way for the new attitude toward nature conceived of as the way things are rather than as the origin of things. One can almost hear Whitehead remarking at this point how readily the intellectual positions prevalent in one age appear to be establishing the groundwork in unsuspected forms for the assumptions and derivative positions of another. Nature is by implication clearly reliable in Ramus; encountering nature was to him simply an intellectual affair, as it was for his age and much of that which followed. Whitehead however observed that the reliability of nature was essentially a medieval idea, which would mean for present purposes that Ramus was merely modifying or reflecting a conception of the natural world which was already well established centuries before he lived and which must have been endemic in his own intellectual milieu. Father Ong remarks time and again that Ramus was merely working over this or that aspect of his intellectual setting rather than producing anything that was really new.

It is always interesting to speculate what the effect of a teaching emphasis is on an academic or intellectual outlook. It is even a disturbingly modern problem. Miller and Ong both have a good deal to say about it in connection with Ramist doctrine. Ramus became enormously popular as a teacher; his works went through many editions and seem to have proved exciting and challenging to generations of students on the continent as well as in the Puritan complex in America. Since so much of his work consisted of textbooks for students Ong implies that this may have led to some of the over-simplification of which Ramus later stood accused, and have added momentum to his determination to kill off the Aristotelian syllogism and its associated logical baggage. Ramus appears to have felt that he had made a major new discovery in the methodological field. Understanding of the nature of things could be achieved more simply, more readily, and more effectively through his method of judgment.

Again for the educational historian the Ramian dialectic holds a notable place among the compelling ideas of Western thought. It is as if dialectic, interpreted as discussion, the contrapuntal exercise of disjunctive viewpoints, contained within it a kind of irresistible force in the long struggle of the human mind to reach archetypal truths. Reason partook of this compelling power, at least by implication, as it participated in the dialectic and as it began to be conceived of as the intellectual force which it would become in the 18th century.

In Ramism, therefore, there appears again to be reflected one of those swiftly moving, transitional periods in which the major intellectual elements seem not to be able to maintain themselves for very long, but rather to derive swiftly from earlier times and in subsequent perspective to be preparing with equal swiftness to give way to later developments. In the Ramian situation there would have been two such lines of development, one in the direction of strict rationalism culminating in the 18th century, and the other the observational or empiricist line with which Ramus might have had very little connection and yet which would not fail to thrive on the foundation of the reliable universe which Ramus apparently took from the Middle Ages and passed to succeeding times.

Later ages would set aside the archetypes; emphasis would fall more immediately upon observed natural phenomena; reason would be delimited, perhaps unduly, to the status of servant or tool in the management of this or that restricted problem in the continuing examination of the natural universe. That is, it would occupy the place of a step or stage in what came to be called ''scientific method,'' the means whereby the information-manager could proceed from point A to point B, all within the observational context in which man the receiver (in the Lockeian sense) essentially recorded data and yet was privileged to work out intellectualistic phases of a problem in the interest of leap-frogging what might otherwise be a monstrous process of unending classification of data. All of this would involve the conception of human nature as essentially derivative from the envelope of the natural Real, and it would have to wait upon the slow discovery that observation of the natural world alone was in itself a limited process before some reassessment of the nature of reason could become practical or tolerable.

Dialectic would experience several rebirths in the 19th and 20th centuries, one for example in the Hegelian-Marxist configuration and one in the Deweyan bio-social metaphysic. Each of these suggests that dialectic partakes of natural process in the sense that it reflects or refracts it, depending on the degree of intellectual involvement: for Hegel it seems to be an effort of the human mind to reach and en-compass natural process; for Marx the nature of dialectic appears to have been transferred out of mind into natural or social process. Hegel and Marx, as has been often enough observed by the historians of ideas, seem in retrospect to have been very close. Dialectical process was somehow for both, in different ways, the substance of natural process in a form which could be comprehended intellectually and which at the same time was reliable enough to be used as predictive ground. For Dewey dialectic conceived of as discussion involved a complicated set of assumptions concerning human personality, almost as givens, though based in a bio-social metaphysic, such that the discussional process could be relied upon to produce something approaching the truth. In a sense Dewey abandoned much of the Western conceptual heritage, yet in a sense also he did not. As he was himself well grounded in the history of thought it is a fair guess that it was not possible for him to give up a good deal of what that entailed. That Dewey's successors have given up his rootage in Western thought may not be surprising but it probably also means that his successors are no longer his disciples.

Extended Idealism as Conceptualism

It is difficult to judge whether the history of philosophy will con-tinue to be written in terms of schools or major divisions as it has been in the past. Solvent forces appear to have begun work in recent times which may have the effect of diverting reflective interests from philosophy cast in terms of this or that viewpoint. Certainly student interest in this area of concern has declined sharply among later institutional generations.

Contemporary foci of interest appear to emphasize problems rather than schools, or less often, systems. All this could be a passing phase conditioned by cultural concern over unresolved moral, ethical, and social dilemmas. It may be that emergence of epistemological and metaphysical concerns at the center of reflective responsibility is the next phase of intellectual effort to be followed in the course of time by re-emphasis on systematic resting points as a consequence.

However that may be, one does not look back over recent centuries from the standpoint of a rising conceptualism without having to take account of the idealistic problem(s). Idealism has in general been concerned to establish the subject-object relation in terms of consciousness and rationalistic awareness, with the consequence that the world-outside was to be known in terms of its effects upon the self-inside. One line of thought asserted that the objective world depended for its existence upon being known by the self. Another escaped from the "egocentric predicament" by positing an objective (divine) mind to stand behind and beyond the strictly human knowing relation. In the latter view, the objective world could justifiably be accepted in its objectivity by individual human perceivers with the assurance that there were other and larger Subject-object relations which served to support the existence of the world independently of people. Thus the semi-humorous, semi-serious anxiety of idealists and anti-idealists over whether a room was annihilated when its single perceiver left it could be obviated by absorption of the issue in the larger grounding of existence in general.

These idealistic currents and counter-currents appear in retrospect to have been the studied efforts of two centuries or more to define the nature of human consciousness and its role in the knowing process and in the subject-object relation. It is awkward now to have to bring these fine distinctions to life for contemporary students whose intellectual lives are so emotionally conditioned away from intellectual exercises of seeming antiquity. Surely the only way to approach the matter from a teaching standpoint is to attempt to breathe life into the students' own awareness relations and to see whether it then becomes important to them to know what the historic researches and experimentations have been in this field.

Elsewhere it has been noted that the new romanticism of the late 20th century, if that is what it is, would most likely be Kantian rather than Berkeleyan in that Kant was willing to insist upon the reality of the thing-in-itself and to attempt to establish the nature of consciousness and of the intellectual or rationalistic process with respect to it, resisting the tendency more prevalent in Berkeleyan derivatives to vacuum up the known world inside the enveloping consciousness of the self. Some have denied that Kant was an idealist himself at all on these grounds, while conceding that he gave rise to subsequent idealisms. The names may pass without arousing undue concern. The point may be well taken, however, and it could in time appear that Whitehead's attempt to describe a system which accounted for the subject-object relation in rationalistic terms while enabling the realistic standing of both ends of the relation has certain family connections with Kantianism. Whether this is an idealism or a realism need not matter from the standpoint of the problem, the elements of which are fairly clear in either case.

It may be interesting to come at the problem from what might be in some instances a student's standpoint. It is interesting to speculate on whether the contemporary cultural interest in drug stimulation and mind-expansion is more nearly a Berkeleyan than a Kantian phenomenon. That is, it might reflect a restricted cultural decision to investigate what have been called the limits of consciousness perhaps with that greater degree of willingness to disregard the question of objectivity which may have been Berkeleyan in its ancestry. Answers to the question might vary with attitudinal commitments and should be left open for the moment.

Transcendental reason conceived of as the individual human capacity to reach beyond the self to apprehend the knowable universe in its essential nature is surely to be considered the primary tool or instrument in the effort to form a viable subject-object relation in the coming period of philosophic concern. Commensurate with the standing reality of the self, the objective universe must similarly be conceived of as having equivalent realistic standing. The inter-relation must be rational; neither terminus must permit itself to be absorbed entirely in the other; neither must be conceived of as limited; neither must be conceived of as necessarily uniform in composition. That is, the self might be partly rational and partly other-than-rational. Other-than-rational in either case might be not necessarily discontinuous with the rational, nor need it be oppositional, logics notwithstanding. In the present view logic will have to wait upon the formulation of the system.

There are perhaps numerous logics, each the methodological servant of a systemic approach. Once this systemic approach is clarified in the course of time, a logical methodology can be derived from it to serve its purposes.

Natural science, it has been observed often enough, whatever else it may be is also a powerful if restricted rationalism. Partly for reasons of its methodological requirements, partly by reason of its observational necessities, and partly by reason of its speculative implications it is surely heavily rationalistic rather than simplistically empiricist. It is enormously interesting to reflect what the effects on speculative philosophy will be of the contemporary fact that man can now exist in outer space and look back at his planetary dwelling from a radically new perspective. If Dewey's emphasis on experience has led his disciples all abroad at points, here most surely its vividness can be expected to exert genuine influence on the development of ideas, if not for mataphysical reasons then more certainly for aesthetic ones. Surely all the old philosophical and religious questions will present themselves anew for restatement in the light of the revised aesthetic context of human existence. The Western religious tradition may be permitted its howls of mirth at the innocent Soviet astronaut who reportedly sailed around in space looking for God out the window of his spacecraft and soberly recorded that he did not see Him. One may hope, out of the great respect which Western society surely feels for the Soviet Union, that the story is apocryphal. As surely the Soviet Union in its turn can recognize that the great questions of human and universal existence are now only inconceivably greater than in times past they have ever been.

Conceptualist Problems

If a conceptualist position is to be evolved today it must then provide for rationalistic and extensional knowing, with mind as creating instrument, creation and selection being synonymous in a realistic context. The nature of reason will be seen more or less as ganglion subsuming intuitional and constructional awarenesses. The self will be defined as the individual and personal amalgamation of subjective and objective elements emergent from the ground of being and eventually resorbing into it. The objective universe, although perhaps hardly ''objective'' in the traditional sense of the term, is surely to be regarded as unlimited from any human sense, as other-than-finite, the manifold

126

nature of which has only begun to be studied in its earliest and simplest appearances.

The problem of universals as presented in the history of thought again seems, in these new perspectives, to be, as so many such problems do, slightly thin and threadbare. Nevertheless it is necessary to suppose that the reality of universals may need to be reconsidered and restated in fresh, new ways for the very reason that the metaphysical problem involved is recurring in new forms and indeed cannot be expected to do otherwise. It is as if the successive stages in the history of philosophy have comprised preliminary examinations of recurrent fundamental problems in thought and understanding and as if the problems which were represented in them must be expected to recur normally in succeeding ages, oftentimes in differing forms.

Concerning the Ultimate, it is only the more difficult to do otherwise than note the Kierkegaardian character of its essentiality in a conceptualist stance. If the natures of philosophical systems are at all describable, each must terminate in a root outside of itself. The root is therefore indescribable in terms of the system, except in this curious Kierkegaardian foreshadowing, the incidence of which is so high among variant existentialist and phenomenological positions. It is, then, quite like the shadow that falls over everything, the nature of which cannot be described although its existence is undeniable:—there is indeed something there, though it is impossible to say what it is.

XII Education and Valuation: A Metaphysical Predicament

American society tends to worry about education. Certainly social thought and communal energy focus around education at all levels. At times the concern is reflected in thought without energy; at other times social energy is applied without thought. The cultural concern, however, is clear enough and is constantly demonstrated in one way or another. Perhaps it was inevitable when a new society began to form itself in the great new continent of the West that a central anxiety should inhere around the way that society should think of itself, define its objectives and purposes, and ensure that its rising forces should emerge in an historical continuity and a promising thrust toward the future.

Every major question in educational thought and practice, when pushed, resolves itself into a problem of philosophic definition. Always and again the generic question is—What is Education? The basis for answering the question has therefore to be philosophic. What every theory of education does is answer that question, if not explicitly in philosophic terms, then implicitly. The final or fundamental definition of education implied or involved in an educational theory is necessarily based on a metaphysical proposition. For present purposes a metaphysical proposition is an assertion concerning the nature of the real, that is, that category of descriptive understanding which is fundamental in the sense that it does not reduce to anything else. The nature and setting of human life, the composition and dimensions of human nature, the natural universe, theory of knowledge, and at least some implications concerning the Ultimate would be fundamental questions expressions concerning which will be made in a theory of education. Every educational theory will then imply a relatively complete metaphysics, and every metaphysics will imply an appropriate theory of education.

The confusion which exists in American thought today is an inevitable consequence of the lack of metaphysical clarity. A necessary open-endedness in philosophic statement deriving from the need to pursue natural knowledge in a multitude of ways and on vast scales has encouraged the notion that fundamental principles cannot readily be pursued and that assertions concerning them are unwisely made and should be withheld. In short, metaphysics is out of fashion.

This has nothing to do with the requirements of philosophical operation. A philosophic system worth its salt must be anchored somewhere, somehow. It has been sufficiently remarked elsewhere that systems do not provide complete self-explanation within their own frames of reference. For a system to work there must needs be a principle, a substance, a fundament or ground outside of itself to serve as its base. The connections between the parts of a system then may follow readily enough.

In actual practice there is a great deal of loose philosophic thrashing-about without benefit of metaphysical landmarks. Much of this confusion develops in educational thought and practice in American communities where philosophy is considered a peculiar creature which ought to be confined to the yards and groves of Academe. Educational confusion in the lay community does not in any wise limit or restrict the energies which the community expends on educational decisions. Indeed, issues in education are pursued with a remarkable energy in very diverse types of community in this country. This fact is most revealing of the profound concern which American society attaches to education as a focus of valuation. Perhaps few social concerns, not even national political issues, produce such clouds of anxiety and emotion on so many levels.

Since decisions are being made all the time in educational areas, not the less readily for the absence of metaphysical clarity, it follows that they are made within restricted ranges of understanding. Policies can be pursued vigorously for a period of time, a few months or a few years, on the basis of past precedents, recent history, popular social, natural, or political understandings, without serious risk of departure from well-trodden paths. Educational practice can vary within practical ranges and can be expected to work reasonably well without any pretense of philosophic profundity and without raising very significant philosophical questions.

The history of education within a given period, considered institution by institution or level by level, can then be expected to consist of variations on traditional themes. Curricular segments can be sliced in different ways, divisions of knowledge can be redivided and recombined to give fresh foci to intellectual address, inter-disciplinary studies can be developed or permitted to decline—all without seriously approaching or affecting any fundamental philosophical question within the reflective framework of a particular society or segment of society.

Innovation eventually became such a great word in American educational thought that it was reflected in federal educational policy, a sure sign that discussion of the issues in the hinterlands had been extensive. The education profession is not without its acidulous philosophers, and some were heard to observe that much alleged "innovation" consists in the moving about of old chessmen and not of anything that matters very much nor of anything that is in any sense new.

Another way of saying this is that American education has become pervaded by pragmatism. In this latest of its numerous incarnations since its inception in the brains of C. S. Peirce and William James educational pragmatism can be described as the resolution of problems and issues in relatively short ranges of perspective, that is, largely within the terms of the problems and issues themselves, and essentially without principles of a very general nature or explicit metaphysical fundaments. Under the pressure of daily affairs in American higher educational institutions it is inevitable that many types of practical problems constantly get settled in pragmatic ways. It is not necessarily a bad thing that this is so; short-range educational problems have to be solved in great numbers in brief periods of time, and this is a way of doing it. Nevertheless, it is also true that fundamental questions in education do not get attended to very often in broad ranges of awareness and concern. To say it differently, educational questions too often tend to get settled in pragmatic modes, that is to say, modes of convenience, rather than to be considered in the depth and breadth which their nature deserves. The difference between a fundamental philosophic position and a pragmatic position then lies in the element of fashion; it is fashionable not to ask profound or far-ranging questions, and undeniably it is easier not to do so. Philosophy in its genuine nature does not, however, permit such slackness. Fundamental questions ought to be considered wherever they are relevant, and restricted (pragmatic) solutions to educational questions ought to be made available within the context of general principles.

No doubt one of the reasons why organized religion in American society in the late twentieth century appears to be suffering from disuse derives from this condition of philosophical vacuity. Part of the business of religion is to raise fundamental questions and to comment on them appropriately in the major areas of human concern. If it is unfashionable to raise general questions in the first place, and if the American churches insist upon raising them, the consequence should be at least predictable and not surprising.

The continuum of tradition and relevance is significant at this point. Any society which has the fortitude to concern itself with educational questions, whether in long-range or short-range dimensions, deserves some sympathy. It is under the necessity of engaging in the valuational process when often it does not have sufficient grounding in philosophy to enable it to do so effectively. Thus does educational thought come at once upon the difficult problem of valuation. Education and valuation are so much and so nearly heart and soul of each other that they might well be considered to be laminated pillars of identical cultural constructs. How can a society decide what is relevant in its own days and what speaks to the condition of its young people? If fashion is a problem and condition in education, what is sure to be produced is social pragmatism and reliance upon ''the big vote.'' Upon what grounds is a community to decide an educational issue? On traditional experience? Upon some new reading of social or individual valuation? How is this issue to be resolved?

It is often convenient, and it must be added, that it is often the habit of philosophers when attempting to decide such questions, to look about and see what it is that people are doing. Great amusement once descended on a college class in psychology when the teacher observed that psychology was what psychologists do. This entertaining operational principle of a generation or so ago in the social sciences has now been generalized so that it is no longer unusual. Philosophers use it, too, though they like to pretend they do not because it is not a dignified or quite proper ground for epistemological decision. But the fact is, they do use it. This is one reason why it is so intensely interesting and so necessary for students of philosophy constantly to raise the question with respect to any philosophical position at all—how does this position or this person know what it or he claims to know?

Tradition is after all a residual set of decisions as to what works for human nature and what is true within the convenient limits of human understanding. The chances are that the sources of certainty were formerly either the same as now or not so very different for earlier periods of human experience than at present or in days or ages to come. What are these modes of understanding?

Again the cultural problem comes to the fore. In the late twentieth century we are prone to say that the great new source of relevance and of truth is social in nature, or even more generally, that reality is of the nature of process in both physico-natural and social realms of thought. The modes of awareness and understanding in any age are probably about the same: rational, intuitive, socio-experiential, sensational, and traditional-experiential. There may not be very many other ways of knowing; these few ways may rise and decline, inter-weave, be periodically active or recessive, and yet in the main may all be present and operative all the time. Valuation must be based upon metaphysics. Judgment will follow upon actuality. That which is worth or dis-worth, which is to say that in which value or disvalue inheres, is that which obtains in a metaphysical sense in the judgment of a particular age.

Perhaps then one must again say, in a particular time and place, that valuation is a function of prior metaphysical decision and that the responsibility of an educational institution is to clarify its metaphysical position based upon epistemological assertion leading to a harmony of systematic thought.

Exercising the philosophic function then amounts to forcing the metaphysical issue. The risk is always that educational philosophy will amount to policy-making in a metaphysical vacuum. Every educational institution ought to be examinable in its metaphysical stance, approached by way of (1) its epistemological method, and (2) its valuation. Later in this discourse it will be possible to turn to several examples of institutional philosophy in higher education and see how valuation fares in the light of a particular metaphysical position or philosophic system.

Another aspect of the problem of tradition and relevance in the general context of valuation lies in the continuity or discontinuity of philosophic generations, that-which-is-assumed as an integral part of that-which-is-proposed. Conveyed in this notion is the fact of thematic continuity from one philosophic or intellective generation to another. That is, a philosophic position clearly held in one period of time can be conceived of as having certain philosophical assumptions on the basis of which it is constructed; these assumptions may however and often commonly are forgotten or taken for granted, so that they become unspoken assumptions of the dominant philosophic mood, exerting profound influences on the thought of that time.

The crucial period of change in valuation occurs between a given philosophic generation and the next, where unspoken assumptions cannot readily be carried on or passed on to a succeeding generation because of the very reason that they are taken for granted and are rarely discussed. This leads to thematic discontinuity between the first and second philosophic generations and a loss of reflective understanding between generations as a consequence of assumptional discontinuity. The problem is not so much that a particular position ought necessarily to endure from one reflective generation to another, but that metaphysical awareness and choice ought to be provided for between the generations to avoid the risk of inadvertent philosophic drift. The problem of philosophic drift has been considered earlier.

Prior to this point the intent has been to define the relations of metaphysics and valuation, to clarify the taking of a position on this interrelation such that valuation is clearly a consequence of metaphysical decision or assertion and that valuational positions taken in higher education can be reasonably seen as deriving from prior decisions concerning the nature of things. An implication would be that wherever valuation is to be a focus of attention the prior metaphysical position involved will be relatively explicit with respect to the nature of human nature, the nature of the natural universe, the nature of knowing, and the nature of the Ultimate. As noted earlier, it appears to be entirely congenial with the American mood in social questions to conceive of education as often at least pragmatically close to the center of individual and community concern. It becomes a very practical exercise in considering a relation of education and valuation to reflect upon what different higher educational institutions have asserted with respect to valuation, and to move back and forth with relative freedom between metaphysics and valuation to clarify positions the institutions may have taken with respect to one central factor or another.

Instances of Educational Valuation

It should be useful now to turn to comparative descriptions in each of several institutional cases. A convenient pattern of questions suggests itself as follows: What basic statements are made by the institutional literature? That is, what statements are made in (1) metaphysics, (2) valuation, (3) the theory of learning and knowing, and (4) policy applications or organization of higher education within the institution? What implications are involved in each part, in each institutional case? Are there appropriate summary positions in metaphysics and valuation by each institution? Is there openness (open-endedness) as an appropriate institutional position, as distinct from a unilateral institutional position? Some questions apply with some institutions and not with others. The summary conclusions if not explicated may have to be surmised.

Different institutions begin at different points in the wide range of educational philosophy. No doubt this is in part a function of the experience and stance from which the institution emerged or, if it is an old institution, a function of its tradition through a substantial portion of its history to the present time.

Assumptions are made by each of the subject institutions of higher education. In attempting to determine some commonalities among them even in the midst of their differences and divergences, one must remember that assumptions are everywhere, as much in the approach of a particular study such as this one as in the assumptions of a subject institution. Most of the instances to be examined are relatively new; Raymond College was founded in 1962 as a new departure on the campus of the century-old University of the Pacific. Johnston College, opened only in 1969-1970, was a new departure on the campus of an established and considerably older institution, the University of Redlands (California). The State University College at Old Westbury (Long Island, New York) in its first phase planned to open formally in 1970 but actually began its on-campus deliberations among students and faculty in 1968-1969. Prescott College (Arizona) inducted its first class in 1966-1967 after a five- or six-year period of planning and intention. Receiving its first provisional charter from the State of New York in 1965 and from the Regents of New York State in 1968, Friends World College, Huntington (Long Island, New York) therefore entered only recently on its new dimension of higher education. New College,

134

Sarasota, Florida was almost as new. Among the older of the newer institutions, Goddard College (Plainfield, Vermont) was founded in 1938, metamorphosing an older secondary and junior college institution into a new four year college. Certain of these institutional examples have since moved into later phases of development. This need not affect the study, which takes for its focus the articulation of ideas and their institutional expression. If some historical and developmental significance inheres around these later changes it can best be understood in vertical accounts appropriate to each institution. Johnston and Old Westbury have each undergone such alterations. More gradual changes will naturally have occurred in other instances.

A formative influence is no doubt applied to a study of higher education when five or more of its subject institutions are drawn from colleges and universities founded since 1960 or so, and from others no earlier than 1935. For this reason it may be useful to introduce a control institution from an earlier epoch the effectiveness of which appears to be undiminished in the present day.

Raymond College

Raymond College, Stockton, California, may appropriately come first since in some respects it appears to be the last revolutionary and perhaps even the most traditional of a group of new and different institutions. It should be clear that there is no intent in this sketch to attach a positive value to radical or revolutionary ideas or practices. Valuation, after all, remains to be defined, and its relation to education, here especially higher education, is still to be made clear. It is simply that in some respects it may be easier to see what certain of the elements in the situation are and what functions are being performed if a beginning is made with an institution less different and less detached from the common educational experience than might be the case with several others.

Raymond College, then, established in 1962 as among the first of the cluster college patterns earlier begun at Claremont, consisted of a student population of 250 and a faculty of 25, a curriculum of 22 core courses and 5 or more electives, to be spread over a three-year, three-term-per-year calendar variable to four years with added electives, independent studies and practica.

Among the core courses offered at Raymond College in one three-year period the following titles appeared: Introduction to the Modern World, Introduction to the Humanities, Mathematics-Natural Science Sequence, Man and Society in Historical Perspective, World Literature in English, French, or German, Perspectives on Modern European History, Dilemmas in the Developing World, Empirical Approach to Self and Society, Perspectives on American Civilization, Fine Arts, Philosophy, Religion, Cultural Values and Social Structure, Contemporary Political Issues, Philosophical Economics, and sundry Independent Studies or Seminars.

Raymond College classes were intended to be predominantly of the seminar form with 12 to 15 students each to permit active discussion by all participants. No majors or concentrations were offered in the traditional sense. Instead the intention was to provide broad, solid foundations for subsequent specialization.

To point the metaphysical question, it was evidently not the purpose of Raymond College to embark on a radical departure in defining the real. That is, all of the traditional modes of understanding were enabled in this curriculum; the standard modes of learning and understanding (knowing) were similarly provided for. While valuation did not come in for specific address in the institutional literature which was disseminated to the inquiring public in this period a general acquaintance with educational approaches of this kind suggests that it inherited a good deal of attention as a legitimate subject of inquiry in the student's three years or four years at Raymond. This is to say, valuation normally inheres in all of the traditional as well as all of the new standard modes of understanding. The foci of educational attention would be those of most colleges and universities and no radical statement concerning the nature of Man, the nature of the real, the nature of learning and knowing, or the nature of the Ultimate should be understood. Rather, all doors would be open in each of these major areas of concern. The individual student or faculty member could move in any direction he saw as justified, always granting that his grounds were reliable and his documentation defensible.

With respect to policy application, which is to say, educative practice, a new and fresh approach appeared at Raymond College. If the great fields of knowledge were not substantially disturbed in this institutional pattern they were certainly realigned, boundaries between them were taken down, courses and studies were organized around questions and issues, in philosophic terms around problems, growing at need in widely diverse disciplines. The principal achievement at Raymond is then to reorganize traditional Western fields of learning for undergraduate educational purposes around problems and issues of immediate and profound significance in the human experience. It probably accomplished this with the help of a devoted and understanding faculty who were able by virtue of past experience to be enthusiastic about the commitment of their institution. This enthusiasm on the part of leadership can make all the difference between success and something less than success in the history of a college or university. Clearly, Raymond College has made a substantial success of what it did. In all directness, it must be acknowledged that traditional Western fields of knowledge can be realigned and reconstructed in a good many different ways with the resultant virtue of freshness and the advantages of new, to some extent constructively upsetting, and fresh approaches to the major fields of human understanding. The application developed at Raymond College was probably somewhat unusual in its selection of problems and issues, in the construction of three years or four years of educative experience surrounding these, and in the peculiar amalgam of experience which if offered to its students and faculty.

Raymond is, as noted earlier, an outgrowth of the University of the Pacific, and it was therefore able to draw on a surrounding university community in Stockton, and certain other California communities in the cases of certain of the graduate schools which had been located nearer to their operational fields, for resources which small colleges alone might not readily expect to have. It is probable that Raymond College emerged from the context of an older university approach as a result of innovative and imaginative thrusts developed among its institutional faculty and associated educators and that a good deal of its educational experience and potential was a natural outgrowth of a traditional organization of the field of knowledge. Institutional history does shed some light on institutional nature. Observers may well conclude that a fresh and distinguished reorganization of traditional fields of knowledge of this type is the most desirable and most reliable form of higher education to he had in contemporary America. Whenever this position is taken it will not be considered necessary to assume radically different metaphysical positions involving human nature, learning and knowing, the real, or the Ultimate. It will simply be necessary to be as fresh, as enthusiastic, as committed, as thorough, as profound, and as open-ended as possible, and thereafter to create a student and faculty community of learners which will absorb the energies and channel the concerns of its members as effectively as a wise selection of problems and issues and a skillful and devoted development of process will permit.

It is worth returning for a moment to the procedural element of small classes and heavy dependence on dialogue and seminar-type discussions at Raymond College. This could have some metaphysical import. It could mean that the individual was regarded as a source of certainty, whether student or teacher, and that the result of a class conducted in this manner in terms of learning and teaching, would be properly unpredictable and yet hold eminent value for the participants not only in an educative sense but also in a metaphysical sense. This is not necessarily the case, and one would not know this about any particular educational institution without extensive experience with it. In the case of a traditional institution organized around lectures by outstanding teachers it is less likely that metaphysical or philosophical open-endedness will be the result or will even be intended to be the result. To be fair, a precise analysis of the lecture process does not at all preclude the dialogic responses of the listener to verbal presentation, such that a genuine dialogue may indeed take place in the students' minds even though it may be unexpressed in the lecture setting and may be implemented only in written papers, examination responses, or in some later forms of student self-expression. Nevertheless, the weight of educational experience involving lectures given in a setting which is essentially a listening experience for students does not tend toward the encouragement of dialogic response on a wide scale on the part of student participants. The fact that Raymond College made a point of organizing its classes around small memberships of 10 to 15 and of developing its educational experience largely in discussional form should mean that relatively great weight was given to the importance and the reliability of individual student development and self-expression.

Thus at Raymond College in this period there appears to have been a highly interesting configuration of traditional Western learning, which included of course the latest in scientific and reflective disciplines, freshly reorganized and realigned around new foci or problems of human interest and concern, most probably producing highly effective educational experiences for students and teachers.

In a setting of this type valuation must necessarily remain open. It is not clear from the literature what the social and community or interpersonal problems are at Raymond; it would be odd if there were not some. Intellection must necessarily receive a very high positive valuation. The achievement or working through of values as a result of intellective endeavor in a great many different fields and around these particular problems of whatever nature must have constituted one of the attractive reaches of the Raymond challenge. That is, the student must be able to work through values on the basis of fresh experience with traditional fields as his spirit and the requirements of his field may suggest. Some guidance will necessarily derive from the disciplines which are clearly interacting around the fresh problems of the Raymond educational experience. It remains unlikely that the world will begin to burn in Stockton; on the contrary, it may begin to improve there.

Johnston College

Again the approach has to be—what was this institution doing and what may those things have meant for its philosophical position in metaphysics and valuation? Without necessarily singling out Johnston College as being responsible for something which the great majority of colleges were doing it is nevertheless convenient to call attention at this point to its emphasis in selection of students.

Johnston described itself in its publications of that period as seeking students with the following characteristics:

> "Above-average intelligence as revealed in high school work; the desire to establish a sound moral and ethical perspective; independence in thought and action with a firm sense of responsibility; evidence of leadership and imagination; the will to live by an honor code in academic and social affairs; willingness to be exposed to a culture other than their own; the desire to help meet the needs of persons and institutions; and willingness to participate in laboratories in personal growth."

Perhaps most colleges like to think of themselves as attracting students of above-average intelligence, but this may be a mis-description of their common point. What they may really want is a gradually rising level of achievement among their students. That would be quite a different matter. The chances are quite good within a few years that the very common institutional emphasis on admitting students of higher and higher intelligence may change in favor of admitting broad spectra of ability as well as preparation with a view to providing on-campus representation of as many ability levels and personality types as possible. Existing selectivity on the admissions front is likely to become selectivity with respect to institutional and group modes. If institutions can be said to have personalities, and perhaps they can, this may be the crucial reference point for admissions purposes within a reasonable time. The recent debate over ''open admissions'' has had a legitimate point to make: student abilities often cannot be predicted with any assurance when considered apart from family, community and school experience.

Admissions officers in their candid moments acknowledge that for the most part they have no idea what they are doing; often they proceed in accordance with rules of thumb which appear to be appropriate for a particular college or university, allowing perhaps for secondary school accomplishment as shown in school records as a central touchstone. Johnston College did not therefore in this descriptive item distinguish itself markedly from other institutions nor did it assert anything very clear about its nature. In the end, every institution wants to feel good about itself and what it is doing and probably some vague notion of uplift in the area of student intelligence contributes to the sense of institutional well-being. It may be noted and passed by.

In valuational areas of its self-description Johnston College took definite form and assumed a direction. It desired a student group which would work at establishing a moral and ethical perspective; along with independence in thought and action it wanted students with a firm sense of responsibility; in this context leadership and imagination clearly would not be expected to lead to ethico-moral disintegration; the determination to live fully would be balanced by an honor code in academic and social affairs which would have the effect of channelling that life; intercultural interests, the wish to help meet personal and institutional needs, and participation in personal growth laboratories would have valuational import of some significance.

Conceiving of itself as ''an interlocking establishment'' with flexibility of functions in people and buildings, Johnston College went on to describe its College community as one in which all members would participate in a government serving in areas where each had a primary

140

interest. This approach to college life and campus organization had been pioneered a generation and more earlier by Antioch in Ohio and Bennington and Goddard in Vermont. No doubt it took many forms in later years and may take still others in years to come. Johnston at that time conceived of administrators and teachers as functionally inter-operational and not as mutually inclusive, as Goddard did. It described living centers for students who were to merge social and academic processes. It desired that each student experience an on-campus "home" which would be an academic environment promoting an atmosphere of inquiry and intellectual interchange in a variety of ways. It envisioned off-campus programs to relate campus experience to the larger society; cross-cultural living, working and conference centers might be established to provide inter-cultural exposures. Independent study was planned as a prominent feature of student experience to balance group study and seminars.

Among institutions moving directly to the heart of some campus social concerns, Johnston College advanced the idea of an honor community. Prescott College, as will be seen later, did and said similar things. An honor community would evidently be a corporate body of responsible individuals. A college should, Johnston said, have its own life style based on "close association of colleagues." Each person should assume responsibility for his or her own behavior and its effect upon the community. The community was intended to support and guide; "it may also be personally demanding and not appropriate for every individual." The College community as a whole would formulate collegiate life principles, intending to do justice to individual integrity without negating the integrity of others.

By way of commentary, educational institutions may be subject to a peculiar hazard. They must encourage growth and development; they find it difficult to define bases for channelling or restricting growth and development. Presumably one may grow to become a skillful and dedicated horse thief. In some societies it might be defensible to do so. If today it appears otherwise, educational institutions must then discover what kinds of growth and development are desirable and on what grounds. Johnston had only the usual difficulties in this respect. If some very general contexts of ethico-moral movement can be established it may be hoped that the resulting moral encouragement will be in the direction of positive valuation and not in the direction of more dedicated and highly skilled horse thievery.

An honor code approach to this problem is an obvious effort to establish channels for ethical and moral growth and development. Where is the code to originate? If an institution has a church or general religious connection, even if vague, it may help to establish its directional context. If its field of reference is entirely social, which is to say, if it depends upon direct readings of American society for its moral landmarks, the problem may be quite a different one. Goddard faced this problem a good many years ago and refused to adopt an honor system. Harvard College under Dean LeBaron Russell Briggs took a similar position in a more restricted context in earlier years of the century. Such positions imply either that human nature ought not to be asked to control itself in situations of a tempting nature (Harvard) or that whatever the human individual wants to do on a bio-social basis has some value and ought to be subtly encouraged and tolerated (Goddard).

The stance of Johnston College was clear enough; it intended to move toward greater interpersonal understanding and human intercommunication; it intended to sharpen and deepen the intellectualization of human life in all fields; it intended to provide socially constructive settings for the development of values; individual and community involvement were to be considerable; it did not at all intend to encourage the disintegration of individual or group value-systems. It made clear provision for the exclusion of individuals whose styles of life, thought, and commitment were not appropriate to the Johnston experience. If it did not explicitly state what the metaphysical grounds of its institutional position were with respect to the fields of valuation, there need not have been any great mystery about them. The grounds were implicitly present. When an institution talks a good deal about values without being explicit about its metaphysical footings the chances are that it is distilling an accepted cultural and moral position on the basis of an existing and fairly standard philosophical system. If Johnston College was doing this one should observe, lest these remarks be misinterpreted, that this is an eminently respectable position to take and procedure to follow, that it surely lies close to the heart of Western experience in the fields of intellectual and religious history, and that probably enough the great bulk of cultural progress will take shape in channels of endeavor very like these. In considering the educational system of Johnston College in its first period one does not then move very far or very radically apart from the mainstream of Western educational history and thought. It is entirely proper that one should not, and one may assume that the student and faculty experience at Johnston developed in a highly exciting and attractive way, especially in those early and fresh years of its being, with notable promise for intellectual and philosophical progression. One further range of comment remains to be made.

If Johnston College moved in the direction of overcoming interpersonal barriers by establishing forward-looking centers of educational living and learning, it also accepted certain hazards in unmapped regions of social relations. Its honor code was its effort to meet this problem. In another respect also it moved to overcome interpersonal barriers. It encouraged ''laboratories of personal growth;'' it intended to innovate by ''integrating disciplines around dimensions of living and learning which relate directly to problems of human survival and growth;'' it opened its first college years with a 10-day mountain retreat to involve the entire community in evaluating and relating to institutional guidelines and to establish an environment for personal understanding and sense of community; among its several program dimensions were the ranges of personal-interpersonal, cultural-intercultural, and national-international. These are evidently extrapolated and deepened applications of the old problem of the one and the many. Johnston College went further in encouraging ''awareness'' sessions reminiscent of the general semanticists, the devotees of Esalen, and a wide range of mystical cults developing in one form or another in these years. Johnston no doubt conceived of itself then as eminently respectable by virtue of its rather substantial historical, religious, and intellectual context. Experimenting with reference to established landmarks is quite a different matter from experimenting without landmarks. Johnston had landmarks. They were generally traditional landmarks and they might have provided the institution with frames of reference to secure the most positive results from its periodic flights of moral and intellectual imagination.

Old Westbury

By way of an introduction, the State University College at Old Westbury, New York represented the effort of the New York State

143

system to engage in a high level experiment in college and university education. The first head of this institution, Harris Wofford, a lawyer and former associate director of the Peace Corps, was brought up, educationally speaking, with the Great Books and brought his unforgettable experience with the Arts and Letters of the ages to the new institution. His interest in law, actively as well as philosophically, and his experience in the Peace Corps gave him added dimensions of an activist sort. Old Westbury was then to innovate; it was to break tradition as might be necessary; it was to create a new approach to higher education or at least to see if a new approach ought to be created. So read the charge for Old Westbury by the then State University Chancellor Samuel B. Gould, a former head of Antioch. How was this to be done? Mr. Wofford told this story in an amusing address recorded from a Danforth Foundation Conference on Liberal Education at Colorado Springs. To make a long story short, the college came to be built on a principle of organic growth; that is, it would gather interested persons, faculty and students, to work out the first problems and the first approach and thereafter it would grow in accordance with the perceived need of whatever entity emerged from that process. This was what happened, except that it did not happen quite as anticipated. 1968-1969, the year of its first deliberations, was a highly turbulent year on American college and university campuses. Old Westbury felt the waves of unease immediately on its doorstep. Perhaps the attractiveness of an institution in process of being born was more than eager young human nature could be expected to ignore. Students came to deliberate, expecting to decide all the questions and to make Old Westbury their special college. There was a long struggle from which the institution emerged still living and in fair health, and wise for its experiences, but inevitably leaving in its wake the decapitated hopes of some of its student planners. Some of the most colorful language in recent English prose characterized one description or another of that phase of the College at Old Westbury.

For its first year Old Westbury chose to center its activities around the problems of poverty and urban affairs. In time this emphasis became more formally the College of Urban Affairs. Also in time, a College of Disciplines was separated off and established on its own; the intention was that other colleges would separate from time to time and carry on as long as they were useful, focusing around one or another problem area.

It was not to be required that these colleges continue indefinitely; they might decline in interest and be discontinued or replaced by others. Common student and faculty participation in institutional affairs was intended to continue, even though some dissatisfaction was felt by disappointed students in the early months.

Mr. Wofford, well-rooted in the great literatures of the past even while he involved himself forthrightly in contemporary affairs, appeared to have effectively raised the question of the essential nature of a college or university. Against the desire of some of the first student participants to organize the entire college around problems requiring activist intervention as part of the study experience, he seemed to expect serious consideration of the differences between a college or university on one hand and a crusading social institution on the other. A college was, after all, a place for study; life stretched out well beyond graduation, with endless opportunities for whatever the young graduate might wish to pursue in the way of activist endeavors. There would be a special function for the educational institution,—to encourage the life of the mind, to merge in it arts, letters and the achievement of intellectual maturity. Its aim was not necessarily to resolve social problems by direct intervention.

From a valuational standpoint the College at Old Westbury presented a fascinating picture. If the outsider may judge from the various literatures, and without personal involvement, the first student participants in the founding discussions arrived with a heavy valuational commitment in the social realm. That is, their social values were largely established, at least for the moment, and the problem was to create an institution which would permit them continuing expression. The student group was 20% or more black, substantially militant in all its groups, drawn by the possibility of immediate involvement in the creation of an original institutional form, essentially activist and committed to social change. The administrative and faculty pioneers arrived not necessarily on the opposite side of any imaginary fence, but sensitive to the need for creating an institution which could continue to provide the excitement of involvement in intellectual disciplines and histories, and perhaps most of all, aware of the need of constructing an institution which would be responsive to new needs of new times, not only of today but of tomorrow, an institution which would permit and encourage the application of the most effective distillations of the Arts

145

and Letters of the ages to the growing and changing problems of modern man.

The drama of Old Westbury in its first years seemed to be that of the struggle of intellectual endeavor and social activism. It was not that the originators of Old Westbury were opposed to social commitment, for they were not; rather, the first center of institutional commitment was urban problems, and this focus continued as emphasis of the first cluster college. Nor would it be accurate to say that the students were opposed to intellectual endeavor; on the contrary, the students were probably so competent intellectually in the first place that in most instances a heavy social commitment was superimposed on an intellectual history long enough to equal that of any college or university student in the country. There is indeed some risk that students in a mood to give themselves wholly over to social expression, if even only for the moment, may lose their sense of proportion, indeed, may lose touch with a sense of the real so that in the end they are blown about among the winds of good causes resulting in a loss of steerage and a penalty in social accomplishment and valuational expression.

It is probable that the metaphysical issue as contemplated in these observations did not arise at Old Westbury in the form being sought here. It would have been interesting if it had. That it did not is a supposition based not on immediate experience but on fair guesses on the basis of the origins of persons involved. In addition to the Great Books input there would have been a heavy Antioch infusion, both in the original inception and in subsequent contributions from friends and students. Goddard was there; other institutions of a socially sophisticated sort were also there in the persons of participants. Metaphysical questions are not commonly raised in those circles; they are taken for granted. Intellection is extremely sharp. Social commitment is decisive, somewhat acidulous, and wide-ranging. Personal self-awareness and interpersonal communication is on a high level. Social sophistication may be the highest of any American student group. From a philosophic standpoint, what then was going on at Old Westbury?

Heavy social commitment on the part of students and institution encountered equally heavy and determinative institutional commitment to genuine and effective intellectual endeavor, the resultant institution to center itself around major contemporary problems of life in the 20th century. This was really a notable drama; the longer-range view probably won; participants were expected to survive with a fair degree of mutual respect, though Mr. Wofford stated with wry resignation that some students named him the "Green Slime" and considered that he had torpedoed one of the great educational possibilities of modern times. The determination with which Old Westbury moved into its next phase argues to the contrary. It could not in its later commitments avoid being socially relevant; its subsequent history suggested that it would continue to be intellectually and educationally competent. If it needed something, that may have been some overt attention to metaphysical questions. Like so many of these sophisticated and intellectually competent institutional scions of the American mid-twentieth century Old Westbury appears to have taken for granted the grounds on which it was proceeding. Why are these social values so important? Which is to say, what is real? Nevertheless Old Westbury was doing a difficult thing and doing it remarkably well. Observers from the educational scene may well appreciate having all this hard work done so effectively for them.

Prescott College

Prescott grew out of a concern of the town of that name in Arizona where a college may have been desired, to put it bluntly, as a phase of community development. A number of colleges have been founded on just such a practical base. At any rate, substantial support was forthcoming from the community and a Congregational Church survey in 1960 indicated its feasibility. In 1963 a Ford Foundation-Fund for the Advancement of Education Symposium gave rise to the Prescott philosophy of curriculum. The student desire was to create a new institution which would link the great established institutions "with which it shares a common heritage" with the opportunity to relate dynamically to "the emerging 21st century" with all the needs and opportunities to come, the demands that this changing period of history would make on colleges seeking to serve in the training of leaders.

So far, then, Prescott appeared to be not unlike Old Westbury. It respected the great intellectual traditions of the West; it hoped to relate its institutional life to the equally great contemporary problems of the late 20th and 21st centuries. It proposed to do this by establishing a distinguished group of faculty minds and inviting in an equally distinguished group of student minds to gather in four major educational centers, Anthropological Studies, Language, Systems, and Civilization. Each was to define a particular approach to liberal educational goals and all were to be inter-related and staffed on a disciplinary basis. Anthropological Studies included biology, anthropology, sociology, ecology, and geology. The Center for Studies in Language included, rather curiously, not only literature but religion, philosophy, history, the creative arts, theater, dance, writing, painting, sculpture, photography, and choral music. Concentrations offered in the Center for Studies in Language were to be literature, philosophy, and religious studies, with individual programs to be available in other fields. The Center for Systems included economics, mathematics, chemistry, technological systems, and natural philosophy. The Center for Studies in Civilization included social studies and political science. Evidently some highly individualistic philosophy of traditional education had been at work here in which the classical fields of knowledge were reformulated in accordance with a pre-conception of interrelations of the major fields. To the philosopher from outside, the fundamental reflective questions remained notably open and unanswered in the Prescott approach. Another way of saying this may be that answers to the fundamental questions were assumed or taken for granted rather than explicated and that as a consequence educational attention in the Prescott system was devoted simply to working out programmatic details.

Some attention was given to problems of group life, a valuational field. Prescott devised the ''Honor Conscience'' as a way of maintaining social order. House rules were to be self-established. Individual integrity in the conduct of studies and related fields was assumed. The individual was required to take responsibility for his role in the community and to consider the well-being of others in the context of a common purpose of academic study. The central reference point of the Honor Conscience was stated to be ''in the end, basically an academic commitment, a rewarding manifestation of induction into a mature academic community.'' This suggests that if the individual could maintain diffuse or divisive behavior without affecting either his own intellectual achievement or the intellectual achievement of his fellow students in a negative way he would be free to do so. Was the fundament of the Honor Conscience then primarily intellectual or social? It appeared to be intellectual. No metaphysical reference point was provided, nor did the official literature of Prescott suggest a philosophic grounding other than traditional intellectualism. Philosophy was evidently regarded as a language, so that metaphysical reality inhered elsewhere, not specified, but perhaps equally in the Centers of Anthropological Studies (human nature), Language, Systems (science studies), and Civilization (social and political science). What was the valuational system represented by the Prescott educational approach?

A modern intellectual renaissance may have been what Prescott College intended to provide. It was sensitive to valuational problems and it clearly devoted some thought to devising an internal system for meeting the moral problems of the day. It is not clear what the philosophy of human nature was which underlay this system nor what the metaphysical system was, other than involvement in the intellectual tradition of Western thought. This could be exciting enough in its own right. Prescott was established in a dramatic region of the country. The southwestern desert of Arizona and those other parts of the country such as the lower Pacific coast and the mountains and lakes which Prescott involved in its expectations of students are dramatic in their own right. College publications suggested that Prescott represented simply a highly intellectualized, fortunately situated and vigorously established expression of traditional Western thought reformulated for the times around new and perhaps unusual foci which may have been those of a group or individual responsible for the inception of the institution. Johnston College had been interested in an annual opening 10-day mountain retreat; Johnston College had however an additional ballast of Western religious thought in the formulation of its educational philosophy. Prescott and Johnston appear to have been metaphysically similar, with the foregoing difference, except that their foci of organization were different. The same expectation could be had of both: they should have proven to be immensely challenging and should have provided an educational experience of lifelong value as long as the original enthusiasm of the founding group could be maintained so that the later students met the pragmatic or short-range philosophical expression of the institution as freshly as the first students who attended. Institutions of this type serve a notable purpose in the American educational scene. They point out that traditional divisions of knowledge are not the only ones which are effective. A wide variety of educational and intellectual foci are equally effective in providing exciting

149

educational experiences for students as long as faculty and staff enthusiasm remains of the first order.

Friends World College

If the purpose of this sketch is to identify valuational positions in higher education then with Friends World College (New York) some sort of reward is achieved. Conceiving of valuation as the expression of ethical and moral judgments and the taking of positions on questions in these areas, with Friends World College it is less than certain just what else there is in higher education. Here perhaps a college became almost a valuational instrument.

As is the case with most educational institutions the history of Friends World College is of interest. In 1958 a group of Quakers near New York decided to found not only a new liberal arts college but "a world college." Twenty-two students representing as many countries in Africa, Latin America, East and West Europe and North America came together in 1963 to take part in an experimental program. Following this, and guided by "the Quaker preference for direct experience" the founders adopted a plan proposed by Morris Mitchell, head of the Antioch-Putney Graduate School, enabling students to travel around the world, living and studying for half-year terms in each of several major regions—Latin America, Africa, Asia, Western Europe, the Soviet Union and Eastern Europe, and North America. It was intended that Friends World College Centers would eventually be established in all of these regions. Each would be an educational institute or college under the laws of that region, responsible to a regional board of trustees, subject to basic College policies and standards set by a world board of trustees. At various times several regional centers operated. The College was opened in 1965; its North American center was variously in Westbury and Huntington, New York.

What did Friends World College want to do? College publications spoke of a search for new guiding concepts growing out of the program of world studies and problem studies. The centers intended to draw together "persons developing creative ideas for resolving urgent human problems." There was heavy emphasis on studying social problems— poverty, conservation, armed conflicts—which could "lead to concepts of world education and world government." The College plan provided for a world campus consisting of six-month stops for students at each of the several regional centers with thousands of miles of ''studytravel'' in each region. This was to be the first of three ''revolutionary'' concepts. The second concept provided that the program of study break with traditional subdivisions of curriculum into subject areas so that the student could

''seek the basic unity of all knowledge in common truth, seek knowledge not as an end in itself but as a means to human goals, based on direct and vicarious experience in recognizing, defining, and solving major problems in our crisis culture. The curriculum evolves and grows out of continual reconstruction of experience.''

The heritage from John Dewey is clear enough in these phrases. Indeed, Friends World College and Morris Mitchell, a guiding spirit and its first head, were quite frank about this. The Quaker heritage and the John Dewey heritage may be two principal influences in the emergence of this new concept in higher education.

The third ''revolutionary'' concept was that teaching should

''yield its honored role to the humble one of seeking; the Quaker subordination of the creature to the inner authority of conscience in each worshipper's quest for truth correspondingly makes the faculty and students a fraternity of junior and senior scholars; the object of the quest is those universally applicable concepts which are emerging today as the counterpart of the destructive forces which threaten human survival.''

Friends World College was then a Quaker-based, socially oriented, individually constructed experience in higher education far-flung into the great cultural centers of the earth. Colleges and universities in America invariably intend to bring together on their central campuses a wide cultural and inter-cultural representation from the centers and the byways of American society and, if they are lucky, from remoter countries overseas. Their laudable objective is to provide cross-cultural experience for the student who may meet and live with students from diverse backgrounds and varied experience. Friends World College did this in a new and dramatic way. It sent the students to the cultures, for a year or two or three at a time, with a great deal of travel, a great deal of exposure to social problems of different kinds, and presumably a good deal of careful study of peoples and problems as curriculum. It must have been marvelously expensive. As is the case with most new colleges Friends World College in those early years might well have been periodically short of funds and may perhaps have been a more than ordinarily delicate financial operation. Perhaps it would not have been a genuine Friends program if it were not. The student of religion may wonder what the Quakers would do if they should suddenly emerge as an overwhelming majority in American society. Bewilderment might take the place of critical sharpness.

Friends World College was no doubt subject to most of the then social problems of the American campus. What was the communication between the two colleges in the Westbury towns of Long Island? The college at Old Westbury and Friends World College may have appeared to contend somewhat in the same lists. That is, student groups at both institutions may have been convinced at one time or another that the activist life ought to become the new focus of the American educational experience. The Quakers put this differently; the choice, indicated Sidney Harman, a later head of Friends World College, lies between a school and an intentional community. Mr. Harman was quite clear that Friends World College was a school and not an intentional community, respectable though the latter might be and valuable though its experience could become for participants. An intentional community, he noted, has as its central objective the purpose of being something, ''a place in which people come together with the determination and intent to live together,'' but where the emphasis is on being and on interpersonal relationships. A school on the contrary, he continued, is structured with specific responsibilities assigned to administrators, faculty, and students. There is an institutional commitment to common learning; the faculty too will learn; community is all-important; within the learning community functional roles will be accepted and frankly played to enable individuals to develop their own educational experiences around the major institutional concerns.

Friends World College did have some major institutional concerns. Although there would be no limits on the intellectual sources drawn upon by students and faculty, it was unlikely that students would be dependent on the Great Books, on intellectual prima donnas or local prophets. Rather, someone with a strong social imagination had hurled John Dewey at each of the major continents of the earth to mix the social problems of diverse societies so they could be studied at first hand by students who took the trouble to move from place to place and to live closely with diverse cultural dilemmas. Social reality was to emerge from social problems, reconstructed in the experience of individual students in the context of a learning community. Friends World College was a great idea. Other colleges have had great ideas, and some of these did not amount to much or go very far. The originality of Friends World College lay in its application to inter-cultural, international, even intercontinental studies the method of John Dewey which had been so effectively tried out at Antioch, Bennington, and Goddard. The application ought to work; the question about Friends World College may be only the practical one of how it gets paid for. Travel is expensive. It is after all cheaper to do everything on one campus providing it can be done effectively and providing that students can be persuaded that other places do exist in a real sense.

John Dewey talked a good deal about change and notably his disciples did the same. Change, primarily social change, came to be for him of the nature of the real. If social things are changing, hopefully constructively, the philosopher judges that he is wading in metaphysics. To the disciple of Dewey the matter need not be further explicated; there is a convenient avenue by which the pragmatic philosopher may escape the need for constructional thought. He should, after all, devote his energies to the solving of problems which present themselves to his eager hands and eyes, and from this contextual activity there should emerge a new social metaphysics (read society) which in turn becomes the really real. All this is familiar, interesting, socially productive, and a fertile seedbed for new ideas and new schemes of educational thought. One does not know how much time there is in the schema of pragmatism for a person to sit and think; or how much there ought to be. After all, the world is supposedly burning up and it would be the duty of the disciples of Dewey if not to put out the fire then at least to harness the flames to constructive uses.

Inevitably, in such a view a great deal was taken for granted in the theory of human nature: Quaker thought has sometimes become somewhat mystical about the inner light. There is nothing wrong with mysticism; it is just that it is difficult for it to be explicit. John Dewey intended to be quite specific. He really did not intend to be very much of a mystic, although he had his moments. So here again was an amalgam of sorts: there was the John Dewey brand of educational pragmatism applied internationally on at least a broad (if not a grand) scale; and then there was the special Quaker conviction about the reliability of human nature. If the latter went out of focus from time to time in connection with one or another of the social problems of young people of the period Friends World College acknowledged that it was capable of standing forth as an institution and stating what would wash and what would not. Its choices were predictably those of other college campuses. It conceded where it was convenient, and resisted where it could not do otherwise. It too had to survive, and it did not hesitate to say so.

In the end that which was most real for Friends World College was the social arena of the day, scattered abroad in many lands. The educative effort was to permit new and fresh individual syntheses of experience based upon immersion of the student in a variety of cultures, leading always to the creation of new conceptual reaches through the resolution of those societal and cultural problems which went far toward comprising the college curriculum. Valuation was then close to central in this educative-reflective-reconstructional experience. New social concepts were to emerge, valuational in nature. Metaphysical or ground concepts appear to have been largely settled. In the end a prime question may be whether Friends World College or any college so constituted can refrain from being an intentional community even while it insists on continuing to be an educational community very much on the move, socially as well as geographically.

New College, Sarasota

When an energetic community is possessed of a large estate not otherwise readily disposable, and when community leaders are interested in educational and economic development, one thing to do is to start a college. It promises good use of facilities and it adds to community activity and resources. This may be what happened with New College, Sarasota.

The world is full of New Colleges. Hofstra University on Long Island has had one; there was now to be another, founded in Florida in 1960. New College, Oxford has been a useful institution for nearly 600 years, and it is still called New College. Perhaps the name "New College" is most often chosen not so much because the institution is new as because it is the hope of the leadership that it may always remain new. That was said to be the commitment of New College, Sarasota. The moral may be that an institution should aspire never to grow old, even after six centuries.

New College, Sarasota, could readily be described in the period of the 1960's. It consisted of the Ringling Estate, some new I. M. Pei residential complexes, a frankly selective admissions policy calculated to produce an intellectually capable student group, a curriculum divided into the natural sciences, the social sciences, and the humanities; and a dual-choice pattern for students, contractual or noncontractual, the first closely supervised and the second with relative degrees of freedom in study choice. Grades were not given, but examinations were; several independent study components were built into each program type. There was the usual institutional interest in diversity of students, high level of intellectual preparation, moral and ethical maturity; campus regulations were very carefully spelled out in publications but New College did not feel that there were very many of these.

New College had in its first decade two general objectives, the achievement of wisdom and general knowledge, and preparation of the student to master a particular field.

There must have been some inspiration in New College. Some uplift would surely have been felt from the intellectual austerity of the I. M. Pei dormitories; it can be assumed that faculty members were very sharp, interested in what they were doing and doubtless good at it. The impact upon students would have been strong.

Valuational involvement at New College appeared to have been limited in any obvious way to the observation in the publications that students who entered the College in those days were for the most part known to be relatively set in their characteristic style and standards of life. Therefore New College had little hesitation in granting considerable ranges of freedom to students even while it reserved the right to intervene in behavioral situations or in the handling or non-handling of them by the student courts. If there are other comments on valuation to be made in connection with New College, from the publications at least it is difficult to know what they might be. In practical terms there probably was a substantial degree of student freedom and a genuine reliance of the institution upon the student as self-mover and selector of his educational future. Certainly there would be ample room to move in a curriculum constructed with as much provision for independent study as New College. As with several other institutions in the present group, it is reasonable also to suppose that a very large part of the effectiveness of New College derived from the enthusiasm of its faculty. Perhaps a clearer image of New College can come through after a period of time. At least Sarasota and Bradenton wanted a college, and they got one. That much is good to know, and no doubt these communities are the better for it. It seems not practical at this point to refer to other clearcut philosophical accomplishments at New College. But never mind; if England's New College has had 600 years to develop a philosophy surely Florida's may take its time.

Goddard College

It is difficult to account for novelty and change. Henry Cadbury used to amuse himself at Harvard Divinity School by pointing out that if the New Testament were examined closely enough it was almost impossible to discover anything in it which had not also been in the Old Testament. And yet of course the New Testament was new. Similar comments can be made about many periods and cultural expressions. It is as if the Hegelian notion of the synthesis as something peculiarly new were borne out in the ways in which change occurs. When studied carefully the compositional elements of a "new" phenomenon are likely to appear almost without exception to be those of previous expressions within the same order. And yet, amusement aside, the new phenomenon probably really is new, or at least appears reasonably to be new in some partial or holistic sense.

To review the philosophical natures of a number of higher educational institutions with a particular view to discovering their valuational import and the metaphysical stance from which each import derives is again to be impressed with the peculiar perceptual elision of historical institutions and periods.

A generation ago there were a scant half dozen colleges which were making something of a profession out of doing things differently,—Antioch, Reed, Bennington, Bard, and then, in 1938 in Plainfield, Vermont,—Goddard. To live in the midst of any of these might have been to decide that no particular element in their makeup was radically new; and yet in those days in the Green Mountains something was new. Vermont thought so, and was not entirely pleased about it. Vermont has never been entirely pleased with Goddard, and yet it is a genuinely tolerant state, far less stiff and chilly than the traditional stories would suggest. John Dewey was born in Burlington; University of Vermont philosophers in recent years have even discovered what books he read as an undergraduate based on records of his withdrawals from the college library, so they must have some small interest in him.

Dewey has two living memorials in Vermont,—Bennington and Goddard. If the latter is chosen for discussion it is not at all that Bennington is less significant in educational history; for many years Goddard borrowed ideas and practices from Bennington, until sometimes it seemed that nothing was worth doing unless Bennington had done it first. Bennington, in short, was educationally respectable and if it did something it must be all right. There were even those who thought that Goddard had borrowed things from Harvard and any number of other institutions. On the whole Goddard preferred to borrow from Bennington rather than from Harvard. In later years the staff learned to smile at the name of Harvard and it should be noted that this was progress.

For all that and all that Goddard was indeed something new. It thought so; the community around it thought so; Vermont thought so; the New England Association of Colleges and Secondary Schools thought so; Ralph Flanders thought so, soon after he had helped to found it; in fact, nearly everybody thought so, and almost nobody liked it very much. Goddard enjoyed not being liked. It was young, brimming over with itself, full of energy, politically leftist, socially leftist, educationally leftist, religiously leftist, structurally leftist; and it liked itself if nobody else did. Historically and culturally perhaps none of the compositional elements in Goddard were new and yet Goddard was new for all that. What did Goddard do: What position did it take? What did it believe?

Some earlier history may be in place. The original Goddard Seminary, founded in 1863 as the Green Mountain Central Institute, continued for several decades as one of the old New England academies on the secondary school level, in the years before high schools became common in most communities. It had been developed with informal Universalist Church connections and this later made a difference. It was located in a region not economically burgeoning, and the time came following establishment of a high school in the city of Barre, Vermont, when the private academy struggled, relinquished the secondary area, became a junior college for girls, and then decided to embark on a new application of progressive education theory and practice to the fields of higher education. The Universalists, now joined with their sister

157

denomination, the Unitarians, were always the less pretentious and less fashionable of those two small, impactious churches. Their ranges of belief were similar, but they took their departures from different points. If both viewpoints accorded central place to human nature and human life, Unitarians were inclined to be intellectualistic while Universalists were inclined to partake of sentiment. Church influences on colleges are subtle but pervasive when their fundamental philosophies are probed into the open. Goddard was certainly affected in deep ways by its Universalist heritage, renewed and reapplied in special ways by its longtime president, Royce S. Pitkin, who was born in nearby Marshfield into a family which took pride in being Democratic as well as Universalist. Adequate studies on this institutional and personal amalgam greatly need to be made, and they have not been made. For present purposes it is sufficient to note that President Pitkin was emotionally and temperamentally a Universalist and not a Unitarian; in common with almost everybody else, the Unitarians did not really like Goddard particularly; they did not know what to make of it, and besides, it was not in Boston. Goddard was ornery; it enjoyed not being in Boston; it enjoyed tweaking Unitarian tails; and when the Unitarians replied by ignoring the little Universalist college in the north Goddard continued in its turn imperturbably on its way. Boston may not have known that it was being snubbed; Goddard was not interested enough to make the point.

It follows that Goddard, deriving from a liberal Universalist heritage, emerging from an unmistakably Vermont context, and adopting the educational philosophy of John Dewey and William H. Kilpatrick by way of Teachers College, Columbia, had a special view of human nature and the human individual. The individual student in structural terms was established at the center of his own higher education experience. He was given great freedom, so much so that the surrounding community was wont to assume that he was probably politically Communist and morally reprobate. Probably someone ought to study the psychology of personality with a view to discovering why it is that the granting of freedom to young people is so often conceived of as bringing about their political and social ruin. There may have been all manner of political and social configurations among Goddard students and faculty from time to time; no doubt there were. If Communism

158

never succeeded at Harvard because there everybody cared a great deal that it should not, it should be noted in all fairness that Communism never succeeded at Goddard because there nobody cared one way or the other. One viewpoint had as much scope as its opposite; people slugged out their differences in community meetings, and it developed that the way to defeat the Communists was to turn the tables on them by staying in the meetings until the leftists all got tired and went to bed. Royce Pitkin did that, among a good many other things.

So the individual student stood very much at the heart of the Goddard educational experience. There are hazards in this, and from time to time Goddard became sloppy and wallowed in sentimental regard for the frailties of human nature. Be that as it may, the fundamental respect for individual human personality was always central in the Goddard scheme of things. Curricular offerings, never structures, were set up around the interests of students. After some years the College began to think it knew what student interests were and there developed the usual reluctance to change this or that in the pattern which had become established and well-documented. But at least Goddard was always able to change, though it may have creaked in the doing, and that is more than can be said for many of its illustrious institutional counterparts.

The curriculum was defined as that which students wanted to do. Here then was a college which made no bones of saying that education was just this. Unfortunately, some of the things which students wanted to do were hardly describable in drawing rooms and parlors. It may have been irritating to the surrounding community that Goddard did not appear to blink at socially deleterious behavior. In what has been elsewhere termed the bio-social ethic valuation is conceived to be biologically and socially determined. Goddard became a departure from explicitly Universalist religious conviction: in its educational expression of an older religious position Goddard substituted society for divinity, and when it wanted to know what was right it tended to ask what everybody was doing. It was also possible to ask how people were made up in a more biological sense; John Dewey did some of this, and Goddard did it. But the real metaphysical substance of the Goddard educational approach and consequently the ground of its valuational dimension was social.

There was something special about dialogue at Goddard. Perhaps there still is. But in those days there was a special excitement, a reach of reality, even a substantive matrix, about the dialogue—which is to say, in educative practice, the classroom, the small-group discussion and the roundtable format. Here again was that special Hegelian something, a newness emerging out of well-established elements which really ought not to have given rise to anything original but which did in any case. The possibilities of the dialogue for intellectual challenge are unlimited, as the St. John's-Annapolis and Santa Fe educational experience has surely shown. In a curious way St. John's and Goddard, no doubt quite like St. John's and Old Westbury, have had this highly important element very much in common. The metaphysics of the dialogue and the discussion have been conceived of as central to learning; the effects of this approach have in both cases been superbly successful. If on many American college campuses today the great period of discussional learning has given way to the new Icarian grasping of the solitary in-dividual for the blinding sunlight of the upper sky there is surely no denying that the age of the great discussion, discussion as art, as challenge, as medium, as learning, has become a landmark in the history of American higher education. Goddard and St. John's have been among the leading instances of it. Different though they have been in some respects, and tartly though they may once have spoken of each other, metaphysically and valuationally their divergences may not have been significant.

While the students at Goddard were standing so much at the center of things, and while the educational thought of the institution was being established around the individual learner, defined in terms of his in-terests, constructed out of his actual experiences, what was the faculty doing? Well, the faculty was doing the same things. There ought not to be any mystery about that. In any genuine sense, everybody is always doing about the same thing at about the same time. The alleged gap between the generations is not a real thing. There is some change in the forms in which ideas and forces or vectors come to be expressed, but there are great commonalities which pervade groups, institutions, and societies, so that if a particular idea or form of behavior has appeared in a group it is very unlikely to be an isolated case. One has but to look around and find its sources, counterparts, implicative origins, and actual histories.

A faculty leads because it is on the ground to start with, it is more permanent, and its influences are therefore more pervasive than those of students. But in any institution worth its salt leadership moves around among groups and individuals, so that in a particular class discussion leadership may inhere first in one individual and then in another, and similarly in a college or university, leadership may move from time to time among faculty, staff and students and then return again to faculty.

The faculty at Goddard usually came to Plainfield because they were interested in the opportunities. Faculty members genuinely believed all those things about students; they respected them for the most part, and for the most part the students returned the compliment. If they didn't, the faculty member soon left; his position became rapidly intolerable. There was no hiding anything at Goddard; if someone went off his rocker everybody knew it; half the community would take care of him while the other half called the ambulance. It was a friendly and welcoming society, open to a fault, subject to the exploitations which communities of that sort draw down upon themselves. Faculty members were very much a part of it all. They had all the foibles of students; they sometimes thought and acted like students; and yet withal they were often teachers in the best Socratic sense, conceiving of themselves not so much as specialists insisting upon their uniqueness as various forms of the traditional intellectual midwife reborn in the triumphant era of the small-group discussion. In later years some of this began to unravel, but all movements have their day.

The John Dewey view of human nature, of the ultimacy of society, and of the social metaphysics resulting from dialogue and social communication is then the central philosophic fact of the Goddard experience. Valuation derived from this into a naturalistic, socio-ethical format. In the field of personal relations there was also, coming down from the Marshfield hills, a certain barnyard morality which had the effect of blunting reflective apperception, of turning aside the opportunity to think about valuation in any very fundamental way. A considerable opportunity for moral development was probably lost through this unfortunate configuration.

Institutional as well as individual viewpoints must be understood contextually, that is, with respect to their histories and settings and not just with reference to their main contemporary thrusts. Goddard was part Vermont, part Universalist, part Dewey/Kilpatrick, part progressive, part experimental. It came to feel some kinship with the North European folk high school founded in Denmark a century ago and given great impetus by Bishop Grundtvig. From time to time it extended a year's invitation to a Danish or Swedish folk school teacher, several of whom spent a year at Goddard teaching and counseling. Without exception they were superior persons, highly effective in the Goddard context. Some were magnificent. The folk school has been not so much an historical influence or point of origin for the Goddard idea as a congenial discovery of later times, much as separated cousins of a family line occasionally discover each other with mutual appreciation in their middle years.

Most clearly among all these institutional illustrations, Goddard has had an educational philosophy. Whether it has been right or wrong, it has at least believed something clearly, and if it confused itself and its own community as part of its mode of operation it certainly stood forth in the American educational scene as proponent of a particular reflective position in metaphysics and valuation. It believed in the central reality of social man; it declined for the most part to pose questions concerning the nature of things which went any further than social man. And in all fairness, it has been eminently willing to take the consequences of what it believed. It withstood the onslaughts of the Vermont community, of irate and grievously injured parents, inquiring government officers, educational accrediting associations, and a host of sister institutions most of whom were not quite sure that it was politic to be seen in the company of Goddard.

Goddard has then been a pragmatist institution. If its metaphysics was truncated, as any Jamesian view of the nature of things would have to be, it at least held to it firmly, and it also firmly grasped the valuational nettle. It was therefore consistent in these major philosophic facets of its existence, at least in its major central period.

While the more recent campus scene, with its emphasis on individualism among students and faculty, will need more time for proper assessment it is possible that this so-called ''scene'' arrived at Goddard somewhat earlier than at most American campuses, as social and philosophical movements were accustomed to do. Because everything had to be welcomed providing it came from what was defined as the individual human seedbed of original thought and creativity, the ''scene'' was in turn built into its educational schema. With its arrival the heyday of the Dewey / Kilpatrick discussional system of education may have begun to pass, to be replaced by a new emphasis on mythic intuition, unconventional social idealisms, and extensions of the bio-social matrix—in short, a new romanticism. The Goddard approach had no way of meeting a new input other than that of eventual acceptance, subject to modification by existing campus influences and components. This is inevitable if the metaphysical context and the valuational reference points are entirely contained within a strictly social system. A Goddard-like community tends to construct itself as a small society internally oriented, and to respond only selectively and occasionally to the larger community outside, as for example when under pressure on some embarrassing issue. For the most part there was a good deal of polarization between the campus and the larger community, state or national, and notably so between the student world and the parent world. It must be acknowledged that Goddard, in the persons of many of its staff, gave scope to the conflicts of young people with families or parents. In fairness it often did so on the ground that it was devoting itself to ''saving'' the student; the parents were inevitably seen as the wicked enemy.

There may then be coming over the horizon a curious setting-to-rights of the confused by-products of societally oriented education. It may in time be found that the new break-through of the student, fracturing the systems of law, of social and economical organization, political quietism, and religious calm, the movement somewhat in the direction of violence, of menace, of demands, and of turbulence will prove to be the early stages of the reassertion of individual significance and leadership, not infrequently destructive, negative, frustrating and anti-intellectual, but nevertheless also unmistakably a new determination of the self to understand and to achieve in new ways and new forms. It would be but a small step from this to an on-coming age of powerful individual leadership and intellective outreach with all that that might entail by way of metaphysical recognition and valuational commitment. The chances are that the bio-social philosophic system which went with John Dewey may already have come to an end so that at present the campus confusion, not just at Goddard but also at institutions generally, represents the early years and the confused years of a new philosophical and theological era. John Dewey was personally rooted in the history of philosophy, as shown by the lists of his early

163

readings; thus philosophical and educational experimentation meant one thing for him. The colleges which came after him and emulated him were not rooted in Western history in the same way, and therefore experimentation for them became very much of a different thing. Thus perhaps does every age construct the settings within which it will grow old and decline even while it establishes the conditions under which a new age will emerge. Within its restricted bio-social contexts Goddard believed intensely; beyond that restricted range it believed little. Therefore its values were biological and social, applied at least in an immediate way within the scope of its own community although often not with the consequence of producing a viable on-campus community which many of its members would acknowledge. In the longer view, Goddard was reasonably content residing in the vales and byways of unbelief. Any larger valuational context therefore atrophied or was suffered to endure in the personalities of stubborn community members who held to systems of belief and valuation in the midst of transcendental desolation.

Conclusion: Education as Thought at Work

It should by now be clear that the present position is that, illustrated or not in the foregoing instances, an educational institution, particularly a college or university, is required by its nature to construct and accept a philosophical or metaphysical position, and to derive from it a system of values which will be served by its educative methodology and practice. Some colleges clearly start with valuation or with sets of ethico-moral ideals, perhaps because it is more convenient to do so.

A philosophic stance is indispensable. More than this, it is inescapable. It is entirely possible to take an institution where it is and force it to disclose what its implied metaphysics happens to be. More commonly than not, its reflective system will turn up short. It is not a habit in the late twentieth century for American philosophy to pursue systematic thought with any genuine commitment, or to regard religio-theological involvement as other than an esoteric activity which ought to be confined if possible to tree-shaded institutions. There is also the hazard that if an institution takes an explicit philosophic stance and maintains it, accepting unflinchingly the larger societal criticisms which may devolve upon it as a consequence, it may suffer both internally and externally for its pains and honesty. So may a church. Still and all, it is what the educational institution has to do. Indeed, it cannot do otherwise, for if it attempts to decline its hand will be forced by the nature of things.

Perhaps one reason that many higher education institutions prefer to remain safely within some form or other of Western traditional thought is precisely because these philosophic and social questions can be left unanswered even while they are being studied. Clearly, the great questions of philosophy and theology do have to remain unanswered. It may be a measure of the greatness of an open-ended society that it is able to live comfortably with unanswered questions.

A further range of puzzlement obtains in the unresolved problem of the extent to which valuational commitment is to be implemented on the campus in the face of potential conflict. The American college community has been treated of late years to a rough course of sprouts in the art of listening in time. Those which have not listened have endured confrontations and more likely than not have learned to listen under less than ideal conditions.

The chances are good that violence and confrontation on the campus constitute an evanescent and passing phase on the American educational scene. It may eventually be determined in the longest view that the tide of violence was turned back by the difficult decision made in Cambridge not only on behalf of the university community at Harvard but in some part for all American colleges and universities, —the decision to terminate by force the occupation of University Hall. This is not to say that identical problems elsewhere, or even recurring difficulties at Harvard, necessarily call for an identical response. It is simply to suggest that there was a sense in which Harvard had to speak for the educational community as a whole, and the fact that it did so, with all its attendant difficulties and unpleasant consequences, may have made the difference in the general direction of valuational commitment and implementation on the American campus in years to come. James B. Conant remarked a good many years ago that there were times in the religious and intellectual history of Western man when the judicious use of force made a determinative difference in the future progress of mankind. It may be, in this latest and most difficult decision which Harvard had to make even while other colleges and universities were deciding differently, that that same principle was again observed, that Harvard took the rap for American higher education in a moment of supreme difficulty. From this high point it may yet appear that the tide of disorder turned and thereafter lapped at points farther down the shore. What Harvard said in its moment of decision was that in the end the American college campus cannot be governed by violence, and that if the tide of violence had still to be turned back by force one more time then that would simply have to be done and the consequences borne. As the comments of succeeding years have come to be made there are few American educators who do not subscribe to this, even while they opt for dialogic solutions to campus problems nearer home. It may have been the ultimate decision in Cambridge which provided them with contextual freedom to move in different ways in the midst of their own crises.

While the college-age student has needed to be heard and to be drawn into the active operation of colleges and universities it is probably true that campus turbulence of the late 20th century was in some part a phase of the configuration of Black recognition and of the general adjustment which American society has had to make in the direction of recognizing itself as a younger population than it used to be. This fact alone may require more adequate representation of younger age groups in the governing councils of higher education.

It remains only to observe that while the present general position is that education requires a metaphysical position in order to be valuationally committed, and that if it is valuationally committed it has be implication a readily discoverable metaphysical position, it is also necessary that both types of commitment, metaphysical and valuational, should remain open-ended and that no closed system should ever be regarded as the last which human nature is likely to produce. Even a theological position is tentative in a sense. The position must be taken, the stance adopted, and the implied valuation accepted. And yet in the end the entire system must remain open to modification, superannuation, reconstruction, and reformulation. Perhaps in many kinds of circumstances the nature of human concerns requires that decisions be taken which will maintain and reconstitute the very capacity of the educational community to make such decisions in comparable settings in times to come. Perhaps metaphysical and valuational commitment, for all that they are cast as decisions, require just such a degree of openness. Perhaps the nature of life and thought, of man and of the Ultimate, also require it.

XIII Consortial Thought and Practice I: An Inter-Institutional Admissions Project

The tides of educational fashion are not always clear-cut in their directions or benefits, nor do they invariably show their reasons for existence. Consortial development in higher education, by which is meant the voluntary associating of colleges and universities in presumably helpful educational enterprises, was such a fashion. It was involved in a tidal wash-back in the early 1970's due to the rising costs of education and lack of clarity as to sound bases for continuing or terminating programs which often tended to produce results deferred rather than immediate, and benefits which were educational rather than financial.

A common pattern in the evolution of educational fashion had been for a few institutions to spin off a program type which might be copied by a few other colleges or universities. The Federal government, usually through an office in the Department of Health, Education and Welfare, might then take it up, turn it around, fund it at a few institutions defined as key centers for that purpose, and put it out as a federal program to create models for other educational institutions to follow. Finally, something of a national mood or movement might or might not develop, perhaps in association with supporting federal grants. Educational innovation developed widely, if thinly, in the 1960's as one result of a pattern of private and public support of this type. In the 1970's, a spreading interest in cooperative education appeared to be following a similar path.

Consortia in higher education may have begun to be noticed in the late 1960's as a gathering form of institutional cooperation, the momentum of which was on the make. For a brief period there was a flurry of federal interest in consortia, but it was just prior to one of the government program reductions and not much came of it from that quarter. The preponderance of consortial effort among colleges and universities remained private.

Actually the history of consortia goes back to a number of institutional arrangements of individual kinds in earlier years which may not have been recognized as harbingers of any sort of movement at their inception. The Claremont Colleges in California and similar instances of coordinate institutions, special cases such as that between Teachers College, Columbia and St. Stephens / Bard, not to mention the development of certain state higher education arrangements, may be cases in point. In later instances, however, there was more of a tendency for colleges and universities to associate themselves in partial ways for mutual programmatic or financial benefit. It is the assessment of this latter type of consortial thought and practice which is the present concern.

The Own Turf Problem

Although in the later 1960's and to a degree in the 1970's, there appeared to be a hesitant movement of sorts toward the establishment and encouragement of consortia, significant factors also militated against it.

The so-called "own turf" problem, to borrow a phrase from Antioch sources, refers to the reluctance of faculty and students to leave their own campuses to take part in educational efforts at other institutions. This is evidently a real condition of campus life, at least for some. Tradition may play a part in it; the "old campus" may have strong pulls. Size of group, geographic orientation and individual taste in these categories may be important. Some students and faculty alike feel strongly that their college is right for them, so that anything new should be added to it in its original location. There is often little or no objection to students or visitors who come on campus to attend programs and activities there; but for home-campus residents to go elsewhere for programs and activities may be a horse from another garage.

Development of experimental, off-campus foci of learning activities such as the numerous academic centers operated by Antioch College or other centers of the University Without Walls suggests that there may also be groups or types of students and faculty who reverse the older, "own-turf" preference and actually like to work in new or different settings. Nevertheless, there are strong residual own-turf preferences which can be observed to act as brakes on consortial participation. Over a period of time, with a succession of carefully developed annual programs among participating institutions, student and faculty interest in inter-institutional programs could perhaps be encouraged. There was some evidence in 1971-72 that a five-institution course in radical social change consistently appealed to students from Wilmington, Wilberforce, Antioch, the University of Dayton and Wittenberg in Southwest Ohio, each institution participating by virtue of its membership in the Consortium on Higher Education Religion Studies (CHERS-/CONRAD, Inc.), a live-wire group of colleges, universities and theological schools based near United Theological Seminary. The rotating study course took considerable planning through the summer to enable a successful operation the following winter. Fifty students were involved, varying from 6 to 12 from each institution. Five Saturday programs were held. Meeting places rotated, so that each group served as host once and travelled several times. Each institution selected its own emphasis around the common theme and presented its own program in its own way. Credit was given by each institution to its own students, usually along with a closely related on-campus course with which the consortial program was articulated. There was no requirement of a religious emphasis; one of the church-related institutions constructed its contribution entirely in political science aspects of social change.

The CHERS instance may not give fair weight to the range of difficulty associated with consortial program development. The CHERS/CONRAD organization comprised an extraordinarily high level and quality of imagination and energy, and would have been considered unusually effective among consortia generally. It was able to command heavy investments of time and commitment from participating institutions and its return to them in terms of program originality and conceptual outreach was incalculable. An extensive study should be made of this remarkable consortium.

Nevertheless, even if the consortial ground was far more fertile and more productive in the CHERS/CONRAD case than in most consortial instances, it may be useful to know that inter-institutional studies involving this degree of commitment and reward are possible where conditions are right. Nor should it be concluded that inter-institutional study courses are even close to central in the range of consortial possibility. Rather, this format was among the simpler and more obvious programmatic recourses. The really interesting and rewarding possibilities in consortial operation lie in other and newer regions of common effort.

The own-turf problem remains a serious obstacle to consortial development. Students and teachers in substantial numbers do prefer to pursue studies on their own campuses, ivy-covered or not, and resist going elsewhere for educational programs. This common mood may change, but it has been a real factor in resistance to consortia.

Later developments of non-campus higher educational programs, whether University-Without-Walls, external degree, or similar kinds of decentralized programs such as the Antioch-sponsored Union Graduate School and the Empire State College program of the State University of New York, the latter beginning on the undergraduate level, may modify the own-turf concept. Yet this concept is a complex phenomenon probably involving the psychology of the one and the many, human investments in society and solitude, philosophies of education, commitments to geographies and to traditions, and the self-imagery of generations of people who liked being from such and such a college or university.

Consortial Costs

At first blush, descriptions of consortial efforts pointed toward probable savings in personnel and in operating costs which might result from combining smaller academic units or activities at nearby institutions. In some instances there may have been savings in cost from consortial relations, but on the whole this factor was not large. For one thing, few institutions sought genuine organic cooperation on functional levels which would have permitted cost reductions. Many preferred to struggle along with all their departments and specialties in the face of severely mounting budgetary demands. Some sought limited cooperation in special interest areas, which often meant simply inviting other institutions to send students to established but sparsely populated programs which they wished to maintain. For institutions seeking prestige and standing there were heavy pressures to retain and strengthen rather than to combine, or exchange, or eliminate.

Libraries have seemed decades ahead of other institutional units in arranging organic cooperation. Thus one university library might specialize in European languages or cultures and avoid Latin American acquisitions, while a nearby library by mutual agreement would not purchase in European areas but would spend its funds on Latin American languages or cultures. Each of the two libraries would then supply reader demands of both libraries in its special fields, and would in turn be supplied by the other in the other's special fields. This kind of arrangement is well established now and long antedated the consortial movement of the 1960's. It was by no means remarkable that the formal founding of the noted Dayton-Miami Valley Consortium of a dozen colleges and universities in Southwest Ohio was preceded by well-accepted cooperation among several institutional libraries. Librarians always cooperate with each other and with the clienteles of other libraries; an axiomatic camaraderie appears to exist among librarians which is almost unexceptionally reliable. Quite possibly library cooperation has been the forerunner of numerous consortial arrangements, albeit unrecognized.

Costs involve deceptive questions. The central issue may be and often is: what kind of educational program should be presented? . . . as distinct from the precise question of financial expenditure. The question of cost, . . . what can we afford? . . . is oftener the question which gets asked. Decisions are made on just that basis. But decisions made on that basis are superficial decisions. Rarely is the real question asked as to whether existing programs already being paid for and figured into the budget are worth maintaining, or are better than or less good than another or proposed program. There are sometimes fair reasons why this is so. Underlying every financial question in college or university operation is the educational or program question which is after all the fundamental dimension. Program means simply people doing things. Colleges and universities, like other contracting agencies, become committed to staff and students with respect to programs; it is often not easy or simple to dismantle a program or change it. Indeed the simplest way to run an institution is to leave it the way it is. Sometimes institutions are left the way they are until they die, because their worlds change around them and if they do not also change, their days become numbered.

For the present, it should be assumed that consortia do not save much money, because the types of consortia being established are not the functionally organic kind which would be able to conserve funds by enabling shared services. Consortia in the mid-1960-70 period tended to be founded as inter-institutional additives, external field offices drawing on annual membership funds, as for example $1,000 to $4,000 per institutional member per year, and on the detritus of occasional federal or private grants the administrative and / or indirect costs of which could sometimes be skillfully applied to near-operational needs.

Consortia could be developed in modes which could save expense, but for these to be financially effective it would be necessary for substantially larger administrative roles to be built into them. Thus a consortium might gradually subsume certain hitherto independent functions of several associated colleges, as for example the programming of some learning areas, the screening of prospective faculty, and the central handling of student personnel operations such as admissions, records and financial aids. One such instance of inter-institutional cooperation in admissions will be described hereafter.

The Educational Value of Additive (Non-Organic) Consortia

Critical educators looking desperately for help in funding or administering their piles of creaking machinery are wont to ask: "What does this consortium do for us to be worth the money it costs?" This is, of course, the wrong question to ask.

Consortia are of value to institutional members to the extent that members choose to invest effort and support in them. Program and personnel investment are forms of institutional activity. Consortia are of the nature of activity. Then the match is that of activity to activity, and the forms and modes are those of ideas, emotional drives, professional interests in various regions, and the greater or lesser enrichments and originalities which emerge from the complex. The proper question to ask is not one about the cost, but one having to do with program value for students and faculty. Bear in mind that money is not the coin of this realm, but rather the investment of persons, activities, and times in the consortial range of applicability. The consortial range of effort necessarily has greater freedom of movement and more originality than most institutional efforts do, as it has fewer encrustations to trammel up

172

its consequence. What a consortium really does for its members, if it is a useful consortium, is to alter the context in which educators do their work. Bone simply, the educator performs his task better if he knows how other educators up and down the line are performing theirs. If he joins with others in combining certain functions which can actually be done more effectively in concert than individually, then the effective range of the consortium may be substantially enlarged. The latter, however, is all too often futuristic. For present purposes the point to note is the fundamental conceptual value in consortia in terms of which the nature of the educational task can be constructively transformed up to the limits which institutional members impose as the price of their participation.

The problem which separate institutions have with respect to consortia is not very different from that of nations, churches, or other human movements of comparable function and scale. They all want to live. Colleges and universities do indeed feel the need to survive, the more so as costs rise and survival becomes uncertain. It is easier to proceed cautiously in financial terms than to adapt, adopt or innovate educationally, with all the pulling and hauling within a faculty which that entails, in answer to newly developing educational needs in the wider community to which the institution ideally is responding. There is the tension with the ideal, the tension of the existing institution with the ideal institution, the college or university of today with that of tomorrow. The one must move toward the other. How rapidly? With what parts of its available resources? At what risks to its assurance of continuing existence and safety? It is all too clear that anxious colleges and universities, particularly the financially beset private institutions, will consider this category of question with close attention to practical survival, even at the cost of being unable to respond to new public needs with new educational programs. It also means that colleges and universities will settle for limited and ineffective solutions to educational and operational problems in preference to facing the need for significant change. A case in point, having principally operational and financial implications, is that of an inter-institutional admissions project of several institutions in Ohio and other central states around the Great Lakes.

An Inter-Institutional Admissions Project

A number of years ago it was suggested by Royce S. Pitkin of Goddard College that institutions ought to be able to save operational overhead by combining certain of their administrative functions, notably admissions. This is among the costliest of operational activities for separate colleges since it involves salary for one or more staffers, travel expense for the visiting schools, and substantial related costs. Estimates of cost per admitted student for admissions purposes when when conservatively figured have frequently proved disturbing to college managers who were conscientious about investment and production. To admit (say) 100 students into a small college, against admissions costs of perhaps two professionals and two secretaries, or a salary item of around $35,000 a year, plus travel of $3,000 per professional, less admissions fees of $20.00 per applicant (200 applicants, assuming 50% conversion, which is a very high percentage), could cost about $37,000, not distributing of catalogues and brochures. The last item alone could run from $12,000 up, depending on what was printed and how it was distributed. The total cost might then run, for a small college, around $55,000 to $60,000 a year, or per admitted student cost of over $500, give or take a bit depending on various factors. For a university of larger size, the total cost could be higher; the cost per admitted student might be lower and would be figured according to the factors. Each institution would need to account for its own situation. Notice, too, that there is a difference between cost per admitted student and cost per enrolled student. A college may admit 100 students to enroll 75. The other twenty-five would turn the college down and go somewhere else, or not go to college at all. Costs would vary accordingly. Numerous other cost elements in a complete admissions process, such as student interviewing, school guidance visiting on campus, longer range school relations activities, and on-campus overhead are omitted in this sketch but clearly are real costs.

Thus it is clear enough that Admissions represents a heavy expense certainly for the independent college and probably for most public institutions. Dr. Pitkin was only talking sense when he suggested that a multi-institutional approach to admissions might be helpful. If one admissions person or one team of persons could represent successfully more than one institution, the costs to each institution might be reduced by a third, or by half, or two thirds, or at least by some significant factor. The question was—could such a plan be made to work? Dr. Pitkin thought it could, but the truth was that Goddard was not greatly honored in its own country in those days and other institutions were hesitant about joining it to test the hypothesis. Nearby Vermont colleges were concerned to remain respectable and not to jeopardize their social standing by doing much of anything with the maverick institution in Plainfield, much less let it be known that they dared be associated with it in the supersensitive admissions field. Nothing ever came of the idea in Vermont.

In subsequent years, a new category of admissions professionals developed on the populous Eastern seaboard. Just as multi-institutional representatives appeared in the federal programs area, piloting proposals for funded programs through the labyrinth of federal agencies in search of supporting grants, so there arose at least a small number of professional admissions representatives each of whom undertook to represent several colleges or universities. Their responsibilities were to reach secondary schools, interviewing prospective students and carrying out the numerous public relations operations required to establish relations between potential students and the sponsoring colleges. Not much was said about this development in the professional publications, but the experience gathered by participating representatives was considerable and varied. This range of effort began about 1967. For the moment a note on approximate comparative cost factors may be useful.

In some instances of this type of contractual relation a single year cost to the institutions of from $7,000 to $8,000 a year each, with professional time and all travel costs for that project being included, proved a practical prospect for both institution and representative. With a two-year contract some saving could be effected, costs to each institution then being of the order of $13,000 to $15,000 for the two year period, time and project travel being again included. On the older, single institution pattern, a full-time admissions representative can easily spend $3,000 to $5,000 a year on travel alone depending on amounts of travel undertaken and on the requirements of office duties on the home campus. With full-time salary of say $14,000 to $18,000 a year the multi-institutional cost per institution of about $7,500 per year must be balanced against a single institutional cost per year of from $17,00 to $23,000 per year. The professional time-cost of multi-institutional representation, assuming approximately equal travel, would run about 30% of full-time single institutional representation. These figures may be generally conservative. It will be clear, therefore, that the advantages to institutions participating in multi-representational programs could be substantial, assuming the representation worked well and actually produced students who persevered through the stages of the admissions process from initial exposure to actual enrollment on campus. To figure it a different way, for a small college which might not maintain a full-time representative on the road in addition to a full-time director of admissions who might travel only 30% of his time costs for travel and salary in a multiple arrangement might be comparable to previous expenditures; the institution's gain would then be the 30% of (higher) salary represented in the field coverage from which the admissions director was freed and in the effects of immediate representation in the secondary school field areas and the possibly wider representation, again assuming the latter was effective in producing actual on-campus enrollment.

To turn now to the particular admissions program of multi-institutional representation which is a focus of this sketch, an initial distinction should be made. In representation of several institutions by a single professional who might reside, for example, near New York and might represent colleges located in a number of southern, mid-western and northern states there would probably be no functional association at all apart from the admissions arrangement among the institutions being represented. They would not be a consortium; they would not do things together. They might be, and usually were for sound operational reasons, quite different types of institutions, to reduce or eliminate risks of possible conflicts of interest. If they talked among themselves they would do so merely to establish and monitor the admissions arrangement in which they shared the time of a professional representative.

The arrangement being described otherwise in these pages, among Wilberforce University, Antioch College, and the other members of the Great Lakes Colleges Association, was strictly speaking not a consortial arrangement either. Wilberforce was not a member of GLCA; its association with GLCA members was tenuous and strictly ad hoc, and came about somewhat by accident. The so-called inter-institutional admissions program was a Title III-Developing Colleges project funded as part of annual grants to Wilberforce by the U.S. Office of Education,

Division of College Support. The Office of Education bore no responsibility for the idea or its implementation other than to define it as properly within the range of Title III programs since it was innovative for higher educational administration and presumably worth an extended test to determine its usefulness for higher education in general. Under Title III arrangements each "developing" institution was linked with an "assisting" institution; Antioch College served in this capacity for Wilberforce University from the beginning of the latter's Title III participation about 1966. Therefore it was natural to inquire of Antioch whether it would be interested in taking part with Wilberforce in such an admissions experiment. Invariably game, Antioch was indeed willing; it also drew in the other members of GLCA in which it was an active member.

Wilberforce was of course the well known predominantly Black institution in the Ohio village of that name in Greene County near both Xenia and Yellow Springs. Antioch, seven miles from Wilberforce as the crow flies—if he turns a few corners as most roads do out there—was predominantly White but even then was initiating strong minority programs including admissions. The proposition served both colleges, perhaps for different reasons. GLCA institutions other than Antioch were also predominantly White. Of their number Earlham, the Quaker institution in Richmond, Indiana, took the most interest after Antioch and was the most involved of the remaining group. During one staff leave at Antioch the program was monitored by Earlham on behalf of GLCA participating institutions. General responsibility for the entire program derived from Wilberforce where the program director was Robert A. Thomas, Wilberforce University Director of Admissions and Financial Aids. An assistant director of admissions was appointed to the Wilberforce Admissions staff by President Rembert Stokes under provisions of the Title III grant, so that the multi-institutional representative was always a member of the Wilberforce staff whose time was shared by interested GLCA colleges without added cost other than internal administrative requirements.

The first project appointment was in 1969. Due to a late resignation the following summer the position was vacant for six crucial months in the fall and winter of 1969-70. A strong appointment was made in the late winter of 1970 and lasted for the sixteen months remaining in the program. Its conclusion had to do with changes in

177

personal plans of the staff; it was also felt that what could be learned from the experience by that time had been learned and that some time needed to go by for its implications to be absorbed. The staff incumbents, it should be noted, were Black, as were other members of the Wilberforce Admissions staff. GLCA Admissions staffs were in general White. Later in the program some GLCA colleges appointed full-time Black admissions representatives on their own staffs, and presumably reduced or dropped participation in the common program. Antioch had regularly made minority group appointments to its various faculty and staff echelons and was well in advance of other institutions in this respect.

The Wilberforce-Antioch-GLCA inter-institutional admissions project was therefore a predominately Black effort and was used as such by all participants. For Wilberforce this meant simply a part time addition to its normal admissions program; since White or other minority students were not applying there in any numbers anyway in those years the Title III program served to augment regular approaches in the securing of Black admissions applicants. For GLCA colleges it was quite a different story, although the substance of the program was precisely the same: it served to augment the efforts of predominantly White colleges to secure Black applicants. The effectiveness of the program was probably similarly conditioned. It would have secured additional Black applicants for Wilberforce, as Black young people expected to go to predominantly Black colleges and would have been relatively ready to do so. For predominantly White colleges it would have involved, particularly in those years, an uphill struggle to interest Black young people in attending traditionally White colleges in which they would have continued to be a minority population. Social factors in the project were therefore extremely complex.

Not all GLCA institutions were equally interested in the project or took equal part. Some appeared not to understand it very well; a number made very little use of it. Others put it to varied uses. One or two were positively uninterested.

The years of the program were years of restlessness on campuses generally. Inevitably, a prime aspect of the project was that it involved "the Black-White thing," at least to some degree. No point was ever made of confrontation; no instance of it ever occurred. The purpose was, after all, to develop admissions results among Black high school graduates for a variety of waiting colleges. In general everyone tended to that business. Yet the issue was by implication real, and it remained real in operational contexts.

The total number of colleges involved numbered thirteen, or more accurately, seven or eight when inactive participants were discounted. Either number was far too large for effective representation. Quite possibly the effective number of participants may have been smaller even than seven or eight. Robert W. Jones of Marlton, New Jersey, one of the early professional representatives, without any connection with the present project, remarked that in his opinion four or five institutions constituted a full load for a multi-institution admissions representative. The Wilberforce-Antioch-GLCA experience in this respect bore out his judgment.

Under contemporary conditions of college administration, increasingly so as educators constantly add to their awareness of possibilities and therefore to the range of things that seem to be worth doing or necessary to do, there is rarely time to prepare adequately to do anything. Even the older, conventional things which colleges have always done become more difficult to bring about, let alone the preparation for new programs which may never have been done before under precisely those conditions. In the present instance it was the consistent feeling of some who monitored the program from various vantage points that participating institutions seldom or never had the time to shake out the issues or to study carefully procedures necessary to a multi-institutional admissions effort. It was not anyone's fault; the remarkable thing was that the program went as moderately well as it did and that it produced what moderate results it did. Realistically, it was indeed one more thing for everyone to see to, in addition to all else they had to see to. Innovative programs not infrequently fall into that sort of category.

Nevertheless there were troublesome problems, and these problems appeared to persist. For one thing, admissions practices varied among participating institutions. The representative was expected to work simultaneously in and with variant admissions procedures, perhaps to fulfill differing functions at the same time with respect to different institutions. Wilberforce customarily delegated substantial authority to all of its Admissions representatives in the field. Each was thoroughly grounded in the Wilberforce admissions process and was

179

expected to speak for the institution in admissions matters when it was crucial to do so. An Admissions staffer in the field could guarantee admission to a prospective candidate if advisable in the press of field contacts, and not infrequently did so; it was understood that the home staff would support the judgment made in such cases. The project representative was trained the same way for Wilberforce purposes and was expected to speak for the University and to exercise the same level of responsibility as the full-time Wilberforce representatives did. Other colleges in the project did not expect the representative to operate from any such base of authority. Actual admission of students was by and large reserved to in-house procedures and personnel. The impression received by the representative was of a very limited role without much responsibility or trust. The representative sometimes felt like a distributor of leaflets and little more.

The added complexity of the Black-White thing could not have helped, although the problem was seldom if ever referred to in those terms. For purposes of consortial study the point to note is that these problems of differing modes of institutional operation and different cultural attitudes tended not to be shaken out among the participating staffs. There seemed not to be time or opportunity to prepare ahead of time, and there was no machinery to handle problems which arose in mid-program. Everyone simply had to toggle through as well as possible, doing the work without facing the real issues. Program effectiveness must have been restricted accordingly.

Along with retention of the decision-making process within the home staffs there appeared to be little or no feedback to the project representative on what was happening to the contacts made for various institutions. Participatory understanding and reinforcement were deemphasized. Again the effect must have been to impair the usefulness of the representative. One or two of the GLCA monitors became aware of this and made efforts to deal with it. But the program concluded before results materialized. To handle such a problem would have required careful development of human relations among particular staff members and of procedural machinery among their institutions, and of course this did not occur.

Since this was not a consortium no member staffs were required to talk substantively with other member staffs, though some may have done so from time to time. Certainly the level of understanding which would have been required to resolve the problems was never achieved. Consortial understanding and trust are highly delicate affairs, achieved among institutions only at the cost of much time and trouble, endless dialogue, and long histories of demonstrated reliability. Alone among consortia operating in the Ohio region, the CHERS / CONRAD group in Dayton and southwest Ohio achieved it; some return to this remarkable consortium will be made in a following sketch of consortial thought and practice. It is not remarkable that the multi-institutional admissions project did not approach it. Genuine consortial relations require what could be called a kind of grace in order to be successful. That is, the free gift of concern, dedicated commitment to the consortial idea, and the willing investment of time and dialogue among institutions are necessary prerequisites to effectiveness of consortial effort. And after all that, comparable investments by participating institutions in active programs must be made if real achievement is to be possible.

The program was then a complicated proposition with factors operating in it which might not obtain in other inter-institutional arrangements, consortial or simply mechanical. All such arrangements are complex in differing ways, and probably each one has its own special problems.

Implications for Consortial Thought and Practice

It seems worth remarking that the multi-institutional admissions program might have gone far better than it did if certain depths of association and negotiation had been pursued, as distinct from the more common kinds of casual institutional association which amount to various forms and degrees of exclusiveness. This is to say, if it is worth while to operate a multi- or inter-institutional program at all, to ensure its success it is probably necessary to develop the depth and breadth of a genuine consortial relation. Short of this, not much of any effectiveness can be predicated. There may be some effectiveness, accidentally or through the operation of particular factors, but that is all that can be expected.

Among implications for consortial thought and practice, first, perhaps is the implication concerning mixed cultural groups. The Black-White thing was a factor in the admissions program, but there was never any hope that the monstrous caverns of error characteristic of the geography of that problem could be grasped or redeemed in so brief and so casual an association. Far deeper and more profound efforts would be required for so great a goal, applied over long periods of time, approaching the encounter group level, among persons determined to work hard at the enormously difficult problems involved. It is of the utmost importance to undertake this task, but it must be recognized that other professional and cultural groups much closer in opportunity and in context have declined to attempt it. The Black-White thing has no casual solution. It must have a profound solution or none at all. For a multi-institutional arrangement to run into it as an accidental factor was to ensure a limited working relation at best, with little depth or meaning to it other than that of getting a limited job done in some pragmatic way in a particular set of circumstances.

Then the working procedures should come in for study. These should surely be laid out carefully ahead of time under conditions assuring that participating staff and institutions understand them and are willingly committed to them. This might not be an easy requirement to fulfill. Perhaps no field of college administration is so marked by rivalry, so afflicted with mutual exclusiveness, competition and distrust, as admissions. The future of every college depends on the students who enter. To suppose that colleges and universities would be generous enough to their rivals to work together with them in this most sensitive field is presuming a great deal. In a time of declining enrollments among at least the private colleges and perhaps the smaller public institutions as well it may be absurd even to hope for it; nevertheless one may strive for it as opportunities permit.

The architecture of a multi-institutional admissions project is of significance. As noted earlier, professional experience in the field suggests that a full load for a staff representative is probably four institutions, in any event not over five. The best results have also been obtained with loads made up of diverse institutions—colleges with institutes, two-year colleges with four-year, special institutions with liberal arts institutions, one geographic area with several different geographic areas.

Thoughtful study probably ought to be directed toward what the common representative should be doing. If he is simply a contact man whose responsibility is to hand out catalogues and brochures this fact should be faced by all participants. Projected success in solidifying applicants into enrollees should be recognized in this format as very low.

Handing out literature is a dull job at best, of no real interest to the staffer or to prospective candidates for admission. Some articulation of the staffer into the admissions procedures of his several institutions would undoubtedly produce better results; here the responsibility would fall on the representative to keep his lines clear and to function on a level of mutual trust that would enable him to know institutional secrets and to operate effectively within that knowledge while protecting both student and institutional clients. It could probably be done, but it would be a good deal of a stunt. What is more certain is that without real articulation of the staffer into the various admissions processes several strikes are being visited on the program before it even starts. This is simply to recognize a human thing; no professional staffer appreciates being put down as a kind of personal deliverer of third class mail.

Multi-institutional admissions projects do indeed appear to be viable, in spite of all their pitfalls. If however there are to be serious efforts in this direction it seems clear that such projects should become genuinely consortial in nature so that careful study can be applied to operational problems. Casual relationships are insufficient. If depth and breadth are not applied there is every likelihood that the program will escape into the limbo of the ill-prepared and the poorly-administered.

The present program was presumably useful to various participants in various ways. For Wilberforce it meant simply more students admitted in the usual ways, within the limits of its share of the common staff person. For the GLCA colleges the representative would have been an initial contact person to work in predominantly Black secondary schools. Some GLCA colleges developed travel routes for their own field staffers to follow in the project representative's tracks, in theory picking up on initial contacts made by the representative. This procedure might have confirmed some uncertain contacts; it also gave the impression that the representative was not able to do the job alone, an unfortunate and probably unexpected by-product.

Another consequence noted earlier was that some institutions appointed Black admissions representatives to their own full-time staffs. This argued the need for admission of more Black students but a distrust of the multi-institutional approach to bring it about.

All in all, when the program concluded it had surely run its course. Participating colleges were far from ready for real consortial effort in admissions. Many colleges may be quite unready for real consortial effort in admissions. Two levels of cooperation are open. With careful management by experienced professionals it is possible that clearly useful multi-institutional representation can be carried out at greatly reduced costs. The catch would be to construct the arrangement with enough built-in mutual respect, cooperation and trust so that the representation can be felt to be part of the outreach of the separate institutions; the representative would need to feel his role and his acceptance as a facet of each institutional reality. In theory an arrangement of this type need not be a consortium, yet even in this preliminary description it obviously takes on characteristics of consortial relationships if it is to be effective. The other level of cooperation is the true consortium, in which some degree of partial fusion occurs among participating staffs and procedures. In this also there is major commitment to resolving related and common educational and social problems.

The Wilberforce / Antioch / GLCA admissions program was strictly speaking neither of these. It was perceived variously by various participants. Many would have seen it as simply a specialized working arrangement applied to certain restricted uses. The original conception of it, however, was probably consortial, so that the fact that it did not achieve the level of consortiality may have been a disappointment. Perhaps it did not need to be a disappointment. It certainly produced some students for Wilberforce, and it may have produced at least a few initial contacts for other colleges. This might have been all that was wanted. If so, then the effort was worthwhile.

Some efforts do not themselves produce far-reaching results but have value in that they point to other possibilities. The Wilberforce / Antioch / GLCA program may have been of this order. As a specialized working arrangement it had some limited effect. Beyond this, it pointed to the possibility of differently based, consortial relationships in admissions work, by no means achieved in this instance and perhaps not achievable within the near future in admissions where the own-turf problem has a burning focus. It remains an ideal for the future, when some adventurous pride of colleges may dare the difficult and the unlikely.

XIV Consortial Thought
and Practice II:
The CHERS/CONRAD Phenomenon

Amid the widespread discussion of the pros and cons of consortia, those promising arrangements-for-cooperation-and-mutual-benefit among colleges and universities which have sprung up by the scores in recent years, there can be discerned an elusive something which needs to be remarked in the interest of understanding and operational practicality. The elusive element is that which makes a consortium a success as distinct from a group which limps along halfheartedly, accomplishing little, pulling at the sleeves of its member institutions in an effort to be liked. If consortia are to be effective the elusive something needs to be present in each instance to provide the imagination and drive to carry the association through the administrative entanglements which will otherwise sap its energies and use up most of the resources it can generate, resources which ought to be applied to inter-institutional programs. What is this elan vitale which occurs so rarely and yet seems to make such a difference?

Consortia are set up in various forms and for various purposes. Not infrequently they become something other than they at first were or were intended to be. The first characteristic to note in the study of a consortium is precisely the purpose for which it was set up. A consortium of six institutions on Long Island recently defined its purposes as planning for and meeting the educational needs of the area by (1) sharing institutional resources, (2) avoiding or reducing wasteful duplications, and (3) making fuller use of specialized faculty resources, program offerings and research facilities. These are sound reasons for forming a consortium. In addition much depends on how the reasons are interpreted and on what assumptions the establishment is made.

Of prime importance are the assumptions which institutions make concerning their own natures and their relationships to the consortium.

College and university heads tend to be hardnosed in a financial sense and to want to know the costs of a program as well as its values and advantages. This suggests that costs are commonly seen as a disadvantage, which they may not be, actually. Still, the contrapuntal opposition of programs and costs tend to make up the substance and form of "the consortial thing" as it does with other educational "things."

What does the consortium propose to do? Save money for member institutions? How? If it means that some institutional members may be expected to cease operations in certain traditional areas are further difficulties to be anticipated? The actual nature of an institutional commitment to the consortium should be made clear when the multi-member arrangement is begun. There are after all only a few ways to save money. Existing programs can be eliminated or reduced in size, with corresponding reductions in costs. Are the member institutions actually committed to either of these approaches? Present programs can be amalgamated, joining small efforts of several institutions into larger efforts of fewer or of single institutions. Are member institutions really committed to reduction of some of their existing efforts in the interests of cost efficiency and educational effectiveness? Future programs can be postponed or discarded, cutting back budgeted expenditures by amounts commensurate with the program reductions. Are member institutions prepared to follow this route and limit their reponses to new conditions? The positions which colleges and universities in fact take on all these questions should be made explicit prior to the formation of a consortium; otherwise the purposes and effectiveness of a consortial arrangement may be diverted before the project is well begun.

Observe that educational grounds rather than financial grounds are fundamental for the making of decisions in educational programs. Finances may in the end say whether a thing is done or not done; the support necessary to the operation of a program is either there or not there. But the values involved in an educational program should be educational in nature rather than primarily fiscal, and in long-range educational planning fiscal means should be managed in the interest of educational ends.

Occasional serendipities aside, it is possible to do complicated and difficult inter-institutional things only when participants are genuinely and deeply committed to doing them. The truth is that consortial members are frequently far from committed to making the sacrifices of

186

sovereignty and the contributions of sustenance which are necessary to the realistic operation of a consortium of institutions. It may not be their fault that this is so. The required questions may never have been raised; the workings and requirements of consortial operations are not well understood, and it is not surprising that there should be errors of judgment as to their degrees of advantage and possible ways of implementing them.

There may be some value in looking at the experience of one distinguished association, the Consortium for Higher Education Religion Studies (CHERS), the legal entity of which is the Consortium on Religion: Agency for Development (CONRAD, Inc.), a group of several colleges, universities and seminaries based in Dayton, Ohio from its founding in 1967-68 through 1972 when its more recent history found it spreading to central and northern Ohio.

CHERS / CONRAD: The First Period

Underlying most human movements are ideas; a consortium, which is after all a movement even if on a small scale, is no exception. Probably a more or less vague notion about the values of closer association stands at the root of most consortial efforts. There precision of thought and organizational preparation are apt to end. The early months of the CHERS association reflected these conditions. In a religious context the energy for an action is more easily accounted for than in strictly secular frames of reference. Many nonreligious consortia have grown out of cooperation among institutional libraries. As noted before, librarians seem often to be motivated by conviction in the direction of assisting other libraries and users of libraries, a religious-like psychology, if they will allow the description. In an initially religious orientation the grounds for decision and implementation are more obvious even than with libraries. The point to note here is that a psychology of extra or additive effort is involved in most successful consortia. This is the singular element to which consortial watchbirds should address themselves. While it has implications which will bear further study, it may be the most crucial factor to account for consortial effectiveness.

The first year or so of CHERS / CONRAD activity centered around program grants. The original Foundation funding for a period of three years provided for administration and program activity. For a time it appeared that the chief use of program funds was in small sub-grants for a variety of institutionally based projects. This has been called the "proposal-funding phase" of the Consortium. * The original intent of the Consortium and of the Danforth Foundation had been to support the idea and the possibilities of cooperation among colleges, universities and theological seminaries leading to the development of programs in religion. Cooperation among such diverse institutions was to encompass both institutional resources and opportunities for innovative programs. Due to a series of confusions and consequences of confusions in its first year, the Consortium became in effect a small foundation. It was a misleading experience for institutions, groups and individuals petitioning for grants because it trained them in effect to suppose that the principal aim of CHERS / CONRAD was to give away small sums of program money. There may have been implied dimensions of cooperation in certain of the proposals and some of the grants. Probably there were. Similarly, there was an implication of cooperation in the existence of CHERS / CONRAD and in the procedures and some of the activities of the Consortium. It may be fair to say that everyone concerned in the Consortium at the time meant well and saw in the consortial programs of that time some elements of cooperative endeavor which had not been there before, but that the nature and substance of cooperative programming had not yet been thought through and were not then perceived. It remained for some original thought and programming to set the consortial vectors awash and moving in new directions.

CHERS / CONRAD: The Period of Original Development

In 1969 and following, new currents of thought began to develop in the Consortium. Multi-level cooperation enabled member institutions to take part on various levels of responsibility and involvement. One of the interests of the Danforth Foundation at the time of the grant had been to determine the extent to which educational institutions of different kinds

---

*Cf. pamphlet, "Evaluative Study and Report of the Consortium for Higher Education Religion Studies" (1972), Dayton, Ohio, CONRAD, Inc., 1435 Cornell Drive (45406). This publication by Frederick Kirschenmann and James Legg, co-Directors of the Consortium, provides programmatic and some interpretive descriptions, the general outline of which is followed here for factual reference purposes.

could actively cooperate—public and private, for example, undergraduate and graduate, religious and secular. There were surprising acceptances of steadfast cooperation among diverse institutions and equally surprising refusals to cooperate. Consistently, the advanced levels of interest and energy game from the seminaries. The region of greatest difficulty remained with the public institutions, some of which feared for their image of academic detachment if they remained in the Consortium. This limitation was not universal among the public institutions, for some did remain involved, if variously. Middle ranges of involvement were expressed in attitudes of private colleges which, if traditionally oriented, stretched themselves to greater or lesser degrees either toward the Consortium if it represented more advanced educational thought and practice, or, if more radically oriented, away from it, assuming that its nature appeared to be too traditional to be of interest. All this was to be expected and meant simply that the membership of the Consortium was remarkably diverse and that the diversity gave rise to different attitudes. Non-consortial factors also gave rise to differing attitudes, so that contextual elements were and probably always would be of utmost importance to consortial effectiveness even if they were not themselves immediately consortial in nature. Instances of this would be degrees of institutional self-sufficiency or determined independence which might derive from unrelated or only indirectly related commitments, and similar factors.

Among the interesting programs which developed in this period was the Center for Theological Studies, a mid-week effort by and for seminary members which offered for students and faculty both common content and the stimulation of conjoined intellectual and religious challenge. At about this stage also, educational philosophy characteristically original in nature began to emerge. It involved re-thinking of the matrices of educational process and eventual reconstruction of the organizational personnel functions and relationships to provide for the greatest flexibility and openness at light cost in traditional structure and format. Out of this new educational imagination there came over a period of time more than two dozen different inter-institutional programs in addition to the Center for Theological Studies, administrative support for which derived from CHERS / CONRAD, ranging from content-centered curricular enrichment types through social valuation efforts to a number of special foci. Certain of these were

189

services performed for groups of member institutions such as investigations for overseas programs, development of common summer programs, coordination of schedules and catalogues of resources, and common administration of student aid, field education, and library resources. Program centered types involved workshops and conferences around various themes for differing member combinations, multi-institutional courses offered at and by several colleges, universities and / or seminaries, and certain pivotal special programs centering on foci such as Black Studies and the thought of Michael Polanyi. A third cluster centered around field studies chiefly for graduate students, focusing attention on distribution of neighborhood medical services in church clinics, intercommunication of city and suburb, and forms of pastoral education.

Even more interesting were the "fragments of some imaginings," in the words of the Legg-Kirschenmann Report, in which some of the newer philosophic thought of the period was brought to bear in the CHERS / CONRAD undertaking. Contextual and interprofessional education, intensive short-term scheduling, common administrative elements, Black Studies, interest-centered interdisciplinary studies, released-time faculty sharing, a field education network, inter-institutional course / workshops, and cooperative response to changing educational needs were some of these. In the same period development of standards for judging consortial effectiveness, or "benchmarks," suggested that such effectiveness could best be measured in terms of problem-solving effectiveness, rising levels of interdependence, fund-raising results, strengthened external relations and expanded educational environments, various kinds of enrichment in programmatic and financial dimensions, the tally of institutional drop-adds, and increased student involvement. Each of these points is developed at greater length in the Legg-Kirschenmann report.

For present purposes the central question remains why a consortium, full of energy, imagination and commitment, exists in distinguished dimension when and where it does, and why other consortia may have proved less distinctive.

Elements of Consortial Effectiveness

Among other factors adduced in the Legg-Kirschenmann study a number can be singled out for comment.

CHERS / CONRAD consistently addressed itself to quite difficult educational problems in energetic and often original ways. It was never content simply to operate institutional machinery. Any association of persons or institutions has the effect of developing machinery, some of which is enlarged need for communication: more persons and more institutional segments need to know more things, and someone, not necessarily the consortial staff, has to see that the information is passed from place to place at useful times. A consortial staff can consume itself promoting communication but this is not likely to be its best use of itself. Developing procedures and provisions for communication can on the other hand be very helpful. The key to consortial effectiveness is in general for the consortial staff to assist institutional staff in finding new modes for institutions to work together; it is in general not a good thing for consortial staff simply to perform particular services for consortial members. A pivotal question for an institutional executive to ask is—In what new ways and settings of thought do staff and faculty counterparts carry out their professional responsibilities? The question should rarely or never be—What does the member institution receive in monetary terms from consortial participation?

A consortium to be effective must therefore address itself to real and difficult problems, and it must do so by developing original modes of approach to those problems. It must not be content simply to run machineries of increased communication or even of common programs. Sooner or later other ways will be found of carrying out skeletal services at apparently lower cost than consortia seem to entail. Consortial patterns should probably call for basing continuing activities on participating institutional staffs as a regular thing, and not depending on consortial staffs for any type of routine service. Consortia should assist member institutions to operate in new and more effective ways; they should not as a general thing do very much routine administration except in the still infrequent circumstance that consortial super-structures develop major permanent responsibilities for the operation of college, university and seminary functions as occurs occasionally with clusters of schools conjoined in some sort of permanent symbiosis. Then a consortium may become an administrative umbrella unit with operational as well as developmental uses. Consortial implications surely point in this direction and doors should be left open toward it. The activities under discussion, however, are normally an earlier stage.

Distinctive and gifted leadership characterized the CHERS-／CONRAD consortium in its period of originality and imaginative development, a phase by no means necessarily concluded. At the risk of embarrassment to the Legg-Kirschenmann co-directorship it should be remarked for the sake of simple accuracy that this was a factor in the consortial situation. New ideas on organizational structure, or the replacement of structure as such with open modes of flow and process, marked new levels of consortial achievement. In these years the consortium was aware of itself as an association of public and private colleges, universities and seminaries and a large part of its concern centered on how its constituencies would relate to and work with each other. The first question was often what to do; the second, how to do it. In many a meeting of institutional representatives discussion focused on new functional patterns. Eventually the creation within the consortium of a functional mode of organization implemented this approach and served at the same time to further functional relationships in activities more remotely related to the consortium. Still, much of the originality was lost on institutional members who were quite naturally preoccupied with their own practical survival. The first three years of the CHERS-／CONRAD program were after all based on a grant from the Danforth Foundation; institutional members did not have to establish the consortium, and while membership costs and various types of participation assessments were common at different times substantial parts of operating and program expenses were paid for from the grant. The opportunity for learning was outstanding, but inevitably some of the implications were missed due to limited institutional responsibility for earlier project costs. Staff imagination and leadership continued to constitute the most important factors in consortial effectiveness.

Identification of factors in consortial effectiveness requires a return again and again to the kinds and degrees of institutional support available. Since in most instances institutional support derives from individual support the basic reference is inevitably to the qualities of commitment available from staff and faculty of member colleges, universities and seminaries.

Institutional staff as distinct from consortial staff are not employed by consortial offices and remain on appointments within their parent institutions. Their function for consortial purposes is to relate to consortia and to other consortial members from the standpoint of the institution they serve. Consortial staff presumably have quite different outlooks and are less tied to local member interests even though they may from time to time assume service responsibilities on behalf of member institutions.

Institutional loyalties constitute a difficult problem when institutions are under severe pressures simply to survive. Administrative units within all types of schools, even private institutions with substantial endowments, came under heavy financial stringencies in mid-twentieth century. It was then that James B. Conant and Royce S. Pitkin twitted the doubting higher educational community by forecasting greater reliance of colleges and universities on federal funding for program and research purposes. The period of federal support duly arrived, and both public and private institutions were reprieved by different kinds of federal assistance. Then the pendulum swung against federal support, and federal assistance programs began to be cut. Alert educational administrators had not been lulled for long by their experience with federal largesse. What governments could give they could also take away. The effect of these two stages of anxiety was to encourage understandable uncertainty within school administrations as to how financial survival could best be assured. Tensions resulted. New methods of educational operation were necessary; expenses had to be reduced and educational services delivered in less expensive but hopefully equally effective ways. Might consortial modes contribute to educational futures? This was the question, or at least one significant question.

The financial question is frequently deceptive, and it does not arise in a vacuum. The fundamental question is, what educational modes are most useful, taking into account all of the factors? The financial question follows and does not precede the educational question. Consortial viability therefore presented some dilemmas to institutions committed to established educational ideas and practices and to the financial expenditures necessary to support them. If consortial ideas and operational modes offered sound educational advantages, while college budgets were already taken up with prior commitments, how could promising new modes be paid for? Who could be persuaded to give up an existing program for something new and less well proven? Consortia were under this type of pressure, and the burden was both real and understandable. Federal grants to consortial organizations were a possible answer; the Office of Education gathered a discussion or two around these issues. On the whole, however, federal support for consortial organizations came in later stages, and while it assisted numbers of consortia it did not break much ground not already assessed and validated. Indirect federal assistance by way of grants to inter-institutional programs which were incidentally also consortial provided an impact more subtle because of its incidental nature, and may have been more effective because it tended to show the uses of consortial sharing of institutional resources by requiring it on program grounds rather than as organizational mode. Federal influence on development of consortial relationships was therefore real, but more indirect than direct.

Private funding and operational contributions from member institutions remained as potential sources of support. The two chief consortia in Southwest Ohio went by different routes for initial funding. The Dayton-Miami Valley Consortium of colleges, universities, and associated industries had a small federal grant for part of its initial support, along with institutional contributions and numbers of special service grants often from industrial connections. CHERS / CONRAD derived its initial impetus from the imaginative thrust of the Danforth Foundation, a private funding source with thoughtful people on its staff who could see the forward reach of cooperation among quite diverse educational institutions. These two consortia therefore came into existence with the crucial help of fund support from outside their membership, although there were member contributions in addition. It is doubtful either could have leaped from the starting gate with anything like their initial drives if their beginnings had depended solely on member contributions or on administrative commitments from member institutions.

Against such a background it may be asked why some consortia have more successful build-up periods than others. Consortia obviously could begin simply with administrative determinations. If this happens the evidence suggests that their courses of development tend to continue to be shaped by predominantly administrative considerations. These can of course be dull affairs, though they do not need to be. Imaginative components can be added from a variety of sources. In the CHERS / CONRAD case the institutional parts of imaginative leadership were often supplied by the forward-looking theological seminaries which were members at that time, and to a lesser extent by the religion departments of college and university members. A clue may reside in this pattern. Significant effects and stances-toward may derive from the breadth and depth of religiously connected commitments. These factors were clearly present in the years of the CHERS / CONRAD development, and the CHERS consortium without doubt ran far ahead of comparable consortia.

To enter a caveat, a religious connection alone may not produce the forward look. Indeed, it may be associated with stiffness and unwillingness to change. Perhaps not all seminaries in all periods of their history would provide the degrees of creative imagination comparable to the several inputs into the CHERS / CONRAD configuration. What may have to be said is that the religious connection is a significant ingredient but that it needs to be associated with creative imagination, an element which religious commitment may or may not carry with it.

Most of the clues to the singular promise and effectiveness of CHERS / CONRAD are comprised in these notes, except that the element of staff creativity should be further remarked. This is a delicate matter to convey, in part for reasons of personal consideration and in part because it is inexplicable except quite simply in terms of who was where and when. It may be most courteous to proceed largely in impersonal terms as long as it is understood that this passage cannot be prescriptive.

The two co-directors of the pivotal middle period came from seemingly diverse sources. James Legg, originally a seminary graduate from the East, had spent many years in administrative and business management of eleemosynary institutions. Frederick Kirschenmann, a North Dakotan philosopher of religion, had been in college teaching. In the course of time, while one had come for financial administration and one for programming, they formed a co-directorship and became interchangeable. Each learned the other's job; either person could and often did do either kind of work, according to convenience. It was an instance of experimental design in organization along functional lines with appropriate re-design and re-casting of staff roles. Operational and functional fluidity might be a way of describing it.

Why do things like this happen? What is their impact when they do happen? Quite simply, what happens in this wise depends on people. Imaginative developments in organizational thought and practice derive from particular staffers thinking and moving in new ways. Why do people think and act in new ways? The question is bootless. Why is anything? For consortia looking for new spheres of effectiveness the necessary advice is not very helpful: go out and find an imaginative staff. Look for a personal situation which carries with it not only the awareness of imaginative new roles but also the capacity to structure and function in new ways.

In the CHERS / CONRAD case it is imperative to record the observation that a veritable stream of new ideas, organizational and programmatic, flowed from the staff into various consortial receptacles. The other side of the coin was a fair receptivity for new ideas among member institutions, and a significant configuration of institutional membership.

Antioch College provided an almost measurable quality of adventurous programming, being always willing to try new things or to help other schools to try new things, even if in later phases it was occasionally bored by the succession of meetings with less adventurous counterparts. Wilmington and Earlham Colleges, both of Quaker derivation, contributed in individual ways. Wilmington's Department of Religion, led by Canby Jones, was interested in building on a base of traditional academic excellence in the direction of outreach into cultural change. Earlham's graduate School of Religion, of which Wilmer Cooper was head in this period, participated as a seminary, often preoccupied by problems of internal direction yet remaining with the consortium as a way of testing the value of consortial relations. Wilberforce and Central State Universities and Payne Seminary were predominantly Black institutions clustered in the village of Wilberforce on the eastern fringe of the then consortial ring; Wilberforce University was private and church-connected; Central State was a member of the Ohio public university system; Payne was a graduate seminary. Wilberforce had the greater freedom of movement, in the nature of things; Central State was distinctive in continuously representing the public educational sector in the CHERS membership, though it was inactive for occasional periods due to unconnected internal concerns; Payne had a difficult role to play as the only Black seminary in a constellation of quarterbacking regional seminaries. Dean Handley Hickey, it should be recorded, held up his end skillfully in that complicated situation. Two Roman Catholic institutions were longtime consortial members—St. Leonard's College in Centreville, with Cyren Maus and Ronald Nunlist as successive academic heads, both of whom served the consortium as well as their own institution, and the graduate Department of Theology of the University of Dayton, often represented by the wisdom of Matthew Kohmescher and Harold Fox. Wittenberg University's membership varied in intensity of involvement, reflecting institutional concerns. Hamma Theological Seminary, an institutional associate of Wittenberg in the city of Springfield north of Dayton, was heavily involved in programmatic and managerial aspects of CHERS, providing some of the strongest contributory support, understandably, since it was a leader in developing community-related seminary programs. Frederick Wentz and Luther Stirewalt were the principal figures in Hamma's involvement in CHERS. United Theological Seminary, with John Knecht and Newell Wert as heads, provided irreplaceable imaginative and practical leadership; without this, little or nothing might have happened at all; with it, the entire history and development of the consortium became possible.

In each case of effective institutional involvement there tended to be a team of staff and faculty supplying institutional commitment and practical member contributions. There may be no substitute for multi-person participation in educational program development. Presidential involvement among college and university members was limited to normal internal administrative awareness and approval; institutional chief executives other than seminary heads were necessarily board members of the Dayton-Miami Valley Consortium. CHERS tended to subsume the related and somewhat specialized faculty and staff interests of colleges and universities. Seminary presidents, rectors, and deans, however, were commonly in CHERS. This is a point worth reflection. CHERS was more programmatically and less structurally oriented than DMVC. It seemed able to move rapidly on program needs and to gather multi-level support from compact institutions of small size. College and university heads were naturally involved with a variety of institutional problems beyond the scope of CHERS interests. For prescriptive purposes, it probably follows that an effective consortium requires significant levels of member institutional commitment, whatever these levels may be in particular cases.

All this is not to say that the operation of CHERS / CONRAD was always smooth or encouraging or free of trouble. It had indeed its share of problems and its periods of discouragement and disillusion, even its crises. But the present point is not so much to detail the operation of the consortium as to identify factors in consortial achievement.

The pattern of consortial composition and operation may now be emerging from the CHERS / CONRAD experience. It remains to refer to the problem of human relations in the consortial setting.

In any multi-personal situation, across institutional lines or within them, the confidence that people have in each other may decide the success or non-achievement of an undertaking. Probably some institutions are indeed controlled by sets of ideas or established stances-toward. More often they may be influenced by individuals, persons complete with individual histories, deep feelings, capacities to understand and accept, inabilities to do the one or the other. Trust is perhaps the central conception.

Trust, according to an early Empire State College formulation of educational philosophy, is the capacity to lay oneself open to others without fear of being hurt. The definition covers many types of cases. In most of them individual trust or the possibility of it is at stake. So sensitive and delicate is the phenomenon of trust that it can be built up only very slowly and in full awareness of the enormous dangers involved. In its earliest stages trust involves faith in the other person, group or institution. It never ceases to have this dependence, but in later stages it grows to a pervasive relational structure in which dependence changes to interdependence in the best sense. It comes into being at great cost in personal investment, at great labor, and only with unremitting constancy through diverse mutual experiences. Its reward is the grace of a special brand of freedom, respite from judgment, from anxiety, from fear of exposure of the self to ridicule, attack or other injury—the entrance into the rarest kind of peace.

It is essentially the assurance that the other person, group or institution is ultimately reliable, that there will never be a betrayal, that the other participant(s) can be depended upon without break or hesitation to wish the relation to endure, even in adverse circumstances. It does not argue entire or continual agreement on all possible points. It does argue the willingness to be open in the relationship, above and before all things to be ready to talk, interminably and repeatedly as necessary, about potential differences and commonalities, basic understandings, and the grounds of relation. To do less than this is to risk reduction or destruction of the interdependence. To work against it by omission is to invite great danger to it. To move actively against it is to destroy it utterly. Trust once recognized as broken cannot be assumed to be recoverable.

CHERS / CONRAD developed, perhaps remarkably, a network of relationship which approached just such trust, allowing for inevitable individual differences. In several seasons of substantial difficulty it went through the interminable and repeated discussions, often with no immediate resolution of issues, with no decisions made for long periods, their outcome being in the realm of experiential process, their substance the labor of developing common understandings, piece by piece, part by part. It was as if the purpose of the discussions had been not to solve the problems but rather to educate the people. In effect, this was precisely the point, if unintentionally. The result of several years of it, with a good deal of participant staff continuity, the perverse and invaluable reward of difficult problems deliberately approached and tolerated so to speak as if in disregard of actual resolutions, was to produce a cadre of communicators who felt trust in each other, who understood from the briefest telephone exchange a host of unspoken factors which bore upon the topic, and who could move toward solutions to problems by way of commonalities laboriously achieved.

Again for prescriptive purposes, consortial effectiveness will be found to require the careful nurture of relationships of trust, encouraged over periods of time, protected against exploitation, articulated with goals genuine and consistent, sustained by a nearly total intrinsic dedication.

* * * *

There was happily no conclusion to this story at the time of writing, as the consortium continued into what appeared to be a promising third phase, not necessarily even then a concluding one. The seminaries of Central and Northern Ohio were making arrangements to join, as were some of the private colleges at a considerable distance from Dayton. A second consortial office was being opened in Columbus to provide balance in administration and services, and the staff, while maintaining its co-directorship pattern, was dividing itself between the two centers. Among the most significant aspects of the new phase, however, was the recognition that compatibility of purposes and function transcended geographic convenience, and that institutions at a radius of a hundred miles or more from either center could be practical cooperators. The question was basic and bone-simple: what had the members decided to do? If they had decided to cooperate it was possible and practical to cooperate. If they should decide it was not practical to do so, that would be the end of it for the institutions so deciding. Any institution had the power to choose or decline success in cooperation.

A great many things were learned from the CHERS / CONRAD phenomenon in the 1967-72 period; others would evidently be learned in the years 1973- and following. Perhaps among the primary lessons of the entire story was that of the original question centrally posed by the Danforth Foundation when it made its initial grant: Could public and private colleges and universities and private seminaries cooperate effectively with each other?—The answer was clearcut with respect to all three categories: they certainly could if they chose to. Not all institutions chose to. One or two private colleges withdrew at points in the experience. One seminary which could have usefully joined never quite did so. Of three nearby public universities in the Ohio State system, one did not join in the beginning, one withdrew in midstream, and one maintained its membership continuously. There may have been anxiety in some public university circles lest the reputation of academic detachment be shadowed by association with seminaries.

The problem of church and state as it affects higher education should be taken up by itself in another place. There is a deal to be said on it, some of it a bit sharp. For present purposes there can be no doubt of the conclusion: Public and private colleges and universities and theological seminaries can indeed cooperate. They have only to decide to do so. The way to begin is simply to walk on to each other's campuses and begin. The details can be handled in the course of time. To discover this, well against the common assumption of American higher education, five years and more of effort on the part of many people must have been well spent.

XV Journey Among Mountains

"Dwindling mountains are they on a dwindling planet,
These that look so solid, these that show so fair;
Wind and rain and frost and hail set tooth to granite,
It wastes like smoke into air."

—*Abbie Huston Evans* *

In retrospect passing through a great divide in the history of thought seems less momentous than might have been expected. The land indeed tips downward; high points shift somewhat among their fastnesses; waters run in new directions; the heights appear to fall away with unexpected gentleness toward the plains. The great peaks which in anticipation looked so vast and final against sky now stand aside, elbowing each other as cliffs and sidewalls do along roads which wind among them, finally receding, unmet and unapproaching, having marked the great division in the characteristics of an age, suddenly at last retiring, displaced and of only historic interest.

Yet even so familiar an experience of changing perspectives as this passage through a continental divide does not tell how completely a set of relations in the realm of ideas can shift. Turning aside from a roadway to ascend some noble peak the climber may discover that the grandeur of its summit seen from a distance becomes on closer inspection a rounded pile of crumbling sedimentary wash, thrust upward aeons ago out of the primordial sea, but now wholly engaged in rushing back down again—at breakneck speed in the scale of geologic time.

Movement among ideas is rather like this. For centuries men may live so to speak in the foothills of some towering arrangement of apparent facts, deferring to them, ordering existence in accordance with their characteristics, denying themselves the freedom to scale the

---

* Abbie Huston Evans, *Outcrop.* New York, Harper, 1928. P. 5. Reprinted by permission of the author. Cf. also *Collected Poems,* University of Pittsburgh Press, 1971; p. 5.

heights which appear impossible, so imposing severe limitations on their own capacities to do what in fact they are well able to do. Social and practical benefits can derive from self-limitations of this kind, and it is useful to remember what these are. Inexorably, however, the forward movement of history, whatever its grounds, impels the minds of men to challenge the great heights, and when at last they do so it can happen that the barriers are not there.

Since the beginning of the modern period the predominant outlook in the West has sought its immediate certainty in the objectivities of detached facts. Immediate certainty has always to be sought somewhere, and the nearer at hand the better. It may be found in some formulation of real essences subsisting within and through things; it may be found within unattached essences if the mind is willing to make the necessary extension of itself. More recently certainty has been located in the simple properties of things by themselves, without essences, so that the properties of a tree which anyone could plainly see made up a tree were measurably thus and so and might even be neurologically accounted for in the operations of the perceiver, at least for the time being.

Conceptions of nature and of human nature inevitably tend in the long run to correspond. A transcendental view of human nature will go with a transcendental view of nature and reality. Conversely, in the period of simple-minded empiricism when an object was conceived to be what it obviously was, cut up and weighed out as best it could be, the nature of the perceiver was also conceived to be an aggregate of properties corresponding to the perceivable properties of the perceivable range of (other) objects. Perhaps it was actually conceived to be just noticeably brighter than if the correspondence had been exactly one-to-one, or subject-to-object, since this would permit readier accounting for consciousness or awareness of objectivity, but not enough brighter to have introduced a qualitative theoretical gain on the human side of the correspondence.

It is impossible to overestimate the influence on our time of this simple intuitive derivation from the seventeenth and eighteenth century view of the objectivity of nature. The point to be made here is that while this philosophic heritage from an earlier time had certain clear intellectual and social uses in the development of Western thought in the intervening centuries it has now been superseded by a re-positing of the pivotal role of the perceiving subject as a determining factor in human awareness and conceptualization of the world of things and events. The consequence is simply enormous, but as the movements of thought are typically very slight and changes in perspective slow-moving and elephantine, much as are the sliding perspectives among the heights of nearby mountains as one moves among them, so these changes are often difficult to see and more difficult still to gauge with any precision. It has been suggested before that the real subject of considerations of this kind is the nature of movement among centers of gravity in the realm of ideas. The implication will be that the essential movement among ideas, granted to be relatively slight, will obtain among conceptual foci, while the outer reaches of each constellation or universe of thought, where the local motion may be relatively large especially with respect to corresponding or even non-corresponding regions of other constellations, are simply borne along in the total change.

Some evidence also derives from typical patterns in thought development. What happens in philosophic history is that theories of nature and natural process proceed comfortably for longer or shorter periods of time accounting for additional ranges of data in some familiar way, as for example in an empiricist way or a phenomenological way, until suddenly at some edge of the ranges of awareness being considered a tiny part of the section under study persistently gives results just a little out of focus. Then the assessment of the entire system must be called into question.

As everyone is well enough aware, this is happening at the present time. By extending substantially the ranges of data being accounted for by scientific process it has gradually become clear that at least beyond a certain point of investigative precision, and in ranges of size of subject-data smaller than had hitherto been possible to consider, the influence of operations and instruments employed in investigation have decisive influences on experimental results. All this is familiar enough. The implications of this new condition have now to be entered on the record.

When a procedural limitation is reached in this way quite evidently a generalization from the new condition is necessary. In the present case the generalization would read somewhat as follows:

—Since it is clear that operational procedures and instruments affect significantly the results of scientific investigation in the sub-atomic range, and since the influence of the perceiving subject appears also to be contributory in less precise and more generalized perceptual ranges, probably allowance must now be made for subjective perceptual contributions, that is, for the conceptual nature of awareness, not only in the ranges in which it most immediately appears but as well over all the ranges of perceptual possibility. Implied in this is a change in the descriptive formulation of the nature of perception, heretofore frequently given in terms of correspondences of subject and object, with various theoretical neurological connectives and with provision for uncertainty in particular instances by introduction of statistical probabilities, to an articulated or gathered conception of the awareness-relation in which contributory subjective prehension provides a grounding of metaphysical connection, that is, an organic conceptualization of object-regions of study.-

Knowing therefore becomes entirely conceptual in nature, even in those ranges of awareness in which subjective contributions appear to be slight or are taken for granted, or in which the effects of contributory components of knowing are negligible. The comment to be made here is that the nature of knowing-in-general has now to be revised because of the implications of certain extreme cases-in-particular. To include the latter aggregation of cases within the general principle is to leave no way to avoid modifying the generalization.

What difference does this make?

As has been indicated, in customary perceptual ranges the pattern of knowing will not appear to be affected at all, because of the minute effects of subjective components. The general nature of knowing will, however, be different. At least, it can only be properly described as determinative, even though its contributory effects do remain infinitesimal in normal ranges. To have all this make sense it is necessary to conceive of the human being as a total instrument, and of various human perceptual and conceptual components such as sense and mind as likewise of instrumental or sub-instrumental orders. It is in addition necessary to allow for the fact that some effects of perceptual activity within the daily range are similarly felt in a strictly operational way, even when these are indistinguishably small.

Knowing in all possible ranges then becomes operational or instrumental in character, depending in part for its consequences on the instruments brought to bear on particular ranges of data. Although in ordinary perceptual ranges the components of subjectivity are most often not noticed simple experiments can be readily devised to show that different eyes perceive different shades of a colored surface, or different shapes or other characteristics in near-identical regions of examination. But for the most part the effects of instrumental perception are overlooked within normal ranges. For the mischief of it one might conclude that if millions of persons should stare all together at the western side of the leaning tower of Pisa the combined weight of their gaze might serve to push it over. For obvious reasons it is difficult to measure this since the displacement of a single gaze borders on the intangible. The necessary assumption has to be, however, that there are effects on the ''objective'' world-in-depth as a consequence of human perception, which combine impressions and substance to construct the definition of the objective-real which is judged to constitute the world in which man lives.

Although it is difficult to measure the quantities of influence deriving from perceptual process which impinge on the world around, there can be no doubt now that knowing must be conceived of for the time being in this prehensive way over its entire range, which is to say, in all the discoverable ranges of human knowing—cultural, scientific, religious, or whatever. ''Perception'' as a term has either to be abandoned as inapplicable, presumably to be replaced by conceptual knowledge to provide for contributory components which stem from the knowing instrument, or else must be restricted by definition to the ordinary sensory ranges which have hitherto been ''normal,'' where instrumentation has been ignored by reason of practical, approximate agreement on epistemological method and assumptions.

The consequences of this conceptual change, this slight movement among intellectual centers of gravity, are as has been observed simply enormous. It may be of use to sketch in what these have of necessity to be, working in reverse order from the nature of the real to the origination of the real, the nature of the knowing relation between subject and object, and the nature of the human self as it corresponds to such conceptions of the real.

Reality has now to be conceived of in what might be termed a depth-metaphysic. Simple objects as they appear to be, objects strictly known to sense, once so useful a notion for clarification of the subject-object relation, are long since gone. The entire, obvious world-of-facts is likewise forever dispatched. A perceived fact as defined heretofore is merely the thin skin of reality, the middle and farther depths of which cannot even be approached with the conceptual tools and schemas at man's present disposal. Furthermore, the depth-metaphysic must be conceived as starting within the individual human self, and so to be extended in continuous relation as far out into the depth-dimension as the self finds it possible with improving capacities to reach.

The nature of the real-in-depth then becomes somewhat involved, but its final nature may perversely be taking on greater simplicity. Whereas in the recent past man has contented himself with "seeing" the surface of a thing or with seeing its surface qualities he may now be compelled to acknowledge the consequence of the conceptual nature of sight, that is, of the combination of sensory reception with intellectual and rational prehension, which consequence is that he must now attend to seeing-in-depth. He must quite literally "see" more profoundly into things, beneath the surface of things, and when at some relatively shallow depth sensory data fade out, as they must do, and so become unavailable, "sight"—as more broadly conceived—will continue its operation, consisting of subsumption of ever larger components of abstract reality. The same can be said of any of the senses. One is reminded of the old story of the farmer who fed his hens on less and less grain and more and more sawdust, so that when a dozen eggs were hatched eleven of the chickens had wooden legs and the twelfth was a woodpecker.

The case in point, however, is not quite so extreme. Notice the implication of sensory perception-in-depth. If the nature of sensation is to be modified as indicated it may mean that sensory reception can be conceived in a sufficiently representational depth-dimension so that it does not need to be discarded as the kind of simpleton's sensing which it has been for so long. Perhaps even the empiricists may begin to stir a little in their winding-sheets. Who can tell what unexpected contributions to perceptual thought may yet be made by visitations from those departed shades?

Objectivity has yet to be defined, and will be a matter of choice. Beyond uncertain points in depth clearly the notion of objectivity will apply, and beyond such points the real-in-depth will continue to extend, perhaps immeasurably, indeterminably, even incomprehensibly. In slightly altered form and perspective, therefore, the givenness of the universe, the problems of the-world-out-there, of creation and origination, remain to be resolved. It is indeed impossible that they should not.

The world in which man lives is therefore properly termed subjective only if the range intended is within the bounds of the conceivable world-in-depth. Beyond the limits of the conceivable the unknown and unknowable world still stretches unprehendably far away. But within these bounds man can truly be said to select and form—even to create—the world in which he lives.

The creation of an immediate world is in part an individual and in part a cultural phenomenon depending on the instrumentation employed, whether highly distinct or commonal, and these potentials only produce the greater variety of contemporaneous instanced worlds. It is necessary to hold, again depending on the instrumentation used, that the establishment of environmental worlds is a selecting process even well within the ranges of the conceivable world-in-depth. That is, there have to be many possible dimensions and structures, many possible logics, many possible reflective systems, each set up with reference to a "partial absolute" of its own. There will then be a total or absolute world-in-depth explicable only in terms of an ultimate, but multiple possible sub-worlds similar in form or structure although of lesser, more immediate, more examinable and often more applicable scales. This rather involved description appears to reflect the present cultural condition.

The issue of truth or falsity will have also to endure re-study. Evidently in a depth-metaphysic a great many systems will be properly termed "true"; the issue may rather be joined on how falsity or untruth is to be delineated. It may be that falsity can only obtain within a particular system which would have to be defined or clearly implied in each truth-statement, or possibly if of sufficient scope, defined with reference to the final absolute, the genesis and ground of the total world-in-depth. Instances of particular aberration are not generally of concern here as they would tend to apply only within given systemic frames. In numerous cases contradictory or partially contradictory positions may be equally tenable in slightly different systems. These are not facile matters; the implications of the stance do not incline toward ready dismissal of divergent points of view. Intellectual understanding is of high significance, and quite evidently the fifty-minute-hour approach, the effort to grasp another viewpoint by assuming it at least tentatively, may be more sound than otherwise.

The nature of knowing, it follows, becomes heavily rationalistic in a metaphysical sense. In some part the depth-dimension becomes known by rational or intellective means. Another way of saying this is that sense-knowledge alters its fundamental composition from simple receptivity of physical data to a more complex and realistic process of physico-intellective relation of subject and object. In this case as in so many others understanding of the general nature of a relation is altered by a particular instance of it in an unusual range of applicability where new characteristics happen to be disclosed. If in a given case of "sensory" knowing, to repeat the point, it is clear that a rational component forms a substantial part of the epistemological relation in one section of the range of applicability, so that knowing depends on the complex composition of the relation, then the simple "sensory" interpretation of the relation must be replaced even in those readier ranges in which it has made fair sense. Thereafter even in the normal ranges of awareness, knowing will be definable only as a complex of components even if the subjective-rational component is often regarded as small in the common Western view; or in another manner of speaking physico-intellectual knowing may be of comparable scope in all possible ranges but the complexity may be observed by the very commonality of accepted conditions of epistemological operation in the Western tradition.

Probably the nature of knowing should be examined from both directions, the rational and the empirical. The two dimensions can surely be developed without assuming that either will be put in the wrong by the other, the resolution being of a certainty a complex resultant of both.

Human nature stands at the root of knowing, and must therefore correspond to the characteristics of the perceived universe. There are two ways to come at this problem, the approach from subjective human nature and the approach from objective data. Insofar as the mid-twentieth century existentialist permits himself to explicate a world-view he does so often enough on the ground of a re-reading of human nature. That is, he decides in the first place what valid human awarenesses are, thereby defining the nature of human nature, and proceeds to define "the-world-out-there" in terms of elements posited in human nature.

There is nothing unusual or especially wrong about this. People have been setting up reflective systems for centuries on the basis of axia as to what human nature really is. No doubt it will continue. Instances of it are found in the several psychological interpretations of reality deriving from the Freudian watershed of the late 19th century, in connection with which observers have thought they were perceiving and recording objective characteristics of the self, and consequently that systems founded on these "perceptions" were soundly based. It would be more helpful and more accurate to recognize that psychological systems, like all systems, provide only very partial and limited grounds for generalization. The social utility of such patterns of understanding can be acknowledged without ascribing to them the validity belonging to more general metaphysical systems.

The present approach in the second of the two dimensions argues from variability of determinacy of data to the operational nature of knowing procedures, and so to the subjective or instrumental character of the subject-object relation.

The implications for the nature of the self are reasonably clear. It suggests that human knowing is a relation heavily intellective and rational in its composition, with varying degrees of penetration into the world outside. Inevitably this position has the effect of also describing human nature in intellective and rational terms; such a description will constitute a metaphysical comment on the fundaments of man's nature. As a special mark of mischievous liberalism in this regard it should be again noted that the empiricist approach is likewise open to further development. The resulting consequence for a description of human nature would correspond to the deepened metaphysic posited from a complicated intellective empiricism.

In general what must be said of the human self is what has been said elsewhere on other grounds, that it cannot relate to the world-in-depth without making the substantive assumptions requisite for a depth-metaphysic, and that these assumptions require the self or soul to be highly rational and intellective, able to extend its substance far out into the comparable substance of the universe, able to judge and to discriminate, able to relate where relation is called for, able to involve itself in systems with the consequence of understanding. It is quite possible that one of the things which is seen to be happening here is the reconstitution of spirit as a sound descriptive entity, the re-description of which in greater detail is an implied necessity.

How different all this is from the universe of the human creature understood as the brief flagellation of biological and social causes. In this bio-social view the great fact on the horizon was the objective world perceived alone in the few poor dimensions of sense, with the consequence that human nature came to be defined as simply the associated latticeworks and sluiceways of sensory reception. On the one side there used to be in the superannuated view of recent centuries this nailed-together pattern of physical lights and shadows, this envelope of liquid life, this collectioned mass of empty skins in the shapes of men waiting to be filled out by the extruded grists of process; and on the other hand there used to be a different kind of mass, equally misleading, but solid, impenetrable, the objective fact, a mountainous range of givenness to which all individual life must bend. Now as if all of a sudden, in part by its own operations, the old world is gone, gone at least in its old format, and with it have gone the tattered judgments of man as composed of oiled and articulated bits and bolts, mechanical product of a mechanical universe cringing around towering obstacles imposed by nature. Man's own imperial being once again has burst the bonds with which he had thought to bind himself, bonds of weakness forged by doubt of self and misplaced awe of natural process. With strength that is slow of self-discovery, but for all its hesitation also irresistible and not to be denied, he has passed through the impenetrable mountains. Already these stand to the rear, fading and crumbling, an illusion perhaps as they were once known, at last become just one more phase in a journey immeasurably long, from lesser to greater understandings.

Bibliographic Notes

Adams, James Luther, "The Changing Reputation of Human Nature." Chicago, *J. of Liberal Religion,* 1942-43.
——, *Paul Tillich's Philosophy of Culture, Science and Religion.* N. Y., 1970.
Altizer, Thomas J. J., *The Gospel of Christian Atheism.* Philadelphia, 1966.

Bahm, Archie J., *Types of Intuition.* Albuquerque, 1961.
Banton, Michael, Ed., *Anthropological Approaches to the Study of Religion.* London, 1966.
Barber, Bernard, Ed., *L. J. Henderson on the Social System.* Chicago, 1970.
Barfield, Owen, *Worlds Apart.* Middletown, Conn., 1963.
Barnard, Mary, *The Mythmakers.* Columbus, Ohio, 1967.
Barranda, Natty G., *Love Unfolding.* N. Y., 1970.
Barrett, William, *Irrational Man.* N. Y., 1958.
Bate, Walter Jackson, *The Burden of the Past and the English Poet.* Cambridge, Mass., 1970.
Benne, Kenneth D., *Education for Tragedy.* Lexington, Kentucky, 1967.
Berman, Harold J. and William R. Greiner, *The Nature and Functions of Law.* Brooklyn, 1958, 1966.
Berman, Harold J., *Talks on American Law.* N. Y., 1961.
Black, Max. Ed., *The Importance of Language.* Englewood Cliffs, N. J., 1962.
Bochenski, J. M., *The Methods of Contemporary Thought.* Dordrecht, Holland, 1965.
Bohr, Niels, *Atomic Physics and Human Knowledge.* N. Y., 1958.
Boorstin, Daniel J., *The Mysterious Science of the Law.* Boston, 1958.
Bowen, Catherine Drinker, *Miracle at Philadelphia.* Boston, 1966.
Bowker, John, *Problems of Suffering in the Religions of the World.* London, 1970.
Brooks, Paul, *The House of Life.* Boston, 1972.
Brown, Delwyn, Ralph E. James, and Gene Reeves, Eds., *Process Philosophy and Christian Thought.* Indianapolis, 1971.
Browning, Douglas, Ed., *Philosophers of Process.* N. Y., 1965.
Bunge, Mario, *Institution and Science.* Englewood Cliffs, N. J., 1962.

Canbaniss, Allan, *Liturgy and Literature.* University, Alabama, 1970.
Cahn, Edmond, *The Moral Decision.* Bloomington, Indiana, 1968.
Capek, Milic, *The Philosophical Impact of Contemporary Physics,* N. Y., 1961, 1964.
Caponigri, A. Robert, Jr., Tr., *Major Trends in Mexican Philosophy.* Notre Dame, 1966.
Cardozo, Benjamin N., *The Nature of the Judicial Process.* New Haven, 1921, 1952.
Carson, Rachel, *The Sea Around Us.* N. Y., 1962.
Channing, William Ellery, *Unitarian Christianity and Other Essays.* Indianapolis, 1957.

Chichester, Sir Francis, *Gypsy Moth Circles the World.* N. Y., 1967.
Chickering, Arthur W., *Education and Identity.* San Francisco, 1969.
Cioran, E. M., *The Temptation to Exist.* N. Y., 1968.
Clark, Kenneth, *Dark Ghetto.* N. Y., 1965.
Cohen, Felix S., *Ethical Systems and Legal Ideals.* Ithaca, N. Y., 1933, 1959.
Cohen, Morris R. and Felix S., *Readings in Jurisprudence and Legal Philosophy.* N. Y., 1951, 1953.
Cohen, Morris R., *Reason and Law.* Glencoe, Illinois, 1950.
Commoner, Barry, *The Closing Circle.* N. Y., 1972.
Conant, James B., *My Several Lives.* N. Y., 1970.
——, *Scientific Principles and Moral Conduct.* N. Y., 1967.
——, *Shaping Educational Policy.* N. Y., 1964.
Cowan, Thomas A., *The "American Jurisprudence" Reader.* N. Y., 1956.
Cox, Harvey, *The Secular City.* N. Y., 1965.
Crane, Ronald S., *The Idea of the Humanities.* Vols. I, II. Chicago, 1967.
Crawford, William Rex, *A Century of Latin-American Thought.* Cambridge, Mass., 1967.

Davis, Charles, *A Question of Conscience.* N. Y., 1967.
D'Entreves, A.P., *Natural Law, An Historical Survey.* London, 195; N. Y., 1965.
De Santillana, Giorgio, and H. von Dechend, *Hamlet's Mill.* Boston, 1969.
De Unamuno, Miguel, *The Tragic Sense of Life.* N. Y., 1954.
——, *Three Exemplary Novels.* N. Y., 1930, 1956.
Dubos, Rene, *A God Within.* N. Y., 1972.
Dugan, James, *The Great Mutiny.* N. Y., 1965.

Eichner, Hans, Ed., *Romantic and its Cognates.* Toronto, 1972.
Einstein, Albert, and Leopold Infeld, *The Evolution of Physics.* N. Y., 1938.
Einstein, Albert, *The Meaning of Relativity.* Princeton, 1946.
——, *Out of My Later Years.* N. Y., 1950.
Eiseley, Loren, *The Invisible Pyramid.* N. Y., 1970.
——, *The Night Country.* N. Y., 1971.
——, *The Unexpected Universe.* N. Y., 1970.
Eliot, Charles W., "A Turning Point in Higher Education." Cambridge, Mass., (1869), 1969.
Evans, Abbie Huston, *Collected Poems.* Pittsburgh, Pa., 1970-71.
——, *Outcrop.* N. Y., 1928.
Evers, Mrs. Medgar, and William Peters, *For Us the Living.* N. Y., 1967.

Fairfield, Roy P., Ed., *Humanistic Frontiers in American Education.* Englewood Cliffs, N. J., 1971.
Feifel, Herman, Ed., *The Meaning of Death.* N. Y., 1959.
Five College Cooperation: Directions for the Future. Amherst, Mass., 1969.
Fleming, William, *Arts and Ideas.* N. Y., 1955.
Forde, Daryll, *African Worlds.* London, 1954, 1965.
Foss, Martin, *Logic and Existence.* N. Y., 1962.
Frank, Philippe, *Modern Science and Its Philosophy.* N. Y., 1955.
Freuchen, Peter, *I Sailed With Rasmussen.* N. Y., 1958.
Friedrich, Carl J., *The Philosophy of Law in Historical Perspective.* Chicago, 1958.
Fuller, Lon L., *The Law in Quest of Itself.* Boston, 1966.

Gardner, Brian, *Mafeking*. N. Y., 1966.
Gardner, Martin, *The Ambidextrous Universe*. N. Y., 1964.
Gierke, Otto, *Natural Law and the Theory of Society, 1500-1800*. Boston, 1957.
Gluckman, Max, *Custom and Conflict in Africa*. Oxford, England, 1965.
Goodheart, Eugene, *Culture and Radical Conscience*. Cambridge, Mass., 1973.
Goss, Gary, *Hitler's Daughter*, Secaucus, N. J., 1973.
Graham, Hugh D., *Violence, The Crisis of American Confidence*. Baltimore, 1971.

Harding, Arthur L., *Natural Law and Natural Rights*. Dallas, 1955.
Hare, R. M., *Freedom and Reason*. London, 1963.
Harper, Ralph, *Existentialism*. Cambridge, Mass., 1948.
Hartmann, Nicolai, *The New Ways of Ontology*. Chicago, 1953.
Hawkins, D.J.B., *Crucial Problems of Modern Philosophy*. Notre Dame, 1964.
Heisenberg, Werner, *Physics and Beyond*. N.Y., 1971.
——, *Physics and Philosophy*. N. Y., 1958.
Hempel, Carl G., *Fundamentals of Concept Formation in Empirical Science*. Chicago, 1952.
Herriott, Frank W., ''An Educational Approach to the Practice of the Ministry.'' N. Y., *Union Seminary Quarterly Review*, 1951.
——, ''Some Concerns of a Christian Educator.'' N. Y., ——, 1960.
Hewitt, Arthur Wentworth, *The McKenzie Memorial Church*. Riverton, Vt., 1970.
——, *The Old Brick Manse*. N. Y., 1966.
Heyerdahl, Thor, *Aku-Aku*. N. Y., 1958.
——, *The Ra Expeditions*. N. Y., 1971.
Hofstadter, Richard, *Anti-intellectualism in American Life*. N. Y., 1969.
Hook, Sidney, *Law and Philosophy, A Symposium*. N.Y., 1964.
Huie, William Bradford, *The Execution of Private Slovik*. N. Y., 1970.
——, *The Klansman*. N. Y., 1967.
——, *Three Lives for Mississippi*. N. Y., 1965.
Hungate, Thad L., *Management in Higher Education.*N. Y., 1964.
Hunter, Edith F., *Sophia Lyon Fahs*. Boston, 1966.
Hunter, Howard, Ed., *Humanities, Religion, and the Arts Tomorrow*. N. Y., 1972.
Husserl, Edmund, *Cartesian Meditations*. The Hague, 1960.
——, *Ideas*. N. Y., 1962.
——, *Phenomenology and the Crisis of Philisophy*. N. Y., 1965.

Infeld, Leopold, *Albert Einstein*. N. Y., 1950.

Jahn, Janheinz, *Muntu: The New African Culture*. N.Y., 1961.
Jarrett, James L. *The Humanities and Humanistic Education*. Reading, Mass., 1973.
Jeffreys, Montagu V., *John Locke*. N. Y., 1967.
Jones, Howard Mumford, *Violence and Reason*. N.Y., 1969.
July, Robert W., *A History of the African People*. N.Y., 1970.

Kaufmann, Walter, *Existentialism from Dostoevsky to Sartre*. N. Y., 1957.
Keeney, Barnaby C., *Judgment By Peers*. Cambridge, Mass., 1952.
Keeton, Morris, *The Philosophy of Edmund Montgomery*. Dallas, 1950.

Kent, Louise Andrews, *Mrs. Appleyard and I.* Boston, 1968.
Kerr, Clark, *The Uses of a University.* N. Y., 1963.
Kierkegaard, Soren, *The Concept of Irony.* N. Y., 1965.
——, *Either / Or.* N. Y., 1959.
——, *Journals, 1834-1854.* London, 1951.
——, *Philosophical Fragments.* Princeton, 1936.
——, *The Present Age.* London, 1949.
——, *Stages on Life's Way.* London, 1945.
Knudsen, Johannes, *Danish Rebel: A Study of N. F. S. Grundtvig.* Philadelphia, 1955.
Koch, Hal, *Grundtvig.* (Tr. by Llewellyn Jones.) Yellow Springs, Ohio, 1952.
Kohler, Wolfgang, *The Task of Gestalt Psychology.* Princeton, 1969.
Kuhn, Thomas S., *The Structure of Scientific Revolutions.* Chicago, 1963.

Lauer, Quentin, *Phenomenology.* N. Y., 1965.
Lee, Calvin B. T., Ed., *Improving College Teaching.* Washington, D. C., 1967.
Leopold, Aldo, *Sand County Almanac.* N.Y., 1949, 1968.
Levine, Maurice, *Psychiatry and Ethics.* N. Y., 1972.
Ley, Willi, *Dawn of Zoology.* Englewood Cliffs, N. J., 1968.
Lieb, Irwin C., *The Four Faces of Man.* Philadelphia, 1971.
Lindhardt, P. G., *Grundtvig.* London, 1951.
Long, Haniel, *Interlinear to Cabeza de Vaca.* N. Y., 1969.
Lord, Walter, *Incredible Victory.* N. Y., 1967.
Lorenz, Konrad, *King Solomon's Ring.* N. Y., 1952, 1970.
Loux, Michael J., *Universals and Particulars.* N. Y., 1970.
Luce, Don, and John Sommer, *Viet Nam: The Unheard Voices.* Ithaca, N. Y., 1969.

Maritain, Jacques, *A Preface to Metaphysics.* N. Y., 1962.
Maslow, A. H., *The Psychology of Science.* N. Y., 1966.
Maxwell, Gavin, *Ring of Bright Water.* N. Y., 1960.
McGee, C. Douglas, *The Recovery of Meaning,* N. Y., 1966.
McGrath, Earl J., *Memo to a College Faculty Member.* N. Y., 1961.
McLuhan, Marshall, *Understanding Media: The Extensions of Man.* N. Y., 1966.
Merton, Thomas, *Conjectures of a Guilty Bystander.* N. Y., 1966.
——, *Disputed Questions.* N. Y., 1953, 1965.
Michener, James, *The Source.* N. Y., 1965.
Mitchell, Morris R., *World Education.* N. Y., 1967.
Montague, William Pepperell, *The Ways of Knowing.* London, 1925, 1958.
Morgan, Elaine, *The Descent of Woman.* N. Y., 1972.
Morreale, Ben, *Down and Out in Academia.* N. Y., 1972.
Munk, Kaj, *Five Plays.* (Tr. by R. P. Keigwin.) Copenhagen, 1953.

Nash, Leonard, *The Nature of the Natural Sciences.* Boston, 1963.
Niebuhr, H. Richard, *Christ and Culture.* N. Y., 1951.
——, *The Kingdom of God in America.* N. Y., 1959.
——, *The Social Sources of Denominationalism.* N. Y., 1929, 1958.
Nietzsche, Friedrich, *Anti-Christ.* N. Y., 1972.
——, *Philosophy in the Tragic Age of the Greeks.* Chicago, 1962.

Page, Bruce, David Leitch and Philip Knightly, *The Philby Conspiracy.* Garden City, N. Y., 1968.
Parrinder, Geoffrey, *African Traditional Religion.* London, 1962.
——, *Religion in Africa.* Baltimore, 1969.
Peaston, A. Elliott, *The Prayer Book Tradition in the Free Churches.* London, 1964.
Phenix, Philip H., *Intelligible Religion.* N. Y., 1954.
——, *Realms of Meaning.* N. Y., 1964.
Pikas, Anatol, *Abstraction and Concept Formation.* Cambridge, Mass., 1966.
Polanyi, Michael, *Knowing and Being.* Chicago, 1969.
——, *Personal Knowledge.* Chicago, 1958.
——, *The Tacit Dimension.* N. Y., 1967.
Pols, Edward, *The Recognition of Reason.* Carbondale, Illinois, 1963.
Pound, Roscoe, *An Introduction to the Philosophy of Law.* New Haven, 1922, 1954.
——, *The Spirit of the Common Law.* Francestown, N. H., 1921, 1947.

Radin, Max, *The Law and You.* N. Y., 1948.
Rapoport, Anatol, *Operational Philosophy.* N. Y., 1953, 1954.
Reichenbach, Hans, *The Rise of Scientific Philosophy.* Berkeley, 1951.
Rensch, Bernard, *Biophilosophy.* N. Y., 1971.
Rickover, H. G., *Education and Freedom.* N. Y., 1959.
Robinson, John A. T., *Honest to God.* Philadelphia, 1963.
Rosenstock-Huessy, Eugen, *The Driving Power of Western Civilization.* Boston, 1950.
Rouner, LeRoy S., Ed., *Philosophy, Religion, and the Coming World Civilization.* Essays in Honor of William Ernest Hocking. The Hague, 1966.
Ruml, Beardsley, *Memo to a College Trustee.* N. Y., 1959.
Russell, John, S. J., *Science and Metaphysics.* N. Y., 1958.

Sandoz, Marie, *The Battle of the Little Big Horn.* Philadelphia, 1966.
——, *Crazy Horse: The Strange Man of the Oglalas.* Lincoln, Nebraska, 1961.
Sanger, Marjory Bartlett, *Billy Bartram and his Green World.* N. Y., 1972.
Scheler, Max, *Man's Place in Nature.* N. Y., 1962.
——, *Philosophical Perspectives.* Boston, 1958.
Schneir, Walter and Miriam, *Invitation to an Inquest.* N. Y., 1965.
Scott, Nathan A., Jr., *Modern Literature and the Religious Frontier.* N. Y., 1958.
(Scott, Robert F.) *Scott's Last Expedition. The Journals.* Arranged by Leonard Huxley. Boston, 1967.
Seth, Ronald, *The Executioners.* N. Y., 1967.
Shuman, Samuel I., *Legal Positivism.* Detroit, 1963.
Sinclair, Andrew, *Che Guevara.* N. Y., 1970.
Singh, Kirpal, *Spirituality: What It Is.* Delhi, 1964.
——, *The Wheel of Life.* Delhi, 1965.
Smith, Buckingham, Tr., *The Relation of Alvar Nunez Cabeza de Vaca.* N. Y., 1871, 1966.
Smith, John E., *Reason and God.* New Haven, 1961.
Snow, C. P., *The Two Cultures and the Scientific Revolution.* N. Y., 1959, 1969.
Spiegelberg, Herbert, *The Phenomenological Movement.* The Hague, 1965.
Stanlis, Peter J., *Edmund Burke and the Natural Law.* Ann Arbor, 1965.

Steiner, George, *In Bluebeard's Castle.* New Haven, 1971.
Strawson, P. F., *Individuals.* N. Y., 1963.
Strolz, Walter, *Human Existence: Contradiction and Hope.* Notre Dame, 1967.
Stuckenberg, J. H. W., *The Life of Immanuel Kant.* London, 1882.
Stumpf, Samuel E., *Morality and the Law.* Nashville, 1966.
——, *Philosophical Problems.* N. Y., 1971.
——, *Philosophy, History and Problems.* N. Y., 1971.
Styron, William, *The Confessions of Nat Turner.* N. Y., 1967.
Sundman, Per Olof, *The Flight of the Eagle.* N. Y., 1970.

Teilhard de Chardin, Pierre, *The Divine Milieu.* N. Y., 1965.
——, *The Phenomenon of Man.* N. Y., 1965.
Tempels, Placide, *Bantu Philosophy.* Paris, 1959, 1969.
Tharp, Louise Hall, *Adventurous Alliance.* Boston, 1959.
——, *Mrs. Jack.* Boston, 1965.
Thévenaz, Pierre, *What Is Phenomenology?* (James M. Edie, Ed.) Chicago, 1962.
Tillich, Paul, *Love, Power, and Justice.* N. Y., 1954.
——, *Theology of Culture.* N. Y., 1959.
——, *The Future of Religions.* N. Y., 1966.
Tolley, Howard, Jr., *Children and War.* N. Y., 1973.
Toulmin, Stephen, *The Philosophy of Science.* N. Y., 1960.

Vahanian, Gabriel, *The Death of God.* N. Y., 1961.
——, *No Other God.* N. Y., 1966.
Van Lawick-Goodall, Jane, *In the Shadow of Man.* Boston, 1971.
Veatch, Henry B., *Rational Man.* Bloomington, Indiana, 1962.
Very, Jones, *Poems.* Boston, 1883. (Courtesy of Frank Reynolds.)
Vidler, A. R., and W. A. Whitehouse, *Natural Law, A Christian Reconsideration.* London, 1946.

Walker, Brooks R., *The New Immorality.* Garden City, N. Y., 1968.
Ward, Barbara, *Faith and Freedom.* N. Y., 1962.
Weiss, Paul, *The God We Seek,* Carbondale, Illinois, 1964.
Wellard, James, *Lost Worlds of Africa.* N. Y., 1967.
West, Rebecca, *The New Meaning of Treason.* N. Y., 1964.
Whitaker, Thomas R., *Swan and Shadow: Yeat's Dialogue with History.* Chapel Hill, N. C., 1964.
White, Amos J., and Luella G., *Dawn in Basutoland.* Boston, 1953.
White, Morton, *Religion, Politics, and the Higher Learning.* Cambridge, Mass., 1959.
Whitehead, Alfred North, *Adventures of Ideas.* N. Y., 1933, 1967.
——, *The Aims of Education.* N. Y., 1929, 1967.
——, *The Concept of Nature.* Cambridge, England, 1955.
——, *The Function of Reason.* Princeton, 1929; Boston, 1958.
——, *Modes of Thought.* N. Y., 1938, 1956.
——, *Religion in the Making.* N. Y., 1927.
——, *Essays in Science and Philosophy.* N. Y., 1947.
——, *The Principles of Natural Knowledge.* Cambridge, England, 1955.
Wild, John, *Existence and the World of Freedom.* Englewood Cliffs, N. J., 1963.

Wilder, Amos N., *Theology and Modern Literature.* Cambridge, Mass., 1958.
Williams, Duncan, *Trousered Apes.* New Rochelle, N. Y., 1972.
Williams, Leonard, *Samba and the Monkey Mind.* N. Y., 1965.
Wittgenstein, Ludwig, *The Blue and Brown Books.* N. Y., 1965.
——, *Lectures and Coversations.* Berkeley, 1967.
——, *Philosophical Investigations.* N. Y., 1958.
Woodham-Smith, Cecil, *Queen Victoria.* N. Y., 1972.
——, *The Reason Why.* N. Y., 1960.
Woodson, Carter G., *The Mis-Education of the Negro.* Washington, D. C., 1933, 1969.

Yarmolinsky, Adam, *The Military Establishment.* N. Y., 1971, 1973.

Zabeeh, Farhang, *Universals.* The Hague, 1966.

Index

Columbia, Maryland, 30
Columbia University, 168
Columbus, Ohio, 200
Communism: on campus, 158-9
Community: as belief-point, 27 & ff. as partial absolute, 35
Community Education, v
Computer: as instrument in Biblical study, 24
Conant, James B., 165, 193
Concentration camp rumor of 1967, 44-5
Conceptualism, 111 & ff.; 126-7; 202 & ff.; theory of knowing, 9, 18, 29; in historiography, 43 & ff.; in history teaching, 46; in constructional thought, 52; broadened, 52; and reason, 52; as extended idealism, 123 & ff.
Congregational church, 147
CONRAD, Inc., 187; (cf. CHERS)
Consortia: college and university, 167 & ff., 185 & ff.; costs of, 170 & ff.; and education, 172 & ff.; as activity, program, 172-3; admissions in, 174 & ff.; grace, 181; principles of, 181 & ff.; purposes, 185; sovereignty in, 186; and libraries, 187; psychology of commitment, 187; originality in, 191; team participation, 197
Consortium on Higher Education Religion Studies (CHERS / CONRAD, Inc.), 185 & ff.
Constructional thought: and reason, 14, 67; religious knowledge as, 29; scientific, 51; and conceptualization, 52, 116; search as, 60; naturalistic, 117
Cooper, Wilmer: Earlham College, 196
Cooperation: among diverse schools, 189, 194, 200
Cooperative education, 167
Cornish, Louis Craig, 12
Crane Review, v
Creativity: as discovery, 25, 207; and the rational, 64
Cuba: as element in extended community, 32

Danforth Foundation, 144, 188, 192, 194, 200
Dayton, 187, 188, 199;—Miami Valley Consortium, 171, 194, 197; University of, 169, 197
Decision(s): individually determined, 9, 57-8
Demonic, 64 & ff.
De-mythologizing: in New Testament thought, 50 & ff.
Descartes, Rene, 10
Deterministic thought, 5, 6,; countervailed, 9
Dewey, John, 77, 123, 126, 151, 152-3, 156 & ff.
Dialectic, 122-3; in Abelard, 120
Dialogue, 160, 184
Discovery: as creativity, 25, 207
Divinity, 32, 34, 55, 159; and the liberal view of man, 57
Division of College Support: U.S. Office of Education, 176-7
Doukhobors, 32
Drama: religion as personal—, 23
Drug culture, 125

Earlham College: Richmond, Indiana, 177; 196
Ecology: of idea-systems, 10, 55, 59, 123-4; of institutions, 99-100
Ecumenism: 21, 26, 28, 35; liberal, 48 & ff. New England approach to, 55 & ff.
Education, v
Education: as idea and practice, 62, 72; and law, 62, 64 & ff.; as tension, 74; vs. the political, 107-8; as metaphysics, 128 & ff., 166; progressive—, 5, 162; and historiography, 46; and the romantic, 59 & ff., 63-4; and the urban education center, 70 & ff., 73 & ff.; multiform, 75; higher, 72; and change, 98 & ff., 103; religion masked in, 106; and valuation, 128 & ff.; as thought at work, 164 & ff.; U.S. Office of, 176-7, 194; federal support for, 193; costs of, 185 & ff.

ff., 93, 169, characteristics of, 30, 35; and secular, 29; foci of belief, 31 & ff.; range of rational-and-romantic-man, 52; significance of individual life, 57, 83-4; function masked in education, 106-7; psychology in consortia, 187, 194-5
Reston, Virginia, 30
Retreats: college, 149
Revelation, 23, 24
Revolution, 102
Rodman Job Corps Center, 74
Romanticism, 5, 52-3, 120, 124, 163; and education, 59 & ff.; nature of, 60 & ff.; and violence, 60 & ff.; demonic, 64: rational, 64

St. John, Gospel according to, 34
St. John's College: Annapolis and Santa Fe, 160
St. Leonard's College: Centerville, Ohio, 197
Science(s): natural, 53; as metaphysics, 87; as rationalistic, 126
Scientific, 54, 111-2; method, 1, 122; thought, 7, 50-1; myth, 15; liberalism, 57; naivete (scientism), 92-3; disciplines and philosophies, 95; rationalism, 120, 126
Secular: as particularistic, 18; reality as religious or, 27; religious and, 29, 57; knowing, 27; influences on education, 98
Selective Service System: grounds for deferment updated, 29
Seminaries: in CHERS, 187 & ff.; 194
Senexet House, vi
Sensory knowledge, 8, 50-1, 208
Slavery, 41 & ff.; and the Black American, 45
Sociology, 94, 95
Soviet Union, 126; as element in extended community 32
Spinoza, Benedict, 6
Spirit, 55 & ff.; 61
State University of New York, vii
Stirewalt, Luther: Hamma Theological Seminary, 197
Stokes, Rembert: Wilberforce University, 177

Structure, 62 & ff.; as rationality, 63
Stylites, Simon, 83
Styron, William, 43
Subjectivity: in knowing, 1, 16, 116, 202; in systems, 114
Systems, systematics, 7, 9-11, 13; belief-points in, 27 & ff.; system consequents, 29; meaning of, 48-9; education, 75 & ff.; nature and limitation of, 77 & ff., 114-5, 202 & ff.; law of extra-systematic referents, 82-4, 91, 129; philosophic concomitants, 95; and ultimates, 96; idea, 111; fundament in, 113; entailed in questions, 114

Taylor, Henry Osborn, 16
Teachers College: Columbia University, 158, 168
Teaching, 124; history, 40; effects of 121-2
Thomas, Robert A.: Wilberforce University, 177
Title III: Higher Education Act of 1965, 176-7
Tolkien, J. R. R., 15
Tradition, 129; in education, vi, 131 & ff.; 168; various institutional expressions of, 136 & ff.; in history, 37
Transcendentalism, 5, 125, 202
Treason: illustrative of belief focus, 32
Trust, 181, 183, 198-9; in consortia, 199
Truth: as constructional 25; 207
Tufts University: Medford, Mass., v

Ultimacy, 28 & ff., 31, 53, 65; 86-7; 90, 92-3; 114; 127, 207; semi-ultimates, 32; awareness of, 55; in law, 80; education and, 94; fundamental question, 95 & ff., 113; various institutional expressions of, 136, 138
Union Graduate School: Yellow Springs, Ohio, 170
Unidimensionality, 27 & ff.; and ultimacy, 28
Unitarianism, 5, 13, 158
United Theological Seminary: Dayton, Ohio, 169, 197

225

Universal(s): 13, 55, 66, 119 & ff.; 127

Universalism, 157 & ff.

Universities: urban, 70 & ff.; as social reform institutions, 72, 75; and settings, 93 & ff.; church-related, 94; "free", 100

University Without Walls: Yellow Springs, Ohio, 168, 170

Values, valuation, 29, 99 & ff. 106-7; education and, 128 & ff.; and metaphysics, 132 & ff.; various institutional expressions of, 136 & ff., 139 & ff., 143, 147, 150, 154, 156

Vermont, 156 & ff.; Civil War invasion of, 38; (cf. Robin W. Winks, "Raid at St. Albans," *Vermont Life* XV, 3, 40-46; Spring 1961); University of, 156

Vienna: as center of philosophic originality, 2

Violence: as romantic force, 60 & ff., 163, 165; extended metaphysics, 61; social pathology, 68; —on campus declined, the Harvard decision, 165-6

Washington, George: Revolutionary War stereotype, 37; as slave owner, 42

Wentz, Frederick: Hamma Theological Seminary, 197

Wert, Newell: United Theological Seminary, 197

Whitehead, Alfred North, 13, 16, 38, 67, 92, 121, 125

Wilberforce University: Wilberforce, Ohio, vi, 169, 176 & ff.; 183-4; 196

Wilbur, Earl Morse, 13

Will, 56

Wilmington College: Wilmington, Ohio, 169; 196

Winks, Robin W., 38, (cf. Vermont)

Wittenberg University: Springfield, Ohio, 169, 197

Wofford, Harris, 144, 145, 147

Xenia, Ohio, 177

Yellow Springs, Ohio: (cf. Antioch College, Antioch-Putney Graduate School, Union Graduate School, University Without Walls); 170, et al.

226

DATE DUE

DEMCO 38-296

Please remember that this is a library book, and that it belongs only temporarily to each person who uses it. Be considerate. Do not write in this, or any, library book.